REFRAMING CHANGE

How to Deal with Workplace Dynamics, Influence Others, and Bring People Together to Initiate Positive Change

JEAN KANTAMBU LATTING AND V. JEAN RAMSEY

PRAEGER
An Imprint of ABC-CLIO, LLC

A B C 🔻 C L I O

Santa Barbara, California • Denver, Colorado • Oxford, England

Library of Congress Cataloging-in-Publication Data

Latting, Jean Kantambu.
    Reframing change : how to deal with workplace dynamics, influence others, and bring people together to initiate positive change / Jean Kantambu Latting and V. Jean Ramsey.
        p. cm.
    Includes bibliographical references and index.
    ISBN 978-0-313-38124-9 (hbk. : alk. paper) — ISBN 978-0-313-38125-6 (ebook)
    1. Organizational behavior.   2. Interpersonal relations.   3. Organizational change.   I. Ramsey, V. Jean.   II. Title.
    HD58.7.L359   2009
    658.4'06—dc22   2009025502

13   12   11   10   09   1   2   3   4   5

This book is also available on the World Wide Web as an eBook.
Visit www.abc-clio.com for details.

ABC-CLIO, LLC
130 Cremona Drive, P.O. Box 1911
Santa Barbara, California 93116-1911

This book is printed on acid-free paper ∞

Manufactured in the United States of America

Contents

Acknowledgments

Writing this book has been a journey. Along the way, we have been aided by many who provided support, guidance, assistance and information—helping us stay on the path we had set. As a partnership, we have several people to thank. As individuals, we have more.

THE PARTNERSHIP: JEAN & JEAN

We are grateful to the scholar-practitioners who provided the foundation on which this work was built: Chris Argyris, Jack Brehm, Daniel Goleman, John Gottman, Elliot Jacques, Rick Maurer, Meg Wheatley, and Peter Senge.

Friends and colleagues reviewed various drafts of this book: Myrtle Bell, David Bradford, Mary Ellen Capek, Darya Funches, Joan Gallos, Mary Harlan, Mark Hays, Diallo Kantambu, Howard Karger, Art Kleiner, Jo Bowens Lewis, Fulkra Mason, Carole Marmell, Nancy Peek, and Dnika Travis. We are grateful for their sage comments and suggestions. Thanks especially to Art, Carole, Darya, Mark, and Nancy for section-by-section commentary and editing. Because of them, the manuscript is much improved.

The other members of our dialogue group—Bill Brenneman, Stephanie Foy, Mary Harlan, Timothy Skaggs, and Betty Sanders—deserve special recognition and acknowledgment. This group has been a mainstay on which we have relied for over ten years. Month after month, the group has created anew a rare and precious jewel: a conversational space in which to explore our deepest selves.

JEAN LATTING WRITES:

I am filled with infinite gratitude toward Maconda O'Connor for providing the bedrock upon which this work has been built. Without her, there would be no book. She is a model of the highest order of social responsibility and visionary thinking. A special thanks also to Gretchen Walters for her zestful approach to life and cheerful support of this project.

My organizational clients and former students provided many of the situations and scenes described in this book. I am grateful for and humbled by their eager willingness to share their stories, triumphs, hopes, and disillusionments. They have challenged me to stretch and grow, and it has been my privilege and honor to do so. Thanks also to the class members who read earlier versions of the book. It has been much strengthened because of their reflective and critical comments.

Spectra Energy, where several of the concepts discussed in this book were developed, welcomed me into the company as Mary Harlan's subcontractor. I continue to be impressed by the company's upholding of integrity and diversity as critical company values during a period of time in which other organizations were not as wise. I am also most grateful to Spectra's human resources department—and especially to Mark Hays and Rohby Mitchell—for modeling some of the most skillful internal consultancy I have ever seen in an organization and introducing me to the powerful listening exercise that was described in this book.

I am grateful to Dean Ira Colby, Karen Holmes, Paul Raffoul, Dawn Hull, Marcia Christ, Lisa Martinez, Yolanda Williams, Carolyn Brooks, and the faculty and other staff at the Graduate College of Social Work, University of Houston for providing the institutional, collegial, and administrative support that allowed us to pursue this work. A special thanks also to the funders, advisory board, staff, and organizational clients of the Center for Organizational Research and Effectiveness where several of the skills described herein were tested.

Eillen Bui, my research assistant, provided indispensable support throughout the evolution of this work. She read every draft of the manuscript, did much of the formatting, conducted numerous library searches, and attended to myriad details that kept us moving forward.

The quality of my life has improved immensely because of emotional clearing technologies developed by several personal growth pioneers:

- Rebecca Rehmeyer (with Mary Harlan), emotional processing
- Transcendental meditation trainers
- Landmark Education trainers and staff
- Star's Edge, especially Cata Low
- Hale Dwoskin, the Sedona Method
- Connirae and Tamara Andreas, Core Transformation
- Elyse Hope Killoran, Spiritual Partnering
- Callahan Techniques and other energy therapies

Family and friends cheered me on through the inevitable ups and downs of writing. My heartfelt appreciation goes to Carol Adams, Roberta Burroughs, Florence Coleman, Valerie Coleman-Ferguson, Darya Funches, Carol Glasper, Meghan Glasper, Victor Glasper, Voris Glasper, Julian Hicks, Nakita Hicks, Tasha Hicks, Rosalind Jackson, Russell Jackson, Marietta Johnson, Nelson Jones, Judith Jones, Amir Joplin, Joan Joplin, Diallo Kantambu, Arvis Latting, Sr., Jo Bowen Lewis, Carole Marmell, Cheryl Miller, Elaine Prewitt, Dnika Travis, Raphael Travis, and members of the dialogue group. They have accompanied me on this sometimes heart-rending exploration through the labyrinth of life. I would not be me if not for them.

Several of my close personal friends are as fascinated as I am with organizational learning and change, personal growth, leadership development, and diversity and inclusion. They deserve special mention here:

- Bill Brenneman of Causal Learning introduced me to organizational learning, root cause analysis, and Elliot Jaques's theory of requisite management. All three concepts revolutionized my thinking about leadership, work culture, and organizational change.
- Darya Funches of REAP Gallery Unlimited was the first to explain to me how releasing the past facilitates envisioning the future. We held a decade-long conversation about the interplay between systemic constraints and personal responsibility that is reflected in some of the thinking in this book and how I now see my place in the world.
- Mary Harlan of Harlan Consulting provided me with the opportunity to subcontract on major diversity initiatives that provided with me a learning-training laboratory in which to explore many of the ideas in this book. She also introduced me to several terms used throughout the book, such as "diversity dimensions" and "emotional triggers." Most especially,

she, along with Rebecca Rehmeyer, provided me with my first riveting introduction to emotional processing.

- The imprint of Jo Bowens Lewis of the Center for Cooperative Change appears throughout this book. She introduced me to the complexity and coherence of transactional analysis as a theory of personality and to her own practice trademark—Principles of Cooperative Living. My understanding of relationships, diversity, and inclusion is far richer because of our numerous discussions over the years. I am especially grateful for the times she has reminded me that there is no need to return to the same dry well.

From the inception of our friendship more than a decade ago, Jean Ramsey has repeatedly reminded me that while I may try to teach whatever I want to teach, students will learn only that which they want to learn. The impact of this simple truth has reached beyond the classroom into all aspects of my life and into this book. Thanks to her, I continue to learn to change what I am able to change, leave alone what I cannot change, and gain a better understanding of the difference. Who knew that when we embarked on this endeavor together, we would become so integral to each other's lives?

Special thanks to—and in memory of—my sister and friend, Judith L. Jones, with whom I discussed many of the ideas in this book during its development. She was particularly helpful in connecting theories and concepts found in this book to Twelve-Step and Recovery, Inc. precepts. One of our rituals was to ask each other, "What is the key to life?" It gives me great pleasure to think that she now knows.

Diallo Kantambu, my husband and life-partner, has been a constant source of devotion and rock-steadiness throughout the conceptualization and writing of this book. He has been there for me through the large and the small—as a sounding board for ideas, my technical guru, and a source of encouragement. Thank you, Diallo, for reminding me of what is possible whenever I forget.

JEAN RAMSEY WRITES:

My appreciation begins with students at Texas Southern University and ends with students at Texas Southern University. I have been privileged to have had several thousand students enrolled in classes I've taught during my 19 years at Texas Southern. All of them taught me a great deal. I especially thank those undergraduate students who took the teambuilding classes during the past six years. By introducing them to many of the skills in the book, I was able to fine-tune my own understanding of them.

Graduate students in the Organization and Management Theory course read several iterations of the book. They discussed the material in class, applied it in their papers and projects, and shared ways in which they used the concepts and skills in their personal and professional lives. Thank you for teaching me so much about what we meant to say.

Several individuals had a significant influence on my learning about clearing emotions and testing assumptions. Micki Fine was the first to help me put all I had read about mindfulness into practice. Debbie Mills improved the quality of my life dramatically by introducing me to yoga. Training in self-awareness and empowerment from Star's Edge and Sedona Training Associates were also life-changing. And once more, day-to-day interactions with students at Texas Southern University provided a rich learning laboratory.

Faculty and staff at Texas Southern also contributed a great deal to my development. I especially appreciate those who were willing to overlook my ignorance and awkwardness in the early days, who expected more of me, and who provided personal and professional support while I learned to be more self-reflective. It is through my experience at Texas Southern University that I have lived the importance of changing one's self in order to change one's relationships and interactions.

I owe a personal, as well as an intellectual debt to colleagues from early in my career: Ella Bell, Lynda Moore, and Stella Nkomo, in particular, who helped me understand that the Women in Management courses I helped pioneer were really "White Women in Management" courses. These individuals pointed out the gaps in my understanding—my blind spots—in ways that were clear yet supportive. Mary Ellen Capek, consummate networker and friend, continues to provide a stimulus for seeing things through different lenses. And Myrtle Bell serves as an ongoing model of commitment and perseverance in doing the work.

Earlier co-authors also helped lay a solid foundation for the collaboration Jean Latting and I experience. I owe a great debt to both Linda Calvert and Joan Gallos for setting a high standard for successful writing partnerships.

Also essential to my participation in writing this book was the growth and development spurred by the 13-year project of building "the cabin." All the family and friends who helped build my mountain home provided yet another opportunity to apply the skills that make up the heart of the book: Betty Arnold, Dave Arnold, Eric Arnold, Justin Arnold, Kristin Arnold, Nathan Arnold, Steve Arnold, Tyler Arnold, Dave Barnes, Linda Calvert, Larry Calvert, Pete Couch, Mary Finan, Belinda Fisher,

Stephanie Foy, Dana Foy, Steven Foy, Andrew Foy, Amy Foy, Alice Greko, Pete Greko, Carol Hunt, Kathrine Mendez, Victoria Ndbuisi, Anita Patton, Barry Peek, Nancy Peek, Bob Ramsey, Kay Ramsey, Ken Ramsey, Mel Ramsey, Tracy Rathe, Kara Shervanick, Johnny Trujillo, Judy Viebig, and Bernice Zimmerman. A special thanks to Steve, Dave Barnes, Ken and Bob—and a special-special thanks to Nancy—for the love and "sweat equity" they have invested through the years.

My deepest gratitude goes to my co-author, Jean Latting. My life has not been the same since you entered it. And isn't that just grand! Our friendship and work together continue to be enriching and learning-filled. I look forward to many more years of rewarding collaboration.

CHAPTER 1

Matt's Story: An Introduction to Conscious Change

The static was so loud during the call that I often asked him to repeat his words. Matt explained that he was caught in an airport on his way home from a conference and wanted to know if I had time to talk. The unanticipated delay had given him some uninterrupted time to focus on a problem he had been worrying about for some time. He had decided to call me because he could see connections between his current dilemma at work and what he had learned in my class on organizational learning and change he had taken a year ago. "I remember some of what we learned," he said, "and I've applied some of the ideas, but it hasn't been enough. I thought maybe you'd be able to help me figure out what else to try."

"You've been at your job nearly six months now, haven't you?" I asked, wanting to get a mental picture of his work situation. I knew the organization was relatively small, and remembered his excitement when he had taken the job: "It's my dream job, Jean," he had proclaimed proudly at the time.

"Six months and two promotions," he said now. "During this time, several managers in our area have left. People keep leaving, and I keep getting promoted."

I waited, knowing he had more to say.

He continued, "The problem is that my director is such an unethical person. She's so manipulative. You wouldn't believe the things she's done." He paused.

Knowing this would be a lengthy call, I put my feet up on the desk. "You know, Matt," I said, "this is the third call I've gotten in the last couple of months from former students who're either unhappy with their managers or the people around them at their jobs. People graduate ready to go into the world and make a difference, and then they encounter what's out there. It can be rough."

He continued, "Well, the whole thing's awful. I keep thinking I should leave, but I'm reluctant to start looking for another job, because I know that if she got a whiff of it, she'd fire me on the spot. That's how unethical she is."

"So, what's happening exactly?" I asked.

"Just yesterday, one of my key staff members came to see me, crying. The director does things to put the staff down; she calls it 'putting them in their place.'"

"Putting them in their place?"

"And that's just the tip of the iceberg. Staff members come to me all the time to complain about her. I sympathize with the unfairness of it all and try to reassure them, but I'm not sure it helps much.

"Jean, you wouldn't believe what's going on. Here's the most recent example. Staff members have glass panes in their office doors that anyone can see through. Most cover the glass with pictures so they have some privacy. Well, she decided that only managers had the right to cover up the panes and the staff should leave theirs uncovered so they wouldn't feel too important."

"Too important?!?!" He was right; I was having difficulty believing it.

"Yes, exactly!" That's what she said two weeks ago when she showed me the memo she'd written about taking down the pictures. When she asked what I thought, I told her the staff needed privacy for interviewing clients, and that they'd feel totally demoralized if she made them uncover the glass. She said, 'Matt, they need to have an office that anyone can look into so they won't feel so important.' I asked, 'But isn't the point for them to feel valued in their work? If they don't feel valued, then our clients won't feel valued either.' She said, 'They already think they're too important, and it's got to stop.' So I said, 'Well, it will make it more difficult for them to do their work.'

"Thankfully, she didn't send the memo—at least not right then. Two days ago, though, when we came to work, all 20 staff members had a memo saying that anything on the glass panes had to be removed by the end of the day or would be taken down for them. I was so angry that I went to her and asked how she could do such a thing. She looked at me as though I was the crazy person and said, 'Matt, I told you staff members were feeling too full of themselves. I'm sorry you don't understand this, but they're just front-line workers. They aren't managers. I can't have them walking around as though they are managers. That has to stop.'"

Listening to Matt's story, I was growing more and more appalled. "So what did you say then?" I asked.

"Well, I told her it was important they feel valued and left her office. I couldn't look at her another second."

"Did you get in trouble with her for speaking up?" I asked.

"Oh, no. I'm still golden. In fact, a few hours later she said she'd been planning to give me a raise and I should expect it in my next pay check. I was furious. She was obviously trying to buy my silence."

"So what do the staff think about your raise?"

"Well, they don't know about it, but they do know about the new computer she gave me just a few weeks before she declared the pictures had to come down. The staff are limping along on computers so antiquated we can't update their software, but all the managers have been given state-of-the-art equipment. She also walks right past the staff without speaking. Here's the bottom line, Jean. She's nasty to them and generous with us. She's promoting divisiveness between staff and managers by taking things away from them and giving things to us. I've tried talking to some of the other managers—asking them not to fall for it, but, sad to say, some of them have! A few agree that the situation is deplorable, but others are doing what they can to win her favor, even at the sacrifice of their own staff. It's demoralizing to watch. Also, the last time I looked our service numbers were steadily dropping, which means our clients are the ones who are really being hurt by all this."

"Why do you suppose she's doing this?"

"Beats me. But she does it all the time. I do know she's really insecure. She constantly asks me if I think someone is mad at her or doesn't like her or something. I'd guess this has something to do with her insecurities, but I don't know what's in her head. Now, here's the kicker. People tell me she's the third director they've had in as many years. I understand each of them was equally oppressive toward staff—each in his or her own way. There's really nothing I can do because I'm not the one with the power to fix it. And I can't afford to quit right now either!"

"Is there anything else, Matt?"

There was a long silence. Then, "Well, yes. I don't know if it's significant or even worth mentioning . . . I mean . . . well, she's not from the United States originally. In her country, people in charge are generally obeyed without question. I sometimes wonder if this is why she thinks she can get away with what she does. I'm trying not to stereotype and it may be nothing at all, but still, I wonder. Not that I would say anything to her about this, of course."

He paused—and awaited my reaction.

PLAN OF THE BOOK

Unfortunately, Matt's story is not that unusual. We hear many examples like this from our clients and students—illustrating how frustrated they are in certain relationships, because people can be *so* difficult. Those who tell us their stories usually have explored a number of options to handle the situation before talking with us. They have already tried to logically explain how right they are to the other person, sometimes again and again; but their reasoned explanations have gone unheeded. They have made overt or covert threats. Some have withdrawn psychologically; that is, given up—only doing what is absolutely necessary. If the situation was bad enough, they might even have left the relationship (quit the job, requested a transfer). A few have taken up sports, yoga, or meditation to manage the level of stress and frustration they have decided is an unavoidable part of their jobs.

Nearly all are convinced that things would get better if others would just listen to them and change their ways; if other people would just "act right," the problems would disappear. Yet no matter how great their efforts to change others' attitudes and behaviors, those others seem incorrigible, unwilling, or unable to see the light. We suspect you, too, have had similar experiences. The greater your efforts to change others, it may seem, the stronger their resistance—and the greater the resultant frustration on both sides.

This book has been written to provide you with options. Matt's story is not an irresolvable situation; in the last chapter, Chapter 8, we will come back to see how he resolved it. But we cannot leap directly there, because, like many organizational issues, his is a complex problem. It takes a variety of acts, at the personal, interpersonal, and organizational levels, to repair this type of dysfunctional situation.

Right now, Matt is doing all he can to convince his director to change her ways. Matt believes the director is using a divide-and-conquer strategy, pitting the managers against the staff, and that some of the managers are going along with it. He is trying to ease his staff's anxiety, encourage his peers to resist buying into the divisive strategy, and convince his director to do things differently. He is worried about the impact of all this on their clients. Though he may not have thought of it in this way, Matt's goal is to encourage three groups—the director, managers, and staff—to work together more effectively for each of their own sakes as well as those of their clients.

It may seem strange to imagine Matt being the one to bring the director, managers, and staff together. After all, he has no clear authority to do so. In the organizational hierarchy, he reports to the director and the other managers are his peers. If he lacks formal power in this situation, is there anything he can do? This book is based on the belief that there is plenty he might do, with or without formal power. Although people with more formal power may find it easier to make improvements in their workplaces, we have found that people lower on the organizational totem pole can also have significant impact—if they are willing to take the risk and use a skill-based approach. The purpose of this book is to describe those skills.

What skills might Matt use in this situation? We begin with the premise that for Matt to accomplish his goals in this situation, he must first be willing to examine and test his assumptions about the director. This is not easy, since from Matt's vantage point, it is his director whose assumptions and behaviors need to change, not his own. Yet Matt's director is not seeking counsel in this situation; Matt is. If Matt wishes to initiate a positive change in this situation, he must first acknowledge that his current thoughts and feelings have helped get him where he now is, and for him to go further he must reconsider them.

The director may not be as unreasonable as she seems—most individuals are well-meaning and doing the best they can with what they have and know. It is likely that some of Matt's assumptions are inaccurate. You will learn as you read Chapter 2 on testing assumptions that perceptions are not always trustworthy, and assumptions about others can sometimes lead to self-fulfilling prophecies. In other words, people often contribute to creating, or keeping in place, the very situations they are trying to change. Learning how to test his assumptions will allow Matt to look at the situation with fresh eyes.

There is also evidence that Matt and others, including the director, have had strong emotional reactions which may be getting in the way of dealing with the situation effectively, and might even be contributing to its dysfunction. We will cover this in Chapter 3 on clearing emotions. Learning how to reduce the baggage of negative emotions will allow Matt to move forward with fewer encumbrances; building positive emotions will give him more positive energy to deal with difficult situations.

If Matt commits to personal change in the form of testing his assumptions and clearing his emotions, he still has the task of forging productive connections among his director, his peers, and his staff. Using the skills of listening, inquiry, openness, and feedback would help improve this—and most situations. Matt would benefit from practicing these skills, and his staff would benefit from seeing him do so, as well as learning the skills themselves. Even if Matt should decide to leave the organization, his staff would be left more protected. No matter the resolution of this particular situation, there will be future situations and relationships that could be more satisfying and effective if these skills were applied. Hence Chapter 4 focuses on building effective relationships.

Matt mentioned that his director was born in another country, suggesting that cultural differences might be adding to their difficulties. Juxtapose this with their unequal power and status in the organization and the situation is ripe for what we call dominant/nondominant dynamics. These dynamics complicate interactions and relationships. An understanding of these dynamics would help Matt bridge what may seem like an unbridgeable chasm between him and the director based on their differing job ranks and cultural expectations. You have undoubtedly encountered situations confounded by differences between yourself and those with whom you are trying to connect—either in terms of demography, hierarchal rank, attitudes, values, or taken-for-granted behaviors. As you will see in Chapter 5, the differences we consider go beyond the traditional categories of race and gender. Becoming more aware of the many ways in which differential status and power divide will help Matt, and you, effectively use known antidotes to predictable dynamics among those more and less powerful.

How might Matt develop a greater ability to influence his director and peers? We don't believe that he is powerless in this situation. He may have limited formal power, but he may have significant informal influence. He has already demonstrated the power of personal integrity and courage, evidenced by his willingness to speak up to the director on behalf of his staff. In Chapter 6 on the conscious use of self, we show how skilled individuals pay close attention to the ways in which their thoughts, emotions, interpersonal skills, personal integrity, and ability to bridge differences affect their interactions and others' perceptions of them. Fortified with this knowledge, they can then make more intentional choices of words and actions to bring about conscious change.

Matt has provided hints that the problems in his organization go beyond the individuals and their interactions with one another. After all, three directors have come and gone over the past three years. Even if Matt is able to work through his current challenges with his director and form a more meaningful connection with her, their relationship may continue to be tenuous unless the organization itself is geared toward promoting constructive rather than destructive relationships. Why did his director feel free to order the staff to remove their pictures? Is there a viable human resources department in this organization? Is there a culture of trust and respect? How might Matt creatively work with his staff and other concerned managers to foster a workplace where people feel valued and even important?

In Chapter 7 on initiating workplace change, we explain how to move beyond a focus on interpersonal dilemmas—especially those involving differences, and most do—to also consider situational dynamics and policies which may be supporting and constraining these dilemmas. We have some suggestions for Matt, and for you, about how to initiate change in the workplace.

The purpose of this book is to help you learn to use yourself more fully and to make more intentional choices about how to draw upon all your resources—your thoughts, emotions, and behaviors—as you seek to influence others and bring them together to initiate positive change.

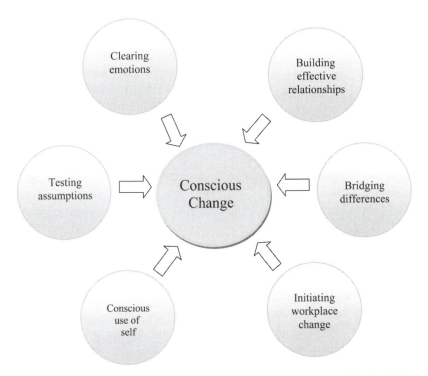

Figure 1.1   © Jean Kantambu Latting & V. Jean Ramsey, 2007–2009.

Reframing change means no longer trying to get others to change, but paying more conscious attention to how you show up in interactions with others. It is about the power of self-change: the potential you have to initiate change by focusing on yourself and the effects of your actions on others.

Demanding that others change often increases resistance and ends up pitting people against one another. Self-change is more likely to plant seeds leading to broader-based change in the work setting—change that may be more sustainable. No matter how powerless you feel in a given situation, you have choices. The ability to choose is a major source of your power to make a difference.

Figure 1.1 depicts what we call the Conscious Change model. The book is organized accordingly.

WHY THIS BOOK?

We, Jean Latting and Jean Ramsey, have spent a combined four decades honing the Conscious Change model and helping others learn it.[1] We have taught and tested this approach in both management and social work classrooms. We have provided training in for-profit, nonprofit, and government settings. We use the principles of this book in our own professional and personal lives. And we continue to gather feedback on their effectiveness.

We wrote this book, in fact, because we found ourselves helping many, many organizational clients and students like Matt. Our goal is to provide a way for those with similar problems to help themselves: to become proficient at identifying workplace dynamics that pit people against one another, and use the influence and power they have, and the skills they have developed, to make things better. There is no magic bullet here. Yet hundreds of organizational clients and students have told us these skills work.

We assume that most people reading this book are competent and already doing pretty well. We know many people like Matt who are quite capable in carrying out their functional work tasks. Work itself is not the source of problems; instead workplace dynamics—what some call politics—are an underlying theme. Referring to these meaty mind-benders as "just politics" belies the complicated nature of what is going on.

Over and over, well-meaning people become embroiled in scenarios they had no intention of creating. Again and again, individuals with integrity and ideals throw up their hands in surrender when confronted with the difficulty in getting from Point A to Point B in their work lives. The message of this book is that it doesn't have to be this way.

Differences do not inevitably lead to conflict. Change does not inevitably lead to resistance.

Our students and organizational clients have told us that, in learning how to consciously use themselves to bring about change in their workplaces, they have achieved:

- an increased sense of personal responsibility and personal choice—they no longer feel powerless to make a difference;
- an increased ability to get more done with and through others—they have learned to appreciate strengths and capabilities in others and be less reactive to others' preferences and moods;
- a workplace climate that is more supportive of them as individuals and employees—they feel more energized and positive, and have experienced improved outcomes;
- an increased comfort with differences—as conflicts arise with others who are culturally different, they feel a greater sense of self-confidence in negotiating that tricky terrain; they no longer feel it necessary to avoid certain people or tip-toe around certain issues;
- resolution of long-standing strain in their lives—they find this reduction in stress improves their physical and emotional well being; and
- a more profound sense of meaning and contribution to the world.

In developing this approach, we used a combination of academic research, self-help tools, and old-fashioned trial and error in our teaching, consulting, and training to identify key principles that seem to have the most impact in helping people improve their work lives. An important condition for what we included was that it be supported by solid social science research. Many self-help books provide valuable assistance based on the authors' own experiences; several such books introduced us initially to some of the methods described. Other self-help books, however, contain superficial, even bad advice. To avoid this, we included self-help references only if they were backed by social scientific research.

Ideas and advice were included only if they met three criteria:

- supported by academic research—conclusions and applications have been tested in research studies, some in the laboratory, others in the field;
- supported by our own experiences—methods proposed have worked for us; and

- reported as useful by our students and organizational clients—feedback has confirmed the practical utility of what we recommend.

We wanted our suggestions and ideas to be backed by academic research because experts who have studied a phenomenon understand nuances far beyond what single individuals might conclude based on their limited experiences. We included only those things we could vouch for personally because we would not impose on readers anything we are unwilling to do ourselves. Relying on feedback from former students and organizational clients was a means of ensuring that our advice was practical and applicable in today's organizations, beyond ourselves, and beyond academia.

In seeking research to support the recommended principles and practices, we cast a wide net, drawing from many disciplines—social psychology, social work, management, organizational behavior, industrial and organizational psychology, relationship and marital studies, public health, sports psychology, education, marketing, and others. We were particularly drawn to the work of positive psychologists who study happiness—a state to which we all aspire. This emerging field seems particularly promising to us as a way to improve our lives, our organizations, and our society.

The format of this book is conversations—between a consultant/coach and her clients, between former students and their instructor, and between colleagues in the workplace. These conversations are loosely based on real situations, with settings and names deliberately concealed. They are intended to make the book more readable and help you apply the ideas to your own situations and lives. We encourage you to stop and reflect as you read—and to use the principles and practices to improve your workplaces, your personal lives, your communities, and the ever-shrinking world in which we all live.

With so much conflict, animosity, hatred, greed, and suffering in the world, people often wonder what one person can do, especially when the individual is not a world leader, or even a local one. Our response is that each of us can begin by doing what we can to improve our own little corner of the world. Indeed, this is happening. Around the globe, more and more people are doing what they can to create peace, to foster human connections, and to share what they have with others.

Using Conscious Change to bring people together is part of that movement. The patience, kindness, compassion, courage, and skills embedded in the model enhance individuals' abilities to significantly influence others. "I feel so much more empowered, I can make a difference," people tell us. The word "empowerment" has become somewhat hackneyed in recent years, but no other word quite captures the glow on people's faces as they report to us, often years later, the results they have experienced from using this approach. We hope you will experience these benefits as well.

Notes to the reader: Throughout this book, in conversations and anecdotes, we have chosen to use the first-person singular: for example, "'You've been at your job nearly six months by now, haven't you?' I asked." Since each story is based on a conversation one of us took part in, we thought it most authentic to pretend there is one "author-Jean" telling the stories. This allows you to benefit from a sense of coherence that comes from one narrator, as well as from the broader perspective and insight that come from having two authors.

We have capitalized the terms "Black" and "White" throughout the manuscript whenever these refer to race. Most people who identify themselves as "Black" are not black in hue nor do most Whites have a white hue. Hence the terms Black and White as we use them are proper nouns referring to ethnicity and not adjectives referring to a particular color or hue.[2]

A parallel distinction exists within the Deaf community. The words deaf or Deaf are used depending upon whether the reference is to an audiological trait (deaf) or a cultural identity (Deaf).[3] In this book, we use the term "deaf" as an auditory trait and hence do not capitalize the term when it is used.

NOTES

1. Ramsey, V. J., & Latting, J. K. (2005). A typology of intergroup competencies. *Journal of Applied Behavioral Science, 41*(3), 265–284.

2. Do we dishonor a people by misnaming them? (1999). *Editor & Publisher, 132*(33), 46; Wachal, R. S. (2000). The capitalization of Black and Native American. *American Speech, 75*(4), 364.

3. Senghas, R. J., & Monaghan, L. (2002). Signs of their times: Deaf communities and the culture of language. *Annual Review of Anthropology, 31*(1), 69–97.

CHAPTER 2

Testing Assumptions

Tyla decided to take a break. As she walked toward the water fountain, she noticed Matthew at the far end of the hall, heading her way. As she raised her arm to greet him, he abruptly turned away and walked back the way he had come.

"What a jerk!" she thought. "It's so childish of him to ignore me just because I critiqued his project this morning."

During the morning staff meeting, she'd suspected her comments had offended him, but hadn't been sure. Now she was certain he was angry with her. Why else would he avoid her like that?

"He should grow up," she murmured under her breath.

How is it that with so little information, Tyla was sure she knew exactly why Matthew turned away from her? In a flash, without conscious awareness, her mind added interpretations of Matthew's intention and meaning to his behavior and both became fact to her. Although it was far from complete, and may or may not have been accurate, her mental model of Matthew's state of mind felt right to her.

MENTAL MODELS: SHORT-CUTS TO PERCEPTION

As you go through life, you form what are called mental models,[1] lenses through which you view all new information. The roots of your mental models were developed during early childhood in response to powerful injunctions by your parents and others about what was possible or not, right or wrong. These injunctions became scripts[2] that governed what you felt comfortable with or even compelled to say or do. As you acted out these scripts, often unknowingly, and others responded to you, you developed more sophisticated mental models about how the world works, what is real, what to expect from others, and what might be easy or hard to do.

These mental models serve as filters through which you take in the world, focusing your attention on what you already believe and drawing you toward objects, ideas, and people that confirm those beliefs. By focusing your attention on a limited part of your environment at any given time, your mental models help you make sense of what is in the world and how you fit into it.

Here are some of the mental models that may have influenced Tyla's perception of her interaction with Matthew. Several times in the past, Tyla's co-workers had given her a hard time for what they called "butting into our business" or "trying to run the whole show." Because of this history, she concluded that coworkers were likely to react negatively to any hint of correction from her. Her sensitivity to her colleagues' criticisms probably had its roots in a script formed in an earlier time: she may have concluded at a very early age that challenging others was unsafe. Now, as an adult, she was unconsciously predisposed to amplify—to pay more attention to—any signal of disapproval, or even ambiguity, in coworkers' reactions to her. Tyla's mental model about what it meant to offer her viewpoint served as a filter for her perceptions of Matthew. She thus interpreted Matthew's action as being motivated by anger.

Even though Tyla was certain she had him pegged, there might have been any number of reasons why Matthew seemingly snubbed her. He might have been daydreaming, not even aware of her presence down the hall. He might not have seen her gesture at all, having turned away just as she had begun to raise her arm. Tyla's mental model, however, prevented her from considering any of these alternative explanations. Instead, she *knew* he was mad at her. And if she took the next step and reacted to him accordingly, that action may well backfire on her—especially if what she believed turned out to be inaccurate.

Understanding Mental Models

Even if reflection causes you to question your mental models, they can still unknowingly affect your behavior. You may not truly believe tall people are smarter than short people, for example, but you may find

No

Rain

In The

The Forecast

Figure 2.1   © Jean Kantambu Latting & V. Jean Ramsey, 2007–2009.

yourself interrupting shorter people in meetings more often than you interrupt taller people.

To counterbalance the effects of your mental models, it is helpful to understand their source and power. Mental models are cognitive mechanisms, active in a wide variety of situations. They often cause you to overlook visible cues. For example, look at Figure 2.1.

Do you see a simple phrase?

If so, your mental model of what you expect has prevented you from seeing a duplicate word in the phrase. Most people looking at this image make the same error. In general, mental models cause people to add information to (or omit information from) a situation so they see more (or less) than what is there. That's why people often think there is a problem when there is none, or fail to see a problem when it is dramatic and important. Tyla could be incorrectly interpreting Matthew's motivation.

Now look at Figure 2.2. What do you see?

If you are like most, you see lines and geometric shapes. Look at the figure more closely. Can you see a letter of the alphabet in three-dimensional form?

Figure 2.2   © Jean Kantambu Latting & V. Jean Ramsey, 2007–2009.

Now try focusing only on the shapes again without also seeing the letter. It's hard, isn't it? Once you see the pattern—the letter F—you may find it hard to simply see the shapes and *not* the letter. That's how mental models affect your perception. Once you impose a mental model on a situation, it is difficult to think about the information in any way other than through the newly-imposed pattern. Tyla is expecting Matthew to be angry because she criticized his project. This is the only lens through which she can see his failure to acknowledge her greeting.

Mental models can also cause you to form judgments about others based on incomplete information or your own personal history. Look at Figure 2.3.

What do you see? Someone wearing eyeglasses? Or a word written in cursive suggesting that someone is not to be trusted?

In Matthew, Tyla only saw someone she could not trust. Only one interpretation of what she saw occurred to her: the most familiar based on her personal history—"Here's more evidence that people are not open to feedback from me." Most people do this; they assume their judgments are correct and act on them as if they were. This can be referred to as being in the answer rather than being in the question.

Figure 2.3   Produced by the SAG Design Guild Team. Used with permission.

BEING IN THE ANSWER

Being in the answer means sticking with your explanation for others' actions and sealing off alternative perspectives. It can be hard to give up your opinions about others. You may pride yourself on being a good judge of character. This skill has, after all, gotten you safely through many treacherous interactions. Unfortunately, many of these initial judgments are flat out wrong and can land you in all kinds of interpersonal trouble.

Does this mean that you never have answers or conclusions about another? No, it does not. Having an answer is quite different from being in the answer. The answer you have may be the most feasible viewpoint based on the information you have at a particular point in time. When you are in the answer, however, you are not open to a new way of thinking about the person. You have decided you know for sure.

What clues might tell you when your mental models are acting as over-zealous filters, causing you to stay in the answer and ignore other possible explanations for people's behavior? Two red flags—two warning signals to watch for in yourself—are either/or thinking and strong emotional reactions.

Red Flag 1: Either/Or Thinking

To view situations through the lens of either/or is to reduce a complex situation to a dichotomy: either it is your fault or it is mine, either I am right and you are wrong, or you are right and I am wrong. This is overly simplistic thinking and an impetus to assigning blame. It is easy to imagine Tyla believing Matthew was to blame and she was blameless. She might have said to herself, "All I did was stand up for the integrity of the project; he was the one getting all huffy about it."

CURIOUS ABOUT THE RESEARCH?

Social psychologists have found that people tend to make self-serving attributions when they use internal, character-based factors to explain their own successes and external, situational factors to explain their failures. With others, they make fundamental attribution errors. They credit others' successes to external, situational factors and failures to internal, character-based factors.

Ross, L., & Nisbett, R. E. (1991). *The person and the situation: Perspectives of social psychology.* New York: McGraw-Hill.

She was in the answer about who was right and who was wrong. This tendency toward either/or thinking underlies several common biases.

The Better-than-Average Bias

Many studies have shown that most people consider themselves as more intelligent, less prejudiced, and better employees than others, yet it is statistically impossible for *most* people to be above average. A better-than-average bias could easily lead Tyla to conclude that she was the only one on the team smart enough to point out the flaws in Matthew's work.

The Consensus Bias

Research has also shown that most people tend to believe others agree with them more than is actually the case. If Tyla held a consensus bias based on the absence of overt disagreement, she might delude herself into believing others agreed with her criticism.

The Self-Serving (and Other-Slighting) Attribution Bias

Most people are quicker to explain events in ways that serve themselves and slight others than they realize. Researchers refer to these explanations as attributions. An attribution is an ingrained assumption about the motives and beliefs held by people—ourselves or others. Tyla assumed her motives were pure and altruistic—she spoke up for the good of the project, while Matthew's response was ego-driven—he detested criticism of his work.

CURIOUS ABOUT THE RESEARCH?

Self-enhancement bias varies cross-culturally. In one study, Norwegians were found to demonstrate less self-enhancement bias than individuals in the United States. Other studies have found that the Japanese were actually more likely to engage in self-criticism than self-enhancement.

Silvera, D. H., & Seger, C. R. (2004). Feeling good about ourselves: Unrealistic self-evaluations and their relation to self-esteem in the United States and Norway. *Journal of Cross-Cultural Psychology, 35*(5), 571–585.

The better-than-average bias, consensus bias, and self-serving attribution bias are called self-enhancement biases. Most North Americans have been socialized to internalize some form of them. But if you have learned this behavior, you can unlearn it, should you so choose.

Red Flag 2: Strong Emotional Reactions

Experiencing strong emotional reactions—often called an emotional charge or being emotionally triggered—is another warning that you may be in the answer. Tyla is reacting fairly intensely to what others might deem an insignificant interaction. Why should a non-greeting in the hall provoke such a disproportionate reaction?

Tyla's rehash of the incident as well as her firm insistence that her criticism of Matthew's presentation was appropriate may indicate the presence of haunting negative emotions. Something had triggered her emotions in a powerful way. Those emotions continue to influence her conclusions as she reflects on the interaction. She had a hard time letting go of her emotional reaction. This may be a warning that something is amiss.

Noticing her emotional reactions—and the possible events triggering them—can help her govern her thoughts, rather than letting those thoughts govern her. For this to happen, though, she must be willing to entertain the possibility that she is maintaining some emotional defenses.[3]

What might have been going on with Tyla beneath her awareness? She may have some unacknowledged doubts about her behavior toward Matthew at the meeting. Her emotional charge may have stemmed from a fear that she had been too critical. Alternatively, Matthew's behavior may have reminded her of unwanted or unacknowledged parts of herself—times when she may not have done as good a job on a project as she could have. Unintentionally and beyond her awareness, she may be projecting the discomfort of these feelings onto Matthew.[4]

CURIOUS ABOUT THE RESEARCH?

Projection is the tendency to impute one's own thoughts and feelings onto others. Attempts to suppress thoughts about one's undesirable characteristics seem to be the culprit here. In one study, people were instructed not to think about their own threatening personality characteristics. Instead of going away, individuals' internal monitors continually checked to see if the thoughts were really suppressed. With their undesirable characteristics right below the surface of their minds, people unknowingly prime themselves to project those characteristics onto others.

Newman, L. S., Duff, K. J., & Baumeister, R. F. (1997). A new look at defensive projection: Thought suppression, accessibility, and biased person perception. *Journal of Personality and Social Psychology, 72*(5), 980–1001.

These are but two possible reasons for Tyla's emotions to have been triggered. Note that neither of these reasons have anything to do with Matthew's intent, or even his behavior; they are about Tyla, not Matthew.

The point of identifying these possible emotional triggers is not to decide which is the most likely provocation, but to recognize the dynamic: some conflict within Tyla, brought to this interaction from her past, is restricting her freedom of thought. Even if Matthew is angry with her, she is ill-equipped to respond effectively as long as she is reacting emotionally. That's because people who are triggered emotionally have narrowed and focused thinking processes.[5] The more narrow and focused your thinking, the less likely you are to think of expanded possibilities and options.

If you are willing to invest some time and effort, however, you can counter the cascade of negative thoughts and emotions and become more fully accountable for your thoughts and feelings.

MAKING UP STORIES

Another cognitive process that may make it difficult for Tyla to respond effectively is the natural and common human tendency to fill in the blanks, that is, to make up a story to compensate for ambiguous or incomplete information.

No one can know for sure what another's actions or words mean; they can only guess based on their experiences. The problem is most people never go beyond their guesses. They make up stories about what things mean and never test whether those accounts are true.

Look at Figure 2.4.

Do you see a circle surrounded by lines? Look again. There is no circle. Only your imagination puts it there.

Tyla's story about Matthew may be about her expectations of how Matthew *should* have behaved ("He should have acknowledged my greeting.") or about *why* he behaved as he did ("He's being deliberately spiteful and paying me back for pointing out flaws in his project."). Professor and management consultant Gervase Bushe suggests that "most interpersonal encounters, especially those in work organizations, are best described as two or more people having different experiences while making up stories about what is going on in each other's minds: stories that are never checked out" (pp. 8–9).[6]

Single episodes like the one Tyla experienced with Matthew might not be problematic, but these experiences accumulate over time. If Tyla behaves like most people, the next time she sees Matthew, she will react to him as if her story about his behavior is true. She is likely to be defensive, angry, or treat him coldly because she believes he is angry with her. This may well trigger Matthew's defensiveness in turn, almost guaranteeing that their next interaction will be a strained one.

Figure 2.4   Produced by the SAG Design Guild Team. Used with permission.

Instead of being in the answer, you can consciously choose to be in the question.

BEING IN THE QUESTION

Being in the question is wondering what things mean instead of assuming you already know. It involves treating your first thought as a hypothesis rather than a statement of truth. Being in the question means being willing to learn something new about the situation. As such, it takes more work—and humility—than being in the answer. It requires searching for alternative explanations for others' behavior.

The first step in being in the question is to consider the possibility that the situation may not be as it seems. Instead, your perceptual filters may be limiting what you see, think, or feel. This willingness to explore your unseen and unacknowledged assumptions frees you to move out of the answer and into the question.

There are several approaches to viewing situations with fresher eyes. Each entails calling your assumptions and beliefs into question, taking different perspectives, and generating alternative explanations for what might be occurring.

Testing Your Initial Assumptions

Ask What If

A simple way to defuse the emotional power of an attribution or assumption is simply to dispute it by asking, "What if it isn't true?"

- What if the other person is right?
- What if I didn't perceive things correctly?
- What if there are cultural differences affecting this situation that I don't know about?
- What if my strong emotional reactions are keeping me from seeing other possibilities?
- What if there is another explanation for the problem?

Asking "what if" and entertaining other possibilities may help jar you out of fixed beliefs and assumptions. What if questions do not deny your original interpretation. Rather, they provoke your curiosity and dispassion. They ask you to live, for a few minutes at least, with an alternative reality in which your assumptions are not correct. Can you imagine a circumstance in which an alternative reality was plausible? If so, what would the implications be?

Tyla might have asked herself: "I think Matthew is angry with me. But I wonder if there could be some other explanation for his failing to acknowledge my greeting? Is it possible he had something else on his mind? Or that he didn't see me? Could I be overreacting?"

Putting Yourself in Another's Shoes

Putting yourself in the other person's shoes, or developing your skill in experiencing empathy, is another way to test your initial assumptions There are two forms of empathy—both are helpful in moving out of the answer and into the question.

One form of empathy is known as perspective-taking, or putting oneself in another's shoes. The other, known as emotional empathy, occurs when a person feels concern and compassion, often spontaneously, for what another is feeling. Perspective-taking is a thought process, while emotional empathy is an emotional process. This distinction is important because research has shown that inadequate comprehension of different cultural perspectives (perspective-taking) lessens feelings of compassion and concern (emotional empathy).[7]

CURIOUS ABOUT THE RESEARCH?

Researchers have found that perspective-takers experience more empathetic concern, are more likely to consider situational context, are less likely to stereotype, and have more positive attitudes toward people in different social groups.

Vescio, T. K., Sechrist, G. B., & Paolucci, M. P. (2003). Perspective taking and prejudice reduction: The mediational role of empathy arousal and situational attributions. *European Journal of Social Psychology, 33*(4), 455–472.

Perspective-taking can be learned. One method for taking another's perspective is called Generating Three Hypotheses. This method allows you to test your initial assumptions and beliefs, and generate alternative explanations or hypotheses for events. The word "hypotheses" is used to remind you that your beliefs about the motivations behind the other person's actions are only educated guesses, something to be tested. By converting your beliefs from assumed facts to hypotheses, you open the door to seeing other possibilities.

The first of the three hypotheses is the negative belief influencing your first reaction. The second and third hypotheses suggest other possible explanations from the perspective of the troublesome individuals. How might those involved explain their actions as right and reasonable?

For the second hypothesis, construct a good intent hypothesis—that is, give people the benefit of the doubt. Even though their actions may have had a negative impact, assume that every individual involved had only the best intentions.

For the third hypothesis, construct an explanation that takes into account the kinds of situational factors that are no-fault; those in which the structure of the situation or the organization has led to negative actions or consequences. In other words, imagine that the troublesome person felt forced into the negative action by circumstances.

To be effective in going beyond your traditional assumptions, the second and third hypotheses must be plausible. As long as you hold the possibility that more than one of the three could be true, you are in the question.

What additional plausible hypotheses might Tyla have formulated about why Matthew turned away from her after she waved to him? She had her negative hypothesis: Matthew was holding her remark in the staff meeting against her. To be sure, she believed it. Still, if she can consider it as only a hypothesis, she might be more inclined to consider testing its accuracy.

One good intent hypothesis is that Matthew had something else on his mind: maybe he was thinking about the conversation he had just had with his supervisor. Remembering something important he had left unsaid, he may have turned quickly to return to his office to share the information before he forgot—and not even have noticed Tyla. This is called a good intent hypothesis because there is no assumption that Matthew intended any harm, even though Tyla's feelings were hurt.

A situational hypothesis is that Matthew is nearsighted but usually wears contacts. His contacts may have been bothering him recently, causing him to take them out. Since he didn't use his glasses for reading, he hadn't been wearing them while working and didn't put them on before walking down the hall. Tyla was just a blur in the distance.

Simply generating multiple hypotheses, especially ones that remove blame and consider other factors, can help you become more aware of your perceptual filters and learn to take the perspective of others. If you attempt to understand others' actions, you are less likely to judge them harshly and more likely to be able to live or work with them effectively.

Uncovering Cultural Expectations

Another method for testing your assumptions is to consider whether events may be caused by differing cultural expectations. Many people are surprised to discover that seemingly simple situations can be interpreted in very different ways by individuals from different backgrounds.

The Case of the Potluck Lunch

A small staff held a holiday potluck dinner, with each person bringing a different dish. At the end of the meal, Yolanda freely fixed herself a plate of all the dishes she especially liked to take home to her family. Although she said nothing, Polly was offended by this, expecting instead that people would take home the leftovers of the dishes they had brought. Secretly, she thought Yolanda's action was selfish and presumptuous. Yolanda sensed Polly's annoyance, but attributed this reaction to the fact that she hadn't chosen any of the dishes Polly brought.

What assumptions might be tested here?

- Polly's assumption: Yolanda was being selfish and presumptuous in creating a sampler of leftovers made by others to take home.
- Yolanda's assumption: Polly was insulted that Yolanda didn't include samples of any of the dishes Polly had brought.

Fortunately, this work group freely discussed cultural differences. A third person noticed the tension between Yolanda and Polly and inquired about it. As it turned out, neither Polly's nor Yolanda's attribution about the other was accurate. That is, Yolanda was not motivated by selfishness, and Polly was not insulted.

Rather, each had different learned cultural assumptions about how potluck leftovers were to be dispersed. The three Whites among the staff, including Polly, assumed each person would either take their own dish home or offer it to others. Yolanda and another Black staff member considered all food community property, so they assumed people would freely choose what to take home from the whole smorgasbord. A third Black person also considered all food community property, but felt the person who organized the potluck should have first choice of what to take home since she was the informal hostess of the dinner.

Note that Polly had no awareness of the cultural assumptions underpinning her irritation. Rather, she assumed her beliefs about the disposition of leftover potluck dishes were universally shared. Under this assumption, Yolanda was obviously acting selfishly. Likewise, Yolanda had no awareness that her behavior offended Polly since she was merely doing what people in her family had done for generations with potluck meals—sharing freely. Unaware of having committed an offense according to Polly's cultural norms, she interpreted Polly's standoffishness with an assumption that made sense in her culture: Polly was insulted because Yolanda hadn't taken any of her food.

Researchers have identified some cultural assumptions that frequently cause conflicts among individuals from different social groups.[8] Table 2.1 contains a few of these assumptions.

Which cultural assumptions in Table 2.1 might have contributed to Polly and Yolanda's differing perceptions?

In Polly's individualistic culture as a White American, since the food was brought by individuals, individuals retained ownership after dinner was over. In Yolanda's more collectivist culture as a Black African American,[9] the community freely shared leftovers. Neither was right and neither wrong—except in the other's culture.

Table 2.1
Cultural Assumptions of Different Social Groups

Cultural Assumptions		Reflection Questions
Individualism	*Collectivism*	In what ways might an individual's behavior be explained by an individualistic vs. collectivist orientation?
Values self-reliance and autonomy; prefers individually based reward systems.	More likely to focus on group interests and downplay individual ones; more satisfied with team-based rewards.	
Competitive Behavior	*Cooperative Behavior*	Does my interpretation of the other person's actions rely on an assumption of the value of competition?
Is highly competitive in social interaction and task performance.	Favors more interdependent and cooperative approaches.	
Individual Causation	*Situational Causation*	Does the individual share my beliefs about people being in charge of their own destiny?
Believes that individuals themselves are the primary cause of events in their lives.	Believes that the primary cause of events is external and often uncontrollable.	
Direct Communication Style	*Reflective Communication Style*	Am I judging someone negatively because their communication style is different from my own?
Speaks directly, assertively, and openly.	Listens reflectively, respectfully, and avoids public embarrassment.	
Task Leadership Style	*Relationship Leadership Style*	Is there a possible conflict here between task and relationship-oriented approaches to this issue?
Is more task-oriented with instrumental emphasis on task completion.	Is more relationship-oriented with emphasis on creating and maintaining strong interpersonal relationships.	
Linear Time Orientation	*Flexible Time Orientation*	Am I using my own view of time as the standard against which I judge the other's behaviors?
Has linear time orientation with emphasis on scheduling appointments, specification of beginning and ending times for events, and use of long-range planning.	Uses more elastic interpretation of time with flexibility in beginning and ending times for events; more emphasis on the present and less on the future.	

There may be an element of competitive vs. cooperative outlook operating here too. Yolanda's hypothesis that Polly was insulted because she hadn't taken any of *her* leftovers may have reflected Yolanda's cultural assumptions about the competitive nature of others.

Note that group differences do not necessarily apply to every individual in the group. In this instance, Yolanda came from a collectivist-oriented background and Polly came from an individualistic one. In another scenario, each of these individuals might have come from families who were exceptions to their traditional cultural norms.

Polly and Yolanda belonged to a work group in which such discussions were held. However, most people don't. You may need to take the initiative in acknowledging or asking about cultural differences.

It is important to note that cultural differences go beyond the obvious ones of national or ethnic origin. All social group memberships influence your assumptions, views, and beliefs—whether they are a result of ethnicity, biology (e.g., gender, age, sexual orientation), hierarchy (socio-economic class, occupation, positional authority), geographic location (nation, region, urban vs. rural) or other factors.

Considering possible cultural factors is another way of testing one's initial assumptions. As Tyla thinks about why Matthew ignored her greeting, she might consider the possibility that cultural differences played a role. If Matthew had a different cultural upbringing than Tyla, he could be angry at Tyla for criticizing him during the staff meeting. He might have been socialized to regard public criticism as unprofessional behavior, personally humiliating, and undermining of respect and personal relationships. Tyla, on the other hand, could have been raised in a culture valuing directness and the concept of "telling it like it is."

CHOOSING TO TEST ASSUMPTIONS

Tyla was certain that Matthew had deliberately ignored her greeting. Under those circumstances, it might be difficult for her to move from being in the answer to being in the question.

> As she sat at her desk stewing about Matthew, a friend called to see if she wanted to go to lunch. During lunch, Tyla found herself blurting out the whole interaction with Matthew and how stressed out she felt by his reaction. Chris listened carefully and then said, "Tyla, didn't we talk about something like this in that seminar we took together? Do you remember? We talked about testing assumptions."
>
> "Are you implying that I may be wrong about Matthew?" asked Tyla. "I don't think so. You didn't see his face this morning."

"Well, I can only tell you what's worked for me since we did the workshop. When I find myself thinking I absolutely know why somebody is doing something I don't like, I stop and notice what I'm doing. Then I consider my assumption as a hypothesis, try to dispute it, and test it. I've tried it in my job and with my family and it works for me enough of the time that I keep trying it. And I'm getting better at it."

By the end of a rehash of the seminar over lunch, Tyla was able to entertain the question of the accuracy of her assumption about Matthew. "I'm at least 90% sure I'm right," she conceded, "but I'm willing to test the other 10%." This was entering into the question, at least on tiptoe. After lunch, Tyla continued to think about the situation. She recognized that her belief in Matthew's anger with her was causing her to feel angry in return. If she wasn't careful, she realized that these feelings could lead to escalating conflict between them. It had happened before. So she pulled out a pad and listed some what if questions. Once she had done that, she felt a little better and decided to go by his office and check some of her assumptions out.

"So, Matthew," she said, "how come you didn't say hello to me in the hallway earlier today?"

"What are you talking about?" replied Matthew, puzzled. "I don't remember seeing you in the hallway. I haven't seen you since the staff meeting this morning."

At this point, Tyla noticed a pair of glasses on Matthew's desk.

"I thought you wore contacts," she asked.

"I usually do, but my eyes started burning right after the staff meeting, so I took them out and have been using my glasses since."

"So can you see without your glasses?" continued Tyla, remembering he hadn't been wearing glasses when she'd seen him in the hallway.

"Only close up. Things are blurry a few feet away, though. Why do you ask?"

Here Tyla began to see another possible explanation for Matthew's earlier behavior, but remained doubtful. Had Matthew really avoided her and was now trying to cover up? She had enough doubt to suspect she would still be uneasy around him unless she surfaced her negative hypothesis. She decided to use the three hypotheses approach. Since he had already given her a situational explanation (he wasn't wearing his contacts), she began with that.

"I asked because I waved at you in the hallway earlier and you didn't respond," she began. "So I wondered if something was wrong. Thinking about it later, I realized one possible reason was that you didn't actually see me, so I'm glad to hear you confirm that."

"One possible reason?" Matthew responded immediately. "What other reason could there be?"

"Well," Tyla responded as she braced herself to continue the discussion, "I wondered if you saw me, planned to wave, but then your attention got diverted for some reason."

Note that this is a good intent hypothesis. It gives Matthew the benefit of the doubt.

Matthew cocked his head to one side, "You've really given this a lot of thought, haven't you? Are you sure you're not being hypersensitive?"

Tyla swallowed hard. She could feel her defenses rising but decided to stay focused on her purpose in the conversation. With a deep breath, she added, "Matthew, I'll be straight with you. I had another thought about what might be going on. I found myself fantasizing that you ignored me because you were annoyed with me."

"You thought I deliberately ignored you because of this morning???" asked Matthew incredulously.

Tyla could feel her heart beating. Staring straight at Matthew, she continued, "It's embarrassing to admit because I don't like to think of people as being vindictive, but yes, I did wonder if that was at least part of the reason."

"Well, if you're going to be straight with me, I'll be straight with you," Matthew replied. "I didn't like the way you jumped on my case this morning. I didn't like it at all. But that had nothing to do with not speaking to you. I didn't ignore you. I simply didn't see you."

There it was, out in the open. Tyla could now separate the two events. She had been correct in sensing Matthew's unhappiness with her actions earlier in the morning, but she had been incorrect in her assumption that not acknowledging her greeting was the result. Furthermore, her honesty with him prompted him to be honest in return.

Matthew was disturbed that she thought he had deliberately ignored her. However, the way she surfaced her suspicions made all the difference. First, she put it as a series of hypotheses about what might have happened. She raised the situational and good intent hypotheses before bringing forth her negative hypothesis. Second, she explained that she "found herself fantasizing" about the idea, clearly framing her negative hypothesis as speculation rather than conviction. Third, she admitted that the idea "embarrassed her" and that she didn't like to think of people as "vindictive." Together, this sequence of explanations made the idea seem less accusatory, even though Matthew did wonder if she were being "hypersensitive."

Her hypothesis about what was going on with Matthew had been partially correct, but not fully so. This is the beauty of overtly testing one's negative hypotheses: often, people sense something wrong about their interactions with others, but misattribute the cause. Even after his missing contacts surfaced as a plausible reason for Matthew's behavior, Tyla remained unconvinced. She had sensed something wrong in their previous interaction. While unrelated to his lack of greeting, her comments during the staff meeting had upset Matthew. They can now begin to discuss this interaction without the overlay of unnecessary bad feelings. By taking the risk to approach him to test her assumptions, Tyla now stands a better chance of repairing her relationship with Matthew.

RETRAINING NEURAL PATHWAYS

Tyla reflected on the close call with Matthew. If she had stayed in the answer and treated Matthew as though he had deliberately ignored her, their relationship could have slowly deteriorated. What about the next time something like that happened? Would she fall back into being in the answer again?

She called Chris. "I've been wondering how you've been able to use what we learned in seminar. You helped me with Matthew this time, but I can't keep calling you every time I have a problem with someone."

Chris chuckled. "First of all, Tyla," he said, "I had strong motivation to start using it. When we took the class, my relationship with Jeremy was rocky. I felt I had nothing to lose by trying it with him at home, so I did. And it worked."

"What made you stick with it?" Tyla asked.

"What got my attention was what we learned about retraining our neural pathways."

"Retraining neural pathways? I don't remember anything about that."

"It's probably in your notes somewhere. The idea is that our habits are held in place by neural connections in our brain. The denser the neural pathways, the more entrenched the habit. Here's why the idea stuck with me. I stretch every morning. I don't consciously decide to stretch; I just roll out of bed, go to the bathroom, come back, get on the floor, and start stretching. It's automatic. But I didn't used to do this. Several years ago, some friends talked me into running a marathon with them. I was really out of shape and knew that if I didn't regularly stretch, I could seriously injure myself. So I decided it was worth my while to deliberately form the habit. It wasn't easy, but after a few months of on-again, off-again stretching, it became a habit. Now, it's so much a habit that if for some reason I can't stretch, I don't feel right.

"So, when we talked about retraining neural pathways in class, I remembered my morning stretching and how I went about cultivating that habit, and thought, 'Well, if I could develop the habit of stretching every day, I can develop a better habit of responding to Jeremy to give our relationship a greater chance of growing into a life partnership.'"

Tyla responded, "Retraining neural pathways, huh? Isn't that a fancy way of saying developing a new habit?"

Chris responded quickly, "Sure, it is. But thinking about it as retraining my neural pathways made it easier to stick with. I realized that the neural pathways connecting waking up with stretching weren't dense enough. Thinking of it as retraining neural pathways changed how I thought about the goal. The new goal was for the neural pathways in my brain to get so strong that I didn't have to think about it, I would just do it."

"And how does that work for you in your relationship with Jeremy?"

"After the seminar, I set a goal of being in the question more. Whenever Jeremy—or anyone for that matter—got on my nerves, I wanted to stop automatically assuming the worst of the person's motives. If I stayed in the question and tested my assumptions, I figured I'd get along better with people. I was right. My relationships with others at home and work have improved."

CURIOUS ABOUT THE RESEARCH?

Jeffrey Schwartz and Sharon Begley coined the term "self-directed neuroplasticity" to refer to the act of deliberately altering how one's brain functions through focused effort and training. People with obsessive compulsive disorder have been taught to resist their intrusive and bothersome thoughts and urges and to stop the frequency of their obsessive rituals (e.g., repetitive hand washing).

Schwartz, J. M., & Begley, S. (2002). *The mind & the brain: Neuroplasticity and the power of mental force.* New York: HarperCollins.

The last two decades have spawned an outpouring of research integrating neuroscience (the study of how the physical brain is structured and operates) and psychology (the study of how and why people think, feel, and behave as they do). With the advent of brain imaging and other sophisticated technologies, scientists have been able to learn much about how the brain is wired and which areas of the brain are involved in processing various types of information. Prior to these studies, it had commonly been assumed that the adult brain changed very little. One of the most exciting findings has been that the brain changes constantly, dropping old and forging new connections between neurons (brain cells) as people encounter new experiences and information. The implications of this are enormous: neuroscientists have discovered that, without surgery or drugs, people can deliberately change the wiring of their brains through what they choose to pay attention to. Neural connections used repeatedly are strengthened, while those not used tend to weaken. The act of learning itself is seen as the key to stimulating new neural connections.[10]

Habits are held in place by particularly strong neural connections linking one set of actions to another. Such habits can be broken over time as people adopt new thoughts and activities and repeat them over and over. With each repetition, the brain develops and strengthens new synapses.

As Chris discovered, getting better at testing assumptions and letting go of initial judgments about others does not happen quickly. Yet with practice, you can learn to consciously choose alternative thoughts—over time it can become automatic. Instead of blaming others, you can learn to notice your either/or thinking and emotional reactions and use them as signals to question your immediate responses and assumptions. As you develop your ability to see others' perspectives, you better understand their realities and see new possibilities for effective interactions and relationships. By repeatedly working to understand others' perspectives in different situations and to distinguish their intentions from the impact you felt, you begin to think more complexly and develop the ability to see multiple perspectives. This allows you to see and feel all sides of an issue, and become more comfortable with contradictions.

"I'm definitely going to try it," declared Tyla. "It seems simple enough, but I can imagine that sticking with it is the hardest part."

"You got that right!" responded Chris immediately. "One way I've found to help keep me in the question is to deliberately build more positive emotions."

BUILDING POSITIVE EMOTIONS

Positive emotions influence both thoughts and behaviors. Something as simple as a broad smile of enjoyment changes brain activity.[11] Twenty years of experiments by Alice Isen and her colleagues demonstrate that when people feel good, their thinking becomes more creative, integrative, flexible, and open to information.[12]

One of the interesting things about these studies is that simple methods were used to induce positive feelings. The most common such methods were to give participants a small (less than $1 value) unanticipated gift, have them watch a funny film, read cartoons, or arrange for them to experience success on an ambiguous task.[13]

> "The studies show," continued Chris, "that it only takes little things to make you feel better—and feeling better allows you to more easily test your assumptions or consider alternative explanations for actions and statements that might otherwise irritate you. A friend of mine told me he uses an image of his toddler nephew laughing and playing to counter negative thoughts."

CURIOUS ABOUT THE RESEARCH?

Barbara Fredrickson at the University of Michigan found that positive emotions such as joy, interest, and contentment broaden a person's options—what she calls an individual's "thought-action repertoire."

Fredrickson, B. L. (2000). Cultivating positive emotions to optimize health and well-being. *Prevention & Treatment* (Vol. 3), Article 0001a.

Tyla said, "Thanks, this has been very helpful. At work, we keep hearing about the importance of taking care of ourselves because our jobs are so stressful. Deliberately building my positive emotions sounds like a good self-care technique to try!"

"Thank *you*, Tyla," responded Chris. "It's been helpful for me to talk about it. Since I've learned to pay attention, every time I pick up a newspaper, I've noticed how many problems or conflicts described are likely to have been started by someone engaged in either/or thinking or making assumptions. The way I figure it, the more people get into testing their assumptions, the better off we'll all be."

NOTES

1. Senge, P. M. (1990). *The fifth discipline*. New York: Currency Doubleday.
2. Steiner, C. M. (1974). *Scripts people live*. New York: Grove Press.
3. Turner, J. H. (1999). Toward a general sociological theory of emotions. *Journal for the Theory of Social Behaviour, 29*, 133–161.

4. Newman, L. S., Duff, K. J., & Baumeister, R. F. (1997). A new look at defensive projection: Thought suppression, accessibility, and biased person perception. *Journal of Personality and Social Psychology, 72*(5), 980–1001.

5. Fredrickson, B. L. (2001). The role of positive emotions in positive psychology: The broaden-and-build theory of positive emotions. *American Psychologist, 56*(3), 218–226.

6. Bushe, G. R. (2001). *Clear leadership*. Palo Alto, CA: Davies-Black.

7. Nelson, D. W., & Baumgartner, R. (2004). Cross-cultural misunderstandings reduce empathic responding. *Journal of Applied Social Psychology, 34*(2), 391–401.

8. Cox, T., Jr. (1993). *Cultural diversity in organizations: Theory, research & practice*. San Francisco: Berrett-Koehler.

9. Cox, T. H., Label, S. A., & McLeod, P. L. (1991). Effects of ethnic group cultural differences on cooperative and competitive behavior on a group task. *Academy of Management Journal, 34*(4), 827–847.

10. Goleman D., Boyatzis, R., & McKee, A. (2002). *Primal leadership: Realizing the power of emotional intelligence*. Boston: Harvard Business School Press.

11. Ekman, P., & Davidson, R. J. (1993). Voluntary smiling changes regional brain activity. *Psychological Science, 4*(5), 342–345.

12. Isen, A. M. (2001). An influence of positive affect on decision making in complex situations: Theoretical issues with practical implications. *Journal of Consumer Psychology, 11*(2), 75–85.

13. Ashby, F. G., Isen, A. M., & Turken, A. U. (1999). A neuropsychological theory of positive affect and its influence on cognition. *Psychological Review, 106*(3), 529–550.

CHAPTER 3

Clearing Emotions

Peg was angry. The team had worked for three weeks to produce a meaningful set of recommendations. They had overcome setback after setback, including the skepticism of a key executive whose approval was critical. Now here they were with the report due by the close of the business day and Jamal had just called to say his computer had crashed, taking with it the latest version of the report document. They had talked about the importance of backing up files and Jamal had promised to send all team members the latest version two days ago as added insurance. But had he done so?

Searching the files on her hard drive, she discovered that the most recent version she had on file was five days old. As team leader on the project, she had handed off the nearly final recommendations to Jamal and his sub-team for them to work on the graphics, check the data, and clean up some of the imprecise writing. Peg glanced at the clock—7:30 A.M.! What could be done now?

Returning to Jamal on the telephone, she demanded to know how he planned to handle the problem. Out came a litany of excuses, explanations, and apologies which only infuriated her more. Instead of responding to his unspoken plea for understanding and forgiveness, she listened silently, hoping the silence would convey her intense disapproval. She repeated her question, "What do you intend to do?", thinking she would really let him have it if he didn't simply answer her question. This time he did, offering to "call everyone and collect the completed sections and put it all together again."

"Since you've blown our deadline, that's the least you can do!" Peg responded, with daggers in her voice. She hung up abruptly before Jamal could say anything else. She knew how angry she sounded. She also knew that in subtle but definitive ways she had broken her vow to always treat others with respect. Instead, she had done her best to make Jamal feel as badly as she was feeling. But he deserved it, didn't he?

Peg had worked hard to involve the team members in the project and believed in strength-focused leadership and empowerment. Yet, the force of her negative emotions was overwhelming her. She hadn't completely lambasted Jamal, but she worried that she might have done real harm to their relationship.

Looking at the clock, she saw that her morning training session was about to begin. "I shouldn't have signed up right before the project deadline," she muttered to herself. Yet she had committed and there was nothing she could do about the situation. She left to attend the seminar.

When she entered the seminar room, the session topic caught her eye: Managing Negative Emotions: Resolving Conflicts within Yourself. "I'm certainly feeling some negative emotions right now," she thought. "So it looks like this is timely."

I was the session leader and since it was a small group. I noticed Peg's agitation as she walked in. This was the third in a four-part training series on conflict resolution. I knew the session might be tough for some because the ideas were likely to be novel to them.

"Today we're going to talk about handling the negative emotions that drive our internal conflicts," I began. "The goal is for you to leave this session with concrete action steps to take when you're so angry or resentful you can't think straight, or you wake up at 3:00 A.M. and can't get back to sleep." They laughed. "Let's start by looking at the first handout (Table 3.1). How might any of it apply to a situation in your own life?"

Peg immediately raised her hand. "I'm glad I don't know anyone here," she began, "because I want to talk about something that happened this morning with a team member."

I interjected, "Thanks for volunteering right off the bat! Before you or anyone else speaks, I ask that we remember that some of the people we talk about today aren't here to explain their side of the story. My request of each of you is to remember that everyone in a given situation may see things differently. Is that agreed?" They all nodded and I signaled Peg to continue.

Table 3.1
Managing Your Emotions

AVOID identifying with your emotions.	START identifying with your values.
AVOID trusting your judgment when you're emotionally flooded.	START considering your impact on others when you're emotionally flooded.
AVOID trying to suppress your negative emotions.	START learning how to recognize and release your negative emotions.
AVOID fixating on what is not working.	START cultivating positive emotions about what is working.

By the time she finished describing her morning conversation with Jamal, everyone was nodding sympathetically. "Been there, done that," said Stefan. "At least you didn't completely blow your stack like I did with my wife this morning."

"You did that and are still able to walk?" asked Robyn with a grin.

"Oh, I called to apologize on my way here," responded Stefan. "I wanted to get in the house when I go home tonight."

Everyone laughed again.

"Peg," I asked, "would it be alright if we use what happened with you and Jamal as an example for this session?"

"Sure," she responded. "I don't seem to be alone in handling things badly when I'm upset, so it's fine."

"Yup. We're all right there with you," chimed in the others.

EMOTIONS AND FEELINGS

"Let's talk first about the neurophysiology of emotions," I began.

"Neurophysiology? What kind of a psychobabble word is that?" asked Stefan mockingly.

"Just hang on for the ride, folks," I responded, acknowledging their skepticism about the jargon. "I'm hoping to make this trip worth it for you."

In recent years, an explosion of research has yielded fascinating information about how the brain functions—how it produces thoughts and feelings and how these interact to affect decision-making, relationships, and even leadership.[1] The field is vast and I knew I could only provide the rudiments of these discoveries. I wanted them to understand enough, however, to give them some insight into their own emotional reactions.

The first step was for them to distinguish between emotions and feelings.[2] Most neuroscientists regard emotions as automatic physiological reactions; not necessarily the product of conscious thought. You may or may not be aware of them. Feelings, on the other hand, result from conscious awareness of one's emotions.

CURIOUS ABOUT THE RESEARCH?

A widely accepted view is that held by neurologist Antonio Damasio: the brain constantly receives signals from the body and processes the signals in the form of neural maps or representations. As the maps are read by the brain and emotional changes recorded, feelings are experienced. Feelings may occur in reaction to real or simulated stimuli experienced by the body. One form of simulation is empathy, occurring when our brains recreate someone else's experience.

Lenzen, M. (2005). Feeling our emotions [An interview with noted neurologist Antonio R. Damasio]. *Scientific American Mind 16*(1), 14–15.

"In other words," I explained, "you can have an emotion without consciously feeling it, but every feeling reflects some emotion."

"Huh?" asked Stefan. "You can have an emotion and not have a feeling, but you can't have a feeling without an emotion?"

"Interesting, isn't it?" I responded. "Have you ever watched someone have a physical response to something—they grimace, blush or jump—yet insist they're 'just fine,' not troubled at all?"

Everyone nodded.

"The individual may not be having the feeling consciously, but their body's showing an emotional reaction.

"Sometimes there's a lag time between our physical reaction and awareness of the feeling. Here's an analogy. If you touch a hot pot, your hand may move away from it before your brain consciously registers 'hot' or 'ouch' or whatever. What makes this important is that you sometimes find yourself taking action before you even think about whether it's wise or not."

Remembering how agitated Peg had looked when she first walked in, I reflected on how all-consuming and overwhelming really strong emotions can be. Because emotions are so compelling, many people have no sense of self as separate from how they are feeling in the moment. A person may say, "I am furious," not "I feel furious." There's a world of difference between those two statements. The first connotes permanent identification with one's emotions; the second describes a temporary state which may change over time.

> "You are not your emotions or feelings," I explained. "You are having an experience with your emotions—one that will go away at some point. You won't always feel this way. Instead of thinking of your emotions as who you are, consider identifying with your principles and values—by standing for what you believe in."

> Peg spoke up, "Being ticked off at Jamal felt all-consuming to me. I was overwhelmed by anger and didn't know what to do about it."

> "What to do when our emotions are screaming at us is the heart of this workshop," I responded. "But before we get to that, I want to provide a little more background about why we have these emotions and feelings in the first place."

From an evolutionary perspective, emotions and feelings developed as part of human survival instincts. Emotions and feelings help you respond to what is useful or threatening to your well-being: a frown on a person's face may prompt you to reflexively move away or signal your readiness to fight back; a smile may draw you closer.[3] These are automatic impulses—a call to action. Feelings alert you to pay attention to these impulses.

> "Just because you have an emotion or feeling doesn't mean you have to act on whatever impulse it produces," I explained. "You may feel threatened by a coworker and want to lay the person out, but that doesn't mean the coworker intended any threat. By paying attention to your feelings, you can learn to consciously choose more effective actions. The first step is to pay attention."

> Robyn spoke up, "But what if there are things I'd rather not feel?"

> "Great question!" I responded. "Most of us have times when we'd rather not feel one way or another. But if you don't acknowledge your feelings, you risk getting stuck in some emotion with your body trying to act while your brain is preventing you from taking action—or even allowing you to feel it. This is part of the stuck feeling. Your body is saying go, but your brain is saying no."

> I turned to Peg. "Are you feeling stuck?"

> "Yes," she acknowledged.

> "You said you're feeling angry. Are you feeling anything else?"

Peg stared at me blankly. "What else am I feeling? I don't know . . . Well, I feel sad, disrespected." She hesitated, "I guess I'm feeling a lot of different things."

"How did it feel to make those distinctions?" I asked.

"Actually, it's kind of strange. I hadn't been aware of the sad and disrespected parts."

"How about trying something?" I asked. "A friend of mine who is trained in transactional analysis says there are four primary emotions, and if you feel stuck, it's helpful to examine which of the four is operating. These four emotions are sad, mad, glad, and scared. Which are you feeling right now?"

CURIOUS ABOUT THE RESEARCH?

Different researchers have come up with different typologies to describe feelings. Claude Steiner, a transactional analyst and theorist, described the four basic feelings as mad, sad, scared, and glad. More recently, Theodore Kemper proposed four primary emotions: anger, depression, fear, and satisfaction. Both Kemper and Steiner suggest that all other emotions or feelings (such as guilt, pride, melancholy, and gratitude) are combinations of these four.

Steiner, C. M. (1974). *Scripts people live.* New York: Grove Press.

Kemper, T. D. (1987). How many emotions are there? Wedding the social and autonomic components. *American Journal of Sociology, 93*(2), 263–289.

"Well, I definitely feel mad and sad," Peg responded. "Glad doesn't register. As for scared . . ." She paused and then took a deep breath, "Actually, I'm terrified." With this, she sighed so deeply her whole chest seemed to collapse. "I'm terrified," she repeated as though aware of it for the first time.

"What just happened?" I asked her.

"It's odd," she responded. "I feel a bit clearer. I'm not sure how to describe it."

I smiled in acknowledgment. Her relief, however slight, was a pleasure to see. "If you want to be able to use your feelings to inform your actions," I explained, "it helps to put labels on the feelings—to name them.[4] When I'm stuck, one of the first things I do is try to ferret out exactly what I'm feeling. I check to see if mad, sad, glad, and scared are in there. More often than not, for me, they're all there."

CURIOUS ABOUT THE RESEARCH?

Research has shown that being able to identify, or differentiate, negative emotions helps individuals regulate them. In a series of research studies, people who focused on and specified their feelings actually experienced less emotional arousal and were better able to problem solve than did those who ruminated about them in a general fashion.

Barrett, L. F., Gross, J., Christensen, T. C., & Benvenuto, M. (2001). Knowing what you're feeling and knowing what to do about it: Mapping the relation between emotion differentiation and emotion regulation. *Cognition and Emotion, 15*(6), 713–724.

Philippot, P., Baeyens, C., Douilliez, C., & Francart, B. (2004). Cognitive regulation of emotion: Application to clinical disorders. In P. Philippot & R. S. Feldman (Eds.), *The regulation of emotion* (pp. 71–97). Mahwah, NJ: Lawrence Erlbaum Associates.

"It did help to name my feelings. But now I'm having another, which is embarrassment," responded Peg.

"I'm not surprised," I replied. "In most work settings talking about feelings—particularly feelings of sadness and fear—is a no-no. As a result, in many workplaces, people claim their decision-making is perfectly rational—no emotion involved. Ironically, researchers have discovered that emotional reactions can aid in decision-making and emotional self-awareness can help you become more effective. Peg is showing us how this is done."

THE EMOTIONALLY FLOODED MANAGER

I looked around. Peg had a more relaxed look and the others were watching with quiet interest.

"Peg," I asked, "when you were talking with Jamal, did you recognize that you were angry?"

"Oh, yes! If he'd been in the room, I might've clobbered him."

"That sounds like anger alright. Strong emotions frequently signal that you need to do something right away. This is a big help if they warn you to jump out of the way of a falling tree limb. But sometimes strong negative emotions lead you to do something that creates danger rather than keeps you out of harm's way. If you'd actually clobbered Jamal, you would've had worse problems than a missed deadline. Having the urge to do that shows how limited you are when you're emotionally flooded."

Peg responded almost inaudibly, "That's how I felt—emotionally flooded."

I looked questioningly at Stefan. He nodded in assent, "Yeah, like I was this morning with my wife."

Peg studied the handout. "It says to avoid trusting yourself when you're emotionally flooded and consider your impact on others instead. When I was talking with Jamal, I wasn't thinking about anything but the trouble we were in. Is this saying I should've recognized that I was emotionally flooded and thought instead about how I was impacting Jamal?"

I stayed silent, waiting for her to finish her train of thought.

After a moment, she continued, "That doesn't make sense to me! Why should I have thought about how I affected him? Wasn't getting the job done more important than his petty feelings?"

"Peg," I responded, "you say you were emotionally flooded. At the time, was it really a choice between his feelings and the job?"

"Of course not," she replied. "All I could see . . . no, I couldn't see anything. I was furious. I knew something was wrong as soon as I heard the first words out of his mouth. I could feel myself getting hot and cold at the same time."

I grinned at her. "That sounds like the fight or flight response, Peg. A whole variety of chemicals and stress hormones were flooding your system, getting you ready to face the danger. A key skill is recognizing when you're emotionally flooded. You felt hot and cold and you can name those feelings, so you're already ahead of the game." I looked at the others, "So what was her response to Jamal?"

Stefan jumped in, "She punished him with coldness—just as I punished my wife with fire!"

"Yes," I responded. "Fight or flight. Some people go hot and respond with fight by lashing out. Others go cold and withdraw emotionally. Both are symptoms of emotional flooding."

I glanced at Peg to see if she was still okay with our continuing use of her example. She was smiling, seeming to await more. This was working for her, so I continued.

During her interaction with Jamal, an everyday miracle was occurring inside Peg's brain. The sound of Jamal's voice entered her ears and traveled from neuron to neuron to the region of the brain known as the thalamus, a gland that processes stimuli from the environment. From there, the information had two possible routes to travel—the long route or the short route. The dominant route would determine her response to Jamal.

In the long route, the information travels from the thalamus to the prefrontal cortex, the part of the brain that analyzes and handles decision-making tasks, and helps inhibit impulsive behavior. In the short route, information goes from the thalamus to the amygdala, the part of the brain associated with hot buttons, based in part on emotional memories from past hurts, abuses, and disappointments.[5] When the short route is taken, information reaches the amygdala so quickly that the prefrontal cortex doesn't have time to analyze or reflect on what to do next.

"Slow down," exclaimed Stefan. "You're using a lot of big words!"

"Yes, indeed," I acknowledged. "There are only three parts of the brain I'm asking you to understand. The *thalamus* receives input from the world, the *prefrontal cortex* decides what to do with that information, and the *amygdala* tells you how to feel about it. Here is a graphic to show you what I'm describing."

"Now obviously, I've simplified this greatly in terms of what actually happens. These three parts of the brain are not the whole story. I'm reducing to bare bones what is, in fact, a complex and intricate web of neural circuits. That being said, let's see how Figure 3.1 applies to Peg."

If the news from Jamal had come a few days earlier when there was more time to recover before the report was due, it might have traveled the long route, reaching Peg's prefrontal cortex with time for her to realize something was amiss and consider how best to respond. The prefrontal cortex and other memory systems in the brain might have reminded her that, despite this mistake, Jamal was an excellent member of the team. She might have remembered praising Jamal the week before for creating a diagram that really enhanced the report. From the prefrontal cortex, the information would have also traveled to her amygdala. Her amygdala and related brain parts might have received an earlier direct news flash from her thalamus, resulting in a momentary reaction of irritation; however, this signal would have been weak, not nearly strong enough to overwhelm her prefrontal cortex as it received the same, but delayed information. All this would have allowed her to put her irritation in perspective and relax.

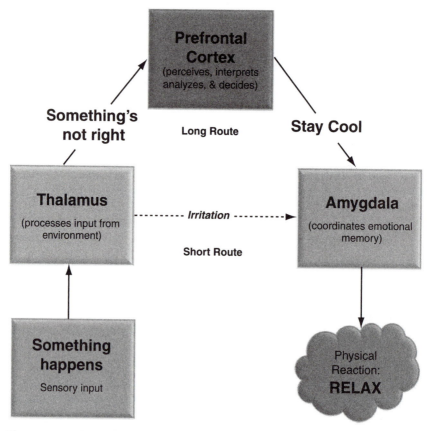

Figure 3.1   © Jean Kantambu Latting & V. Jean Ramsey, 2007–2009.

Stefan studied the figure. "Why does it matter?" asked Stefan. "It's kind of interesting, but I don't know what I'm supposed to do with this information."

"Let me describe the short route," I responded. "Then the answer to your question may become clearer."

He nodded and I continued.

Judging by Peg's actual response to Jamal, the input about Jamal's action did not travel the long route. Instead, only the short route, a fight or flight response, was activated, as shown in Figure 3.2. With the first words she heard from Jamal, the neural information in Peg's thalamus took a short-cut straight to her amygdala where an immediate alarm was registered. This occurred so rapidly that the prefrontal cortex had no time to assess the best way to respond to Jamal, let alone think through whether the incident was a true crisis or only

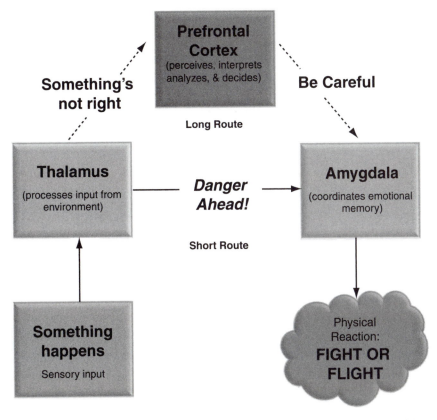

Figure 3.2   © Jean Kantambu Latting & V. Jean Ramsey, 2007–2009.

a temporary setback. The amygdala's immediate reactions virtually commanded Peg's neuromuscular system to issue a cutting—and chilly—response to Jamal.

> What were the hot buttons being triggered for Peg? I internally debated asking her forthrightly and decided to do so. "Peg, you may or may not want to answer this, but I'd like to ask you a personal question."
>
> She burst into laughter at my question. "How much more personal can this discussion get?" she teased.
>
> I smiled in acknowledgement and continued, "Is there anything in your past that made Jamal's actions—or rather, inactions—particularly grating to you?"
>
> She hesitated before responding. "When I was a child, someone in my family was always making promises to do this or to get that and then at the last minute, wouldn't come through. This happened over

and over again." I could see the effort she was making to control her emotions.

"Again, Peg," I responded immediately, "you're ahead of the game. Many people wouldn't be so self-aware. Did you think of this family member when you were talking with Jamal?"

"Not exactly," she said. "But I recognized the sickening feeling in my stomach at being let down once again."

"So you remembered the feeling, but not a specific incident?"

"Yes, that's it exactly."

Hearing Jamal's disappointing confession sent Peg's amygdala into hyperdrive, reminding her of disappointments she had experienced each time this family member had let her down.

As I was explaining this, Peg gave me a wry look. "At least I had enough presence of mind not to call Jamal an irresponsible idiot. But I couldn't resist saying that contacting everyone was the least he could do since he'd blown our deadline." Her phrase, "I couldn't resist" provided only a mild indication of the power the amygdala had gained during the heated exchange with Jamal.

I turned back to Stefan. "You asked why the information was useful. When I'm emotionally flooded and unable to shake a generalized feeling of dread and doom, it's comforting to know that the problem is under my own control rather than someone else's. It's *my* amygdala that's flooded. It's *my* neocortex that's shut down. So, it's *my* job to restore internal balance before I can be effective in that situation. That's what I focus on."

Peg responded quickly, "So how do I turn off being emotionally flooded? I tried telling myself not to be so upset, but that didn't work."

THE MYTH OF SUPPRESSED EMOTIONS

One of the most common ways to try to stop the flood is through suppressing emotions.

I turned toward Robyn. "Earlier you asked, 'What if there are things I'd rather not feel at all?' Would you say more about that?"

Robyn reddened slightly and responded, "I'm listening to Peg lay all this out—how she feels mad and sad and scared all at the same time—and I'm amazed she finds it so easy to talk about her feelings in front of everyone. I'm much more private. I let my feelings out only in private, and then only a little at a time. I don't want things to get out of control."

"You're not unusual in that," I assured Robyn, and others nodded in agreement.

Emotional suppression is a form of flight. Rather than risk painful feelings and in an effort to maintain control, some people try to shut down feeling altogether. They tell themselves it is silly to be so upset, while trying to ignore the churning going on in their bodies. The churning doesn't disappear, though, just through trying to push it away.

> Robyn smiled as I explained this. "That's me," she said. "When it comes to handling difficult situations, I want to be as rational and logical as possible. Sometimes my hands shake, but I just ignore that so I can stay mentally alert."
>
> "Remember the distinction between emotions and feelings?" I asked the group. "Emotions are your complex, unconscious, physiological reactions to things. Feelings reflect your conscious awareness of those sensations. After an upsetting event, you may be able to suppress your feelings, but the emotions and their effects don't disappear. That's why your hands may continue to shake."
>
> Robyn responded, "Maybe the emotions haven't really gone away, but as long as they stay in their box and I can go about my business, I'm just fine. I haven't found anything that works better." With that, we all laughed.
>
> "Well, Robyn," I responded, "if you have a system that works for you, great. Suppressing emotions often brings some short-term benefits; otherwise, you and others wouldn't be trying to do it. However, research shows there are some real disadvantages to suppressing emotions."

Suppressing emotions carries tremendous costs, both psychologically and physically:

- Suppressing emotions can actually be dangerous. For example, if you sense danger and you suppress the feeling and fail to act, you can jeopardize your own or others' safety.[6]
- Suppressed emotions may rebound: though you succeed in holding off awareness of fear or anger for a while, it may return as strong as ever after several hours or a day.[7]
- Ironically, suppressing emotions can lead you to ruminate—replay the same pessimistic scenes and explanations repeatedly. It is as if you are in an endless thought loop. This can sometimes drag you down into depression.[8]
- Your suppressed emotions may leak into your interactions. For example, though you think you are controlling your

resentment, others notice the unconscious cues you exhibit and may form inaccurate attributions about their causes.[9]

- Suppressed emotions may lead you to scapegoat others. You may unknowingly project onto others the emotions you refuse to acknowledge in yourself. ("Those people are so *angry!*")[10]
- When you suppress your emotions around others, people find it harder to connect with you. They experience you as less likeable.[11]
- Feelings build up; you may harbor resentments until you explode, saying things you later regret. A typical pattern of unmanaged emotions is suppression-suppression-suppression-explosion.

Everyone was quiet for a few moments. Stefan broke the silence by saying, "What do you mean 'suppression-suppression-suppression-explosion?'"

CURIOUS ABOUT THE RESEARCH?

The impact of emotional suppression may be moderated by cultural values. One laboratory study found, for example, that individuals with Asian values had fewer negative social consequences from suppressing their emotions than did those with Western European values.

Butler, E. A., Lee, T. L., & Gross, J. J. (2007). Emotion regulation and culture: Are the social consequences of emotion suppression culture-specific? *Emotion, 7*(1), 30–48.

Robyn spoke up again, "Actually, when I think about it, that's close to what happens with me. I put on my headset, listen to my music, and try to ignore what's going on around me until someone finally gets on my last nerve. Then I blow up at that person."

I waited to see if anyone else wanted to add something. No one did, so I said, "There's a reason I provide this training, Robyn. My pattern used to be like yours. I would hold things in until I exploded. Some people thought me a patsy; others thought I had a sharp tongue. How they saw me depended on whether they experienced the suppression or the explosion. It affected my reputation and diminished my ability to really see where others were coming from. Mostly, though, it brought me a lot of stress and cost me peace of mind. I was unhappy, so I sought tools to learn a new way."

"Peace of mind?" repeated Robyn. "No, I can't say I have that," she added softly. Then she shook her head as though shaking off the very thought and asked in a deliberately calm voice, "What do you mean by 'diminished your ability to see where others were coming from'?"

PREVENTING SELF-FULFILLING PROPHECIES

"This has to do with the tendency of suppressed emotions to leak out," I began. "Let's take the hypothetical case of Jane Doe and John Smith. John has done something Jane considers reprehensible. She's so angry she could scream. Yet, she doesn't think she can expose her anger to John, even privately. So she stuffs it. How might that affect the way she treats him in other interactions?"

"It won't," Robyn said. "If she wants to conceal how she really feels, he won't ever know how angry she is underneath."

Stefan shook his head. "I'm not so sure about that. I work with someone who puts on this false smile whenever the boss is around. None of us knows what happened that got him so mad, but we do know his smile isn't genuine. I think the boss knows too, but ignores it. Our staff meetings are becoming more and more uncomfortable, however, because he throws occasional daggers and then acts like he's just joking around. He isn't fooling anyone."

"Stefan's co-worker isn't fooling others, but he may be fooling himself," I suggested. "Our minds play tricks on us when we're emotionally flooded." I distributed Figure 3.3. "Look at the first five steps of this diagram showing the current relationship between Jane Doe and John Smith. What's happening?"

Peg responded, "This is where Jamal and I are headed if I'm not careful. I'm just as angry as Jane Doe—caught up in the flood. I did recognize that as his manager, I couldn't just let him have it, but my anger leaked out when I said, 'that's the least you could do.'"

"How is Jamal likely to respond?" I asked.

"I could tell that he knew I was zapping him. Who knows? He may be emotionally flooded himself—not only because he messed up, but because I wouldn't accept his apology. He's probably worried that I'll be vindictive. Frankly, I think he may be the vindictive one and try to come back at me somehow."

I continued, "If Peg is right and Jamal is also emotionally flooded, then they're both likely to blame the other and respond to each other

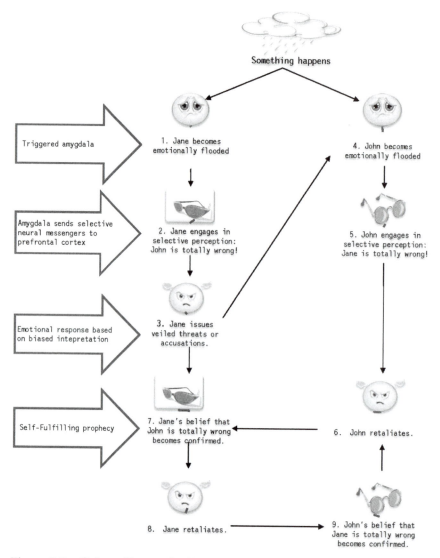

Figure 3.3   © Jean Kantambu Latting & V. Jean Ramsey, 2007–2009.

based on their distorted perceptions—much like Jane and John in the last four steps of the diagram. Each thinks the other is the culprit, and each believes she or he is doing all they can do to make the best of a bad situation with an impossible coworker.

"This is the self-fulfilling prophecy in action: She believes he's inexcusably wrong—and lets him know it through words or behaviors. He believes her behavior is proof positive that she's the one in the wrong—so he responds negatively, confirming her belief that he's impossible to deal with. And on it goes—each living up to the other's negative expectations while believing the other should get their act together."

Peg shook her head slowly as she looked at the diagram. "I can see how this could happen with Jamal and me. But I truly feel that in this situation, he's in the wrong. This is so frustrating," she sighed. "What am I supposed to do?"

"The key to breaking this self-fulfilling prophecy," I replied, "is to drain the emotional flood. Emotional clearing processes are available to help you do this. I'm going to introduce you to a couple of possibilities today."

"Say what?" asked Stefan. "Emotional clearing???"

"Yup!" I responded. "I'm talking about clearing your negative emotions so you can think again. Let's take a lunch break, then this afternoon we'll talk about how to break the self-fulfilling logjam."

CLEARING EMOTIONS: THE PROCESS

When everyone returned from lunch, I could see both curiosity and skepticism on their faces. "Are there really effective techniques for clearing negative emotions?" they seemed to be asking.

From experience, I suspected the biggest hurdle would be their willingness to try one of the approaches. When I had introduced emotional clearing methods in the past and asked people to try them at home, most returned the next day (or week) explaining how they just couldn't get into it. Fortunately, with this group, there was the whole afternoon, so I could ask them to go off privately for a half hour or so and try to put one or more of the approaches into practice.

> I began by explaining, "In the midst of emotional flooding, you aren't thinking clearly. The only information allowed into your consciousness is that which supports your present emotions. New information isn't considered. You're stuck in past memories. When I'm emotionally flooded and thinking I'm in a no-win situation, I take comfort in knowing that I'm not doing it to myself. I realize that my amygdala has taken charge. I can reclaim myself by clearing my emotions.
>
> "First let's be clear about the goal. The goal is to achieve a state of clarity. When this happens and you are no longer churning about the issue, your amygdala is no longer triggered."
>
> "Okay. Think of a problem you're presently wrestling with and write it down. Please don't pick major life issues like whether you should

break up with a partner or sell your house and car and move to Antarctica. This is for practice, so pick something that's bothering you, but won't determine the future of your existence on this earth." They laughed.

Peg asked, "What about the incident with Jamal? Does that qualify?"

"Certainly," I responded. "It's important to you, but not life-shattering, right?" She nodded.

"And everyone knows what I'm going to be working on!" interjected Stefan, stimulating more laughter.

Everyone jotted down an issue.

Even though various forms of emotional clearing have existed for thousands of years, recently some simple, self-directed, and structured methods for emotional clearing have emerged. Most emotional clearing approaches have three steps in common: (a) feel the feeling and intensify it; (b) observe the feeling; and (c) release the feeling.

These three steps are the essential elements of a visualization method described by the Buddhist practitioner T. Tulku as a means of releasing unwanted self-images in order to "become more flexible and open to experience."[12] As he explained:

> First, we need to recognize these fantasies for what they are: images projected by the mind that have no reality in themselves . . . One way to do this is to look directly at a self-image during a strong emotional upset. As the emotions take shape, intensify them, letting them build up until they become very strong and powerful. Make them so vivid and alive you can almost see and touch them. Feel them as fully as you can. Then use this vital energy to arouse your awareness to separate you from your image-making: step back and look directly at the situation you have created . . . When you look at the image directly, it disperses, for it is empty, insubstantial. True, the feeling is there, but as soon as you have lost interest in sustaining the image of yourself, in feeding it energy, its hold power dissolves (p. 53).

Here are the basic three steps:

- Feel the feeling: "As the emotions take shape, intensify them, letting them build up until they become very strong and powerful."
- Observe the feeling: "Step back and look directly at the situation you have created."

- Release the feeling: "When you look at the image directly, it disperses, for it is empty, insubstantial."

"What do you mean, release the feeling?" asked Stefan. "How do you release a feeling?"

"The same way that you release the tension in a muscle," I responded. "Everyone who wants to try it—let's do it together. First, tense your shoulders together and really *feel* that. Now *observe* that feeling—pay attention to what all that tension feels like. Now, relax your shoulders and *release* all that tension. Feel it or watch it ease away."

I watched as shoulders tensed and then released around the room. "Did it work? Were you able to release the tension?"

Nearly everyone responded in the affirmative.

"Releasing an emotion works very similarly. Here's what's going to happen this afternoon," I continued. "I'll explain two different emotional clearing approaches. Both include some variation of the concept of feel the feeling, observe it, and release it."

Robyn looked straight at me, "I don't like the part about having to feel the feeling and intensify it. I don't know what's buried up in here." As she spoke, she tapped the side of her head, prompting chuckles from others.

"You're in control here, Robyn," I replied. "You get to decide how much feeling—or how little—you want to experience. As much or as little as you want to do is fine."

She still looked skeptical, but said nothing, so I proceeded.

Sedona Method

The Sedona Method is used to release unwanted feelings.[13] It closely parallels the three-step process previously described.

CURIOUS ABOUT THE RESEARCH?

A pilot study found that those using the Sedona Method demonstrated an improvement in heart rate, reduction in blood pressure, and reduction in muscle tension compared to a progressive relaxation technique and a control group.

See: http:www.sedona.com/scientific-evidence.aspx

The steps are simple. Think about something troubling you and name at least one feeling associated with it. Then ask yourself the following questions:

- Am I willing to fully welcome this feeling as best I can? (Answer yes or no)
- Am I willing to let it go, just for the moment? (Answer yes or no)
- Will I let it go? (Answer yes or no)
- When? (Answer with a specific date)

I asked, "Who's willing to try it aloud with me?" Hands went up and I was glad to see Stefan's was one of them. "Stefan, do you mind telling us what you'd like to focus on?"

He grinned and said, "Well now, y'all know how I blew it with my wife this morning. I called to apologize, but I don't think the apology was accepted." Even though he continued to grin, I could see the sadness in his eyes.

"Stefan, what are you feeling right now?" I asked, deliberately speaking more slowly.

"Oh, I don't know. Sort of upset, maybe?"

I waited.

"A little sad. A little annoyed. After all, she started the whole thing. I mean, it started when . . ."

I interrupted, "Stefan, in emotional clearing, the story of what happened and how it happened isn't important. What's important is what you're feeling. Let's just stick with that."

"Okay," he replied. "Sad and annoyed. That's what I'm feeling."

"Alright, Stefan, choose one of those. Which one?"

"Sad."

"So now answer the questions. Are you willing to fully welcome this feeling of sadness, as best as you can? To allow yourself to feel really sad?"

He stared at me for a moment, then closed his eyes. After a few seconds, he responded softly, "Yes, I can feel it."

"Are you willing to fully welcome it, Stefan?"

Another few moments of silence. Then, "Yes, but I don't like it."

"Stefan, stay with this. Just stay with the feeling. Are you willing to fully welcome it?"

More silence. Then, "Yes."

"Are you willing to let it go, just for the moment?"

"Am I willing? I'm willing but not able."

"Stefan, I'm only asking you if you're willing. Are you willing to let it go, just for the moment?"

He visibly sighed, "Yes."

"Will you let it go?"

Another sigh. Then, "Yes."

"When?"

He took a deep breath and then his eyes popped open and he looked at me.

"What just happened?" he asked.

"Why don't you tell us?" I asked.

"Well, something changed. I'm still sad, but it's not the same." The puzzlement in his voice and his face were evident.

"Okay, let's try it again. This time, everyone do it along with Stefan with your own problem or concern."

Everyone closed their eyes. I went through the four steps again.

This time, when we finished, Stefan had a slight smile on his face.

"What happened this time, Stefan?"

"Well, when you asked whether I was willing to let it go, I thought, 'Sure, why not? I can at least be willing'. Then when you asked if I would let it go, I thought, 'Go where? Where will it go? I can't let it go.' Then, I recalled the exact words, 'Will you let it go?' And I thought, 'Well, I'll let it go whenever it wants to leave.' So then you asked, 'When?' and I thought, 'Why not right now?' The next thing I knew, poof, it just left. It was very strange."

"How do you feel now?"

"Sort of lighter. I'm still . . . still . . . I don't know, still upset or something, but I'm definitely lighter."

"Great!" I exclaimed. "You have the gist of it. Now that you know what can happen—even to a small extent, you know what to aim for. Now is there any sadness left?"

He closed his eyes, "Maybe just a little, but not as much."

"Good. If we had time, we'd continue to work with the rest of the sadness and then repeat the process with your anger—or annoyance. I think that's what you called it."

He nodded slightly.

"What about the rest of you?" I asked. With that, they started talking among themselves, checking to see how it had worked for everyone. Some had been able to release all or part of a feeling. Others had not and were baffled by it all.

Robyn spoke up, "Nothing happened with me. I couldn't really experience it or let it go."

"What was the feeling, Robyn?"

"Well, I feel really ticked about something that happened last night."

"Okay, so would you prefer to stay ticked off?"

She looked at me for a moment, and then said, "As a matter of fact, yes! Someone's behavior was really sorry and I have a right to be angry about it."

"Yet you chose it for this exercise. Why was that?"

"Well, because I have to interact with the person—a lot—it's a relative—and if I'm to have peace in the family, I have to get along with him." I could see she was becoming uncomfortable.

"That's fine, Robyn. You don't have to tell us the whole story. What you're saying is that you're ticked off, you feel justified in being ticked off, yet you know that if you stay ticked off, you may create problems for yourself in your family. Is that right?"

She nodded.

I said, "Okay, then the feeling to work with is resistance to letting go of being ticked off."

"Resistance to letting go of being ticked off?"

"Sure. Everyone, think of something you're ticked off about. Make it something you feel you deserve to be ticked off about and don't want to let go of because otherwise . . . Otherwise what?" I looked at Robyn.

She immediately responded, "Otherwise I'll be a patsy."

"Good. Okay folks, think of something that ticks you off—either now or in the past— and that you think you deserve to be ticked off about, and if you let go of the feeling you'll be a patsy."

Broad smiles spread across the room. It was clear this struck a nerve. Robyn was smiling too.

I walked them through the four steps.

- Am I willing to fully welcome my resistance to letting go of the feeling of being ticked off?
- Could I let the resistance go?
- Will I?
- When?

A few people looked up smiling at the end of the exercise.

"Let's do it again—on the same thing: your resistance to letting go of your ticked-off feeling."

I repeated the steps, and then suggested, "Now go back to your original feeling of being ticked off and let's walk through it again.

After we finished, I asked for comments. About half the group had been able to let go of some of their resistance. A few had successfully let go of the feeling of annoyance itself.

I went back to Stefan and asked how he was doing.

He said, "That was great. I really wanted to stay annoyed at my wife, but I could feel it being whittled down. I can still feel the upset, but it's not nearly as intense as before. I feel better, but I'm still—what did you call it?—'churning' inside."

Stefan's experience is common. Often when people first try emotional clearing, they are dismayed if they do not experience immediate or complete relief.

I included everyone as I responded to Stefan, "This is a skill—like learning to roller skate. The more you practice, the more proficient you get. So let's start right now. Everyone, please pair up and do a few rounds with one another. Either repeat the same process over and over again or alternate between releasing the feeling and releasing the resistance. The key is to find which combination or variation of a process works for you."

After about 20 minutes, I suggested, "Let's take a break. When we come back, I'll introduce you to another process called Uncensored Journaling."

During break, Peg asked if she could talk with me privately. "Some people are wondering if you're saying that if they just learn to do these processes, they won't have any more upset. What if someone here is seriously troubled?" she asked.

"Thanks for letting me know, Peg," I responded quickly. "That's not the impression I want to give. I'll address it before the end of the day."

Uncensored Journaling

"Keeping a daily journal," I began after break, "is an effective method of getting pent-up thoughts and emotions into the light of day where they can be examined and integrated.[14] One variation is uncensored or 'stream of consciousness' journaling. While focusing on an emotional issue, simply write all your thoughts about it without censorship until you experience a shift and greater clarity. It can take some time."

They looked at me quizzically. "Okay, here's a problem I've been working on for a while and am making some progress with," I explained. I picked up pen and paper and pretended to write while speaking aloud.

Why on Earth am I staying up yet another night knowing that I have to get up on the morning when I should be in bed? I wonder if I left the stove on? My fingers are tired of typing and my arm is starting to hurt. But I can't go to bed right now because I forgot to put in that load of wash. I am NOT going to wash clothes at 2 A.M.! That's ridiculous! I wonder what's happening with that Senate fight? Maybe I'll see if CNN has something on. This is stupid! What am I doing still up? I keep thinking of things to do. . . . If I keep this up, I'll be exhausted in the morning and will fall asleep during my meeting.

I stopped at that point.

"So what happens next?" asked Stefan. "Is that real?"

"Yes, it's real, unfortunately. I keep going until I get relief. It goes on and on like that until, suddenly, I start feeling on edge or even a sense of dread. Then I know I'm getting close to what's bothering me, so I stick with the feeling. Remember from before—*feel the feeling?* If I start getting edgy and tense, I know I'm getting close, so I stay with it and keep writing until something shifts. Then I feel suddenly sleepy or at peace. I did it the other night and then went right to bed."

"You make it sound mystical," Stefan responded.

"For me, it sometimes is," I answered. "But it's also practical. It certainly beats being all bleary-eyed in the morning."

WHAT RESULTS CAN YOU EXPECT?

Everyone agreed to go off and try Uncensored Journaling alone for 30 minutes, or continue practicing the Sedona Method with a partner if they preferred. When they returned, Peg was the first to speak. "I tried Uncensored Journaling, and it worked. This surprised me. At first, I was just letting off steam about Jamal, but then out of no-where, I started writing about my siblings. I'm the oldest of six kids. I was always responsible for the other kids, but had no authority over them. When one of them messed up, I was the one who got in trouble. Even though I couldn't make them behave, I'd be the one blamed. It was so unfair."

The room was quiet. The intensity in Peg's voice matched her expression.

"Here's how I resolved it," she continued. "I realized I was treating Jamal just like I treated my brother Tim. Tim would hardly ever mind me—I would warn him and warn him about stuff and he wouldn't pay me any attention. Then I would be held responsible." As she spoke, she had a delightful lilt in her voice. Her relief was plain to see. "So now I know why I was so confused and upset. I play by the rules and Jamal doesn't and I end up with the blame."

"Exactly! So how can you use this insight? What will you do now?"

"Well, I think I can have a more empathetic conversation with Jamal. I know now that he wasn't responsible for all of my upset. At the same time, he still has to be accountable for his actions. He has to fix the problem and he and the team have to come up with a way to prevent it from happening again. What's wonderful is that this allows the focus to shift away from me and how upset I am to the project, Jamal, and the team. It feels as though my priorities have been turned right side up again."

"Emotional clearing keeps you clean," I agreed. "You can think of it as an anger-management technique."

As Peg was discovering, once you get your amygdala untriggered, you are free to act more consistently with your values. The more emotionally clear you are, the more likely you are to have deeper and more effective experiences with others.

Stefan piped up, "I tried Uncensored Journaling too. I didn't have the breakthrough Peg did, but I did get a little clearer about what set me off this morning. I know my wife didn't intend to have that impact on me. I think I need more time with this."

Stefan was right. It does take time, especially if you have a pile-up of emotions. It's never just one thing; it's an accumulation of things one on top of the other. If you find you are not getting enough relief using one emotional clearing approach, there are many others available.

Some people learn to put unwanted emotions in an imaginary balloon and watch them fly away. Others find that prayer or meditation works. Writing about important personal experiences in an emotional way for as little as 15 minutes a day over the course of three days can bring about improvements in mental and physical health.[15] Once you find a method that works for you, the key is to practice, practice, practice. Practice helps retrain your neural pathways so it gets easier and easier.[16] You may still get knocked down by an emotional two-by-four occasionally, but you will know how to recoup and handle the situation more effectively.

> I looked around the room and saw that the atmosphere had changed. Not everyone in the room had had a satisfactory experience, but most could see the potential. I encouraged everyone to continue practicing, reminding them that self-care skills take time to develop. Remembering my promise to Peg to address those who might indeed have serious personal problems, I offered an important caveat to what we had done so far.

OTHER SOURCES OF HELP

"What we have covered today," I explained, "are self-help approaches for people who feel as though they have a reasonable handle on life. Yet we all go through periods when we're simply overwhelmed. What should we do under those circumstances?"

Stefan responded first. "Well, I'm married to a psychotherapist, so I know the right answer: seek professional help." He grinned broadly—as did we all.

"Yes, Stefan," I agreed. "That's where I'm going. You shouldn't regard anything we've talked about today as a substitute for seeking professional help. There are self-help groups if you want that kind of support. Alternatively, you can seek help from a mental health professional. These are not mutually exclusive. I've benefited from all three—emotional clearing processes, support groups, and professional therapy—whenever I felt my life had become unmanageable or I felt powerless to change on my own."

"You've seen a shrink?" Robyn piped up. "I wouldn't have guessed that about you."

"It would be irresponsible of me to talk about or teach emotional clearing methods if I hadn't addressed my own issues," I responded. "For me, seeing a therapist is more efficient than slogging through emotional sludge by myself. I pay an accountant every year to handle my taxes. I pay a therapist when I'm in intense distress. It's more efficient. Why should I stay bogged down when there are experts who've spent years learning how to help me feel better? Emotional clearing is maintenance for me, not therapy."

The room was quiet. "Should I provide you with references?" I asked.

They nodded.

Passing out a handout listing sources of help, I explained, "The American Self-Help Group Clearinghouse Web site has a searchable database for different types of problems in different geographic areas.[17] The Web site of the National Institute for Mental Health has a description of signs, symptoms, and treatments for various mental health problems.[18] They also suggest where to go for help."

BUILDING POSITIVE EMOTIONS

Positive emotions were last on the agenda. I put the topic last because it is the easiest to explain, although for some, nearly as hard to do and maintain as clearing negative emotions.

"Building positive emotions should be part of your daily repertoire," I explained. "One way to do this is to take a moment to just look around and appreciate what is there to appreciate."

"That sounds like mindfulness,"[19] Stefan interjected.

"It's very much like mindfulness. I know each of you have heard this before, so I won't dwell on it. We're so accustomed to being mindful of what's going wrong. Make a commitment to also notice and appreciate what's going right. Deliberately cultivating positive emotions is especially effective after clearing negative emotions. It's good to fill that freed-up space with positive emotions."

If you think of your emotional well-being as a car in motion, negative emotions are like the brakes, while positive emotions are like the accelerator. Negative emotions provide the red alert—they let you know something is wrong.[20] They narrow your options. Deliberately building positive emotions acts to take your foot off the brake so you can hit the accelerator and go forward to enjoy your day. You have greater freedom to put things in perspective, reach out to others, and take risks. When you feel positive emotions, you feel more creative and see potential opportunities more clearly.

CURIOUS ABOUT THE RESEARCH?

The more positive emotions built up, the more resilient individuals are when negative events occur. Positive emotions also serve an inoculation function by shoring people up against bad times.

Tugade, M. M., & Frederickson, B. L. (2004). Resilient individuals use positive emotions to bounce back from negative emotional experiences. *Journal of Personality and Social Psychology, 86*(2), 320–333.

"So how do we build positive emotions?" asked Robyn. I was glad to see her curiosity piqued.

"I've already mentioned one way—just appreciating what is around you. You can do this several times a day," I responded, "Another way is to simply smile, even when you don't feel like it. Putting on a happy face can really work."

Research has shown that a broad smile of enjoyment does change brain activity[21] and that deliberately following negative emotions with positive ones reduces the cardiovascular effects of negative emotions.[22]

"Another way is to try one of the emotional clearing approaches that we just talked about," I continued. "You have already experienced how this can help improve your mood.

"Yet another method is the gratitude journal." I explained.

Gratitude Journal

"You can begin today. For a week, at the end of each day, write down at least three things that went well that day and their causes. Psychology researchers have found all kinds of benefits from this practice."[23]

"Keep a journal every day?" commented Robyn. "I don't know about doing something like that every day."

"Every day works best," I responded, "but if you can't do that, then something still works better than nothing. Even weekly recording of things you're grateful for will provide some benefit."

"Do you do it?" asked inquisitive Stefan.

"I sure do. And do you know who else does it? Oprah! She's found it so useful that she has several pages devoted to journaling on her website, including the gratitude journal."

"Are you recommending her as a bona fide researcher on the topic?" teased Stefan.

"Not in the academic sense," I responded. "Yet, by all reports, she takes very seriously her worldwide influence over millions of people and the power of her endorsement. If you decide to keep a gratitude journal, please know you're in good company with untold numbers of people who've been influenced by her and apparently found it useful."

Intentionally Hold Positive Feelings

A second method is to simply allow yourself to experience positive feelings. When you receive a compliment, remember a pleasant experience, or see a breathtaking sunset, try holding the positive feeling for at least 60 seconds. Most people have no trouble holding negative emotions by steaming and stewing for that long. However, for many, 60 seconds for a positive emotion can feel like a long time.

CURIOUS ABOUT THE RESEARCH?

Savoring pleasant experiences has been found to be positively correlated with well-being, including increased optimism, a sense of personal control, life satisfaction, and self-esteem.

Bryant, F. B. (2003). Savoring beliefs inventory (SBI): A scale for measuring beliefs about savouring. *Journal of Mental Health, 12*(2), 175–196.

After I finished explaining, Robyn looked up at me, "Now this makes intuitive good sense to me."

I smiled at her honest response. "Are you willing to try it?" I asked.

"I'll think about it."

"Good enough! What about the rest of you? Please pair up and tell one another what you will commit to and what you're willing to think about trying."

In the last few minutes of the session, I asked people to sum up what they'd gotten from the session. Peg leaned back and said, "Over the last half hour, one of my favorite quotes keeps running through my head. It's from Howard Thurman, the famous educator who said, 'Don't ask what the world needs. Ask what makes you come alive, and go do it. Because what the world needs is people who have come alive.[24]

"I came here in a fog, all upset about Jamal. Somehow, after the emotional clearing session and now thinking about the things I'm grateful for, I feel more alive. Earlier you talked about how we should identify with our values. The way I feel now is the way I want to feel all the time. I feel ready to talk with Jamal about his accountability in a wholly different way and my values say that is the right thing to do."

Peg grinned as everyone spontaneously applauded.

NOTES

1. Rock, D., & Schwartz, J. (2006). The neuroscience of leadership. *Strategy+Business, Summer,* 72–81.

2. Lenzen, M. (2005). Feeling our emotions. *Scientific American Mind, 16*(1), 14–15.

3. Plutchik, R. (2001). The nature of emotions. *American Scientist, 89*(4), 344–350.

4. Barrett, L. F., Gross, J., Christensen, T. C., & Benvenuto, M. (2001). Knowing what you're feeling and knowing what to do about it: Mapping the relation between emotion differentiation and emotion regulation. *Cognition and Emotion, 15*(6), 713–724.

5. *See:* Dubuc, Bruno. (2002–present). The brain from top to bottom. http://thebrain.mcgill.ca/flash/i/i_04/i_04_cr/i_04_cr_peu/i_04_cr_peu.htm; LeDoux, J. E. (1995). Emotion: Clues from the brain. *Annual Review of Psychology, 46,* 209–235.

6. Gross, J. J., & Levenson, R. W. (1997). Hiding feelings: The acute effects of inhibiting negative and positive emotion. *Journal of Abnormal Psychology, 106*(1), 95–103.

7. Wenzlaff, R. M., & Wegner, D. M. (2000). Thought suppression. *Annual Review of Psychology, 51,* 59–91.

8. Neff, K. (2003). Self-compassion: An alternative conceptualization of a healthy attitude toward oneself. *Self and Identity, 2,* 85–101.

9. Devine, P. G. (1996). Breaking the prejudice habit. *Psychological Science Agenda, 9,* 10–11.

10. Newman, L. S., Duff, K. J., & Baumeister, R. F. (1997). A new look at defensive projection: Thought suppression, accessibility, and biased person perception. *Journal of Personality and Social Psychology, 72*(5), 980–1001.

11. Butler, E. A., Egloff, B., Wilhelm, F. H., Smith, N. C., Erickson, E. A., & Gross, J. J. (2003). The social consequences of expressive suppression. *Emotion, 3*(1), 48–67.

12. Tulku, T. (1981). *Hidden mind of freedom.* Berkeley, CA: Dharma Publishing.

13. Dwoskin, H. (2003). *The Sedona method.* Sedona, AZ: Sedona Press.

14. DeSalvo, L. (1999). *Writing as a way of healing.* San Francisco: Harper San Francisco.

15. Pennebaker, J. W., & Seagal, J. D. (1999). Forming a story: The health benefits of narrative. *Journal of Clinical Psychology, 55*(10), 1243–1254.

16. Lutz, A., Greischar, L. L., Rawlings, N. B., Ricard, M., & Davidson, R. J. (2004). Long-term meditators self-induce high-amplitude gamma synchrony during mental practice. *Proceedings of the National Academy of Sciences, 101,* 16369–16373.

17. *See:* http://mentalhelp.net/selfhelp/

18. *See:* http://www.nimh.nih.gov/health/index.shtml

19. Baer, R. A. (2003). Mindfulness training as a clinical intervention: A conceptual and empirical review. *Clinical Psychology: Science and Practice, 10*(2), 125–143.

20. Fredrickson, B. L. (2000). Cultivating positive emotions to optimize health and well-being [Electronic Version]. *Prevention & Treatment,* 3. Retrieved May 5, 2007, from www.journals.apa.org/prevention/volume3/pre0030001a.html

21. Ekman, P., & Davidson, R. J. (1993). Voluntary smiling changes regional brain activity. *Psychological Science, 4*(5), 342–345.

22. Fredrickson, B. L., Mancuso, R. A., Branigan, C., & Tugade, M. M. (2000). The undoing effect of positive emotions. *Motivation and Emotion, 24*(4), 237–259.

23. Emmons, R. A., & McCullough, M. E. (2003). Counting blessings versus burdens: An experimental investigation of gratitude and subjective well-being in daily life. *Journal of Personality and Social Psychology, 84*(2), 377–389.

24. *See:* http://www.howardthurmanbooks.org

CHAPTER 4

Building Effective Relationships

"Ahmed, I've been getting complaints about your performance on the Super Win Project," began Gerard, the director of a large project at XYZ Company.

Ahmed, one of Gerard's team leaders, responded forcefully. "I bet it was Marcus. He's mad because I didn't take his suggestion on how to set up the report."

"Actually, it wasn't Marcus. He told me how pleased he was with the format you came up with."

"Then it must've been Christine. I told her three times to check her figures and each time she got more and more upset."

"Actually, I've heard that your attention to detail has been a major part of the project's success thus far."

"Well, if it wasn't them, I can't imagine who it might be, because no one else has been ticked off with me."

Gerard was getting a little annoyed. He took a deep breath and responded, "Perhaps if you'd let me explain, I'd be able to clarify what's going on. This isn't a world-shattering issue, but I thought you'd appreciate hearing the feedback since you've indicated some interest in preparing yourself for additional leadership responsibilities."

Gerard was relating this story to me during one of my regular appointments with him. His company had engaged me to serve as a management coach to him.

"How do you manage folks who are unreasonable?" he asked me. "Ahmed simply won't listen."

"I think the building blocks of effective relationships might be useful," I responded and sketched them for him (Table 4.1).

The goal of these skills is to build more effective, mutually beneficial relationships. Through listening, openness, inquiry,[1] and feedback, you may position yourself for open and honest exchanges with others. The more open and honest the exchange, the more likely it will lead to effective and beneficial relationships.

POWERFUL LISTENING

Conversations such as Gerard's with Ahmed, in which one person is trying to take the conversation in one direction while the other spins it off in another, are common.

> Gerard ruefully shook his head and pointed to the word "listening" on the notepad. "Ahmed was definitely not listening to me," he commented. "He kept cutting me off, thinking he knew what I was going to say before I had a chance to say it."

There are many ways people communicate their failure to listen. Here are some you may recognize:

- *Substituting one's own version of events*: "I know what you're going to say." or "Here's my story, it's even better than yours." The listener may want to correct the facts, reinterpret their importance, or generally show how he is smarter.
- *Immediately disagreeing with what the speaker says*: "No, you've got it wrong! That's not what happened!" In this case, the listener grants special privilege to her own interpretation of events rather than listening carefully to the speaker.

Table 4.1
Building Blocks of Effective Relationships

Listening		
Inquiry		
Openness		
Giving Feedback	Receiving Feedback	Seeking Feedback

© Jean Kantambu Latting & V. Jean Ramsey, 2007–2009.

- *Dismissing or downplaying the feelings of the speaker*: "You shouldn't feel that way!" "Don't cry [be mad, be sad]. Things aren't as bad as they seem." Distracted by the desire to shut down or back away from emotional displays provoking discomfort, the listener may lose the opportunity to learn what is prompting the emotion—and thus miss a significant signal about the current state of the individual or organization.

"Because he kept interrupting me," Gerard continued, "it took me fifteen minutes to explain what should have taken five, and I still don't know if he heard or understood what I said."

When listeners respond as Ahmed did, little of the speaker's message gets through in any meaningful way. Effective listening is not passive, however. Powerful listening is active and can result in powerful outcomes.

"Didn't you tell me about some exercise on powerful listening that you and others did in another company?" asked Gerard. "How did it go? It might be worth trying with my group. Ahmed's not the only one who has trouble listening. We all do."

"Yes, you could do it with your group," I responded.

The exercise had been both fun and fascinating and I was glad for the chance to explain it. The participants had been divided into pairs and asked to choose topics they felt deeply about. It was set up so each person alternated between the speaking and listening roles.

In the first round, listeners were told to give no verbal or nonverbal responses—to just sit impassively. Typically, the speakers started with gusto, talking about their topics with enthusiasm. After just a few moments, however, they usually faltered. The blank stares from their listeners did not shut the speakers down completely, but certainly slowed them down.

In the second round, listeners were told to show active indifference. Some became creative: they glanced at their watches, opened their notebooks, or pretended to be talking on the phone. Others went so far as getting up from their chairs and pantomiming talking to other persons. In response, most speakers simply stopped talking altogether.

In the third round, listeners were instructed to do whatever they could *nonverbally* to demonstrate true interest in what their partners were saying. In nearly all pairs, speakers gathered momentum as they talked and became more animated over time.

Participants were asked to describe what an interested nonverbal response was like. They said things like:

- "She leaned forward and looked me directly in the eye."
- "He nodded his head and smiled while I was talking."
- "As I talked, her facial expression changed in response to what I was saying."

After the exercise, listeners expressed amazement at the power they felt. They could see how their nonverbal behavior visibly affected the speakers. "I never knew I had such influence just in how I listened," said one. "But it makes sense. I've seen my manager react similarly in meetings when no one's paying attention to what she says."

The subtle difference between the first round (when listeners displayed a passive lack of response) and the second (when they displayed active disinterest) also elicited a lot of comments. Passive nonresponse, such as a blank stare, discouraged speakers, but active disinterest usually shut them down completely. One speaker proclaimed, "It [passive disinterest] didn't cause me to quit talking, but I started wondering why I was wasting my time trying to say anything to this person." Active disinterest, on the other hand, felt repugnant to anyone speaking.

> Gerard grew more and more pensive as he listened to my description. "I can see now that much of my frustration with Ahmed was coming from my sense that he wasn't listening. His excuses were really ways of telling me he had no interest in what I was saying."
>
> "Exactly," I said.

How might Ahmed have demonstrated active interest in Gerard's feedback? He could have begun by being quiet—just listening. Meanwhile, he could have communicated nonverbally that he really did want to hear what Gerard had to say, by maintaining eye contact or nodding his head as Gerard spoke.

When you engage in powerful listening, you do not have to say anything. Your power comes from what you elicit from others through your listening behavior. How you listen supports or inhibits what others hope to achieve in communicating with you.

INQUIRY

Inquiry is a natural extension of powerful listening. The practice of skillful inquiry allows you to communicate more interest in what others are saying—and increase your understanding of it. The practice of inquiry goes beyond simply asking questions. Generally, you ask questions to ascertain facts; you engage in inquiry, however, to uncover underlying assumptions and meanings.

"Think back to your conversation with Ahmed," I suggested to Gerard. "Why do you think he responded with 'I bet it was Marcus' and 'It must've been Christine'?"

A look of annoyance flashed across Gerard's face. "He's always defensive like that—or at least most of the time."

"Do you think he believes you listen to him?"

"I listen to him yak-yak-yak all the time."

"My question is not about what you really do, but what he thinks you do. Do you believe he feels heard and understood by you?"

"I don't see why he wouldn't. Whenever I try to get in a word edgewise, he talks over me."

People often get annoyed when someone talks over them. Yet, this behavior may not be a personality problem. It may instead imply that the person has a different understanding of something than you do. For example, if the person is giving you more information than you want about a subject, perhaps he doesn't have an accurate understanding of how much you already know. Or, he may think he has to continue explaining because there's something you don't get.

Gerard stared at me. "Are you suggesting that he talks over me because he thinks I don't understand what he's trying to say?"

"That would be one possible conclusion. How could you find out whether it's for that reason or some other?"

Again, Gerard looked at me intently. "I suppose I could ask him, but what would I say? 'Are you over-explaining yourself because you think I don't get it, or because you're so defensive you don't know when to shut up?' Obviously, a question like that wouldn't work."

We both laughed. "Gerard, are you in the answer or in the question about Ahmed's behavior? Do you think you know why he keeps explaining himself to you?"

Gerard sat back in his chair. "Well, I admit I was in the answer when we first sat down, but now I'm not so sure. I may not know what's going on."

"If you're truly in the question, could you feel comfortable going into inquiry—trying to find out what's going on with him?"

Gerard nodded slowly. "Yes, the more I think about it, the more curious I am about why he does the same thing over and over. But how do I ask him without appearing to jump on his case?"

Skillful use of inquiry has two related but distinct purposes. One goal is to learn more about what others are saying—and why they are saying it. Inquiry also allows you to test your understanding of what the other person is saying. The skillful use of inquiry can help you check your assumptions, even in the midst of a conversation.

What questions might Gerard ask to test his assumption about the causes of Ahmed's behavior?

- He could probe and ask for examples: "Ahmed, when I was trying to explain the complaints I'd heard on the SuperWin project to you, you interrupted to guess who'd given me the information. Would you help me understand what was going on with you at the time?"
- He could ask about Ahmed's reasoning: "I've been thinking about possible reasons for the fact that you assumed the complaint came from someone who was ticked off. Is something going on in the team, or with you, that might make this a concern?"
- He could test his understanding of Ahmed's perspective: "Were you worried that I was going to take their word without giving you a chance to explain your point of view?"
- He could test his assumptions about Ahmed's behavior or motivation: "I'm not sure, but I get the impression you feel defensive about your work, maybe because you think the rest of us don't value your input somehow. Do you feel this way sometimes?"

The tone of voice Gerard uses to ask these questions is critical. If he asks questions in a demanding or accusatory way, Ahmed is likely to respond with even more defensiveness. If his tone signals genuine interest and curiosity, however, Ahmed is more likely to give good information. Gerard has to signal his willingness to listen to the responses to his inquiry in both verbal and nonverbal ways.

In several of the possible inquiry questions, Gerard asks whether his own behavior is somehow provoking Ahmed's defensive reactions. Inquiry doesn't push all the responsibility for the communication onto the other person. Rather, Gerard is willing to acknowledge that he too may play a role in what is not working in their communication.

A companion skill to inquiry is openness.

OPENNESS

Openness requires being as forthcoming as possible about your underlying assumptions, rather than assuming understanding. You seek to provide enough information and context so that both the intent and underlying meaning of what you are saying can be understood. The goal is to be transparent.

What you mean to say may not be what others are hearing. Others may be listening, but through their own perceptual filters. Through practicing openness, you welcome, even invite, others' questions.

"Let's talk about openness in this situation," I suggested.

"I'll admit I haven't been as open with him as I might," Gerard conceded.

"In what way?"

"I get so impatient with his repeated explanations that I just want to end the conversation as quickly as possible. I know I don't fully share my reasoning most of the time."

"Do you think he senses your impatience?"

"It probably makes him try harder to get through to me—in all the wrong ways of course. It's one of those—what do you call it?—self-fulfilling prophecies." Gerard shifted uneasily in his seat. "Okay, I get it. Now what do I do?"

"What if he asks for openness by saying, 'Gerard, why are you asking me these questions? What are you up to?'"

"He wouldn't dare," replied Gerard immediately.

"Maybe not, but let's practice anyway. If you're ready for the tough responses, you can handle the milder ones much more easily."

"If he wants to know what I'm up to, should I tell him the truth?"

"The truth with kindness, yes. How might you respond without accusing or blaming him while not smoothing over the hard stuff?"

Gerard burst out laughing. "I know what *not* to do," he said.

"I'm ready," I responded eagerly.

"Years ago I had a boss who thought I wasn't up to par. Come to think of it, that situation reminds me of this one with Ahmed, only now I'm the supervisor. My manager came down really hard on me and told me I should show more leadership with my group. When I asked him to explain, he wouldn't give me any examples and he wouldn't define what he meant. All I got was that what I was doing didn't fit his definition of a leader, whatever that was."

"You're right. That's a great example of what openness isn't!" I exclaimed. "Now how would you respond in a way that stays focused on Ahmed's strengths, communicates your concern for his welfare, and yet clearly suggests more acceptable behavior?"

Gerard swallowed hard. "I might say, 'Ahmed, sometimes when I tell you something needs to be fixed, you jump right in and do it. Other times, I can't even tell you what the problem is before you seem to be defending yourself. I want to know what brings on these different reactions. If I can understand this, I can better support you in doing your job." He paused and looked at me.

"That's an impressive response," I told Gerard. "In it, you're telling Ahmed what he's doing right as well as what isn't working. You aren't blaming or shaming, and you're owning your responsibility as a manager to support him."

"But what if he comes back at me saying it's my fault he's acting that way?"

"Is it?"

"No, of course not."

"Could there be something you're doing that's aggravating his behavior?"

"That's what I'm trying to find out with the inquiry, isn't it? Is it me? Is it him? Is it something else? What I'm gathering is that if he gets defensive over my inquiry questions, I have to turn around and use openness to explain why I'm even asking him about it."

"Yes, that's it," I responded. "If he understands where you want to go, he can more easily go there with you."

Gerard's responses showed he clearly understood that his job as manager was to create conditions for his employees' success.[2] Being open about what underlies your questions or requests provides a tangible form of support by keeping employees from wasting time trying to second-guess you.

I continued, "Now, if you know it's not all your fault, yet you can see that you could be aggravating his behavior, then you can stay open and responsive to what he has to say—even if he says it imperfectly."

"Says it imperfectly?"

CURIOUS ABOUT THE RESEARCH?

A survey of 1,000 employees found that employees who felt passionate about their work and connected to their organization were far more likely than others to say their manager "sets me up for success" and "is always understanding of me when I make mistakes."

Crabtree, S. (2004, June 10). Getting personal in the workplace. *Gallup Management Journal Online.* Retrieved November 2, 2006, from http://gmj.gallup.com

---

"Sure. You say you haven't responded perfectly to him in the past. If he comes back at you implying it's all your fault, that would be an imperfect response on his part—two imperfect people trying to work it out. Yet you're the manager, not him. You have ultimate accountability for what's working and not working in the department.[3] How could you maintain a state of openness and civility in this situation and model the behavior you want from him?"

He paused for a moment. "I could try, 'Ahmed, I don't want either of us to act as though the other caused the whole thing. If I've done something to put you on the defensive, I want to know it. We both want this project to succeed, and for you to do the best job you can as project leader.'"

Again, Gerard hit a home run. He shunned the blame-shame game. He put the project goal front and center. He acknowledged his responsibility as manager to set the tone. He clarified his willingness to hear what Ahmed had to say.

Openness can require a change in mindset. You must discard the belief that your assumptions are common sense and therefore should be reasonable to everyone. In fact, like everyone else, you have mental models that cause you to make assumptions—assumptions others may or may not share. In practicing openness, you make your assumptions and thinking processes visible.

You want the impact of your words to match your intent. The only way to ascertain whether others understand what you are saying is to ask. Thus, openness and inquiry go hand in hand.

GIVING FEEDBACK

A few weeks later, Gerard requested a telephone conference with me. "I've been using powerful listening, inquiry, and openness as often as I've thought about them," he began. "I've flubbed up a few times, but when I've used them, they've worked. The problem now is that I still have the same issue with Ahmed: his performance on the SuperWin project. When I first brought it up, he was defensive, so I never got a chance to fully explain my concerns. Now that we've started building more trust between us, I want to talk with him about it. But how do I do so without tearing down what I've worked so hard to build with him?"

"You're talking about giving him corrective feedback," I responded. "The better you get at listening, inquiry, and openness, the easier you'll find it to give, receive, and even solicit feedback."

Feedback is a core ingredient of all open, honest, and effective relationships. When you give feedback to others, you usually hope they will use the information to alter their attitudes or behavior in some way. In an organizational setting, when you give feedback to others, you usually expect the receiver to either increase effort (work harder) or use better strategies (work smarter)—that is, to close the gap between desired and actual performance. Feedback helps people adapt, learn, and create new possibilities for themselves and others.

Despite these laudatory goals, most people avoid giving corrective feedback. Similarly to Gerard, you may find yourself wanting to deliver feedback to another but feeling uncomfortable about doing so. Your past efforts to do so may not have had the desired effect.

"In the past, when I've tried to give him feedback," added Gerard, "he hasn't responded the way I think he should. Why isn't he worrying about improving himself instead of my having to figure out the best way to approach him? If he didn't have so much going for him, I'd just let him go. But, for all of his defensiveness, he does have skills that would be hard to replace at this point."

Change occurs only if the feedback receiver accepts the feedback and decides to change. Thus, acceptance of feedback is an important goal. There are ways to increase the probability that others will accept, and act on, your feedback.

Focus on Strengths

Corrective feedback is important, but must be balanced with positive feedback. By emphasizing the strengths people have, you communicate your confidence in their ability to make the changes you suggest. In short, positive feedback draws on the strength-focused stance recommended throughout this book.

CURIOUS ABOUT THE RESEARCH?

Individuals may perceive negative feedback as a threat to their sense of identity. If the feedback deflates their sense of self-efficacy or competence, people may respond by withdrawing rather than increasing effort or developing better strategies.

Ilgen, D. R., & Davis, C. (2000). Bearing bad news: Reactions to negative performance feedback. *Applied Psychology, 49*(3), 550–565.

"I can see how a focus on strengths could be helpful in giving feedback to team members who're really trying. It would act as positive reinforcement, wouldn't it?" Gerard asked.

"Yes, that's right," I replied.

"But where I'm puzzled," he continued, "is how to use strength-focused feedback with team members who never seem to do anything right. Ahmed's not the only person in my group giving me headaches. I have another team member, Sylvia, who's let the team down so many times in the past year that it's hard to remember anything positive she's done."

"So how do you feel about Sylvia?" I asked.

"I'm getting increasingly frustrated with her. I've talked and talked to her. I've pointed out her weaknesses time and time again and she hasn't changed. I'm on the verge of transferring her out of my group."

"Is it possible that your frustration is getting in the way of being able to see any strengths that do exist?" I asked.

"How do I find strengths under all her weaknesses?"

"Identifying strengths isn't as hard as you imagine," I explained. "If you think about it, you already know what hers are. You said she's been on your team for over a year and she hasn't been transferred or fired. So she has to be doing something right. See if you can set aside your frustration with her for just a moment and think about her work as a whole."

The phone went silent and I could almost hear him thinking. Finally, he spoke up, "Okay, I see what you mean. I do know what her strengths are. She's considerate. She obsessively checks to make sure every detail is taken care of. When she hands in her part of the work, it's usually excellent and thorough. The problem is she just doesn't get things done on time. Her stuff is nearly always late. It's a team project, so it puts the rest of us in a jam."

"So what's your goal in giving feedback to Sylvia?"

"I want her to be timelier so the rest of the project isn't held up."

"Is that all you'd like from her? Are you willing for her to decrease the quality of her work in order to get it in on time?"

"No. I really do want her to continue doing what she's already doing well." He paused thoughtfully.

"Okay, I see. That's why I should mention her strengths, so she realizes I want her to continue those!"

"That's part of it," I replied. "Another reason is that it helps increase people's inclination to even make a change."

Three things are required for individuals to hear your feedback and be willing to change. First, they must believe change is necessary. Second, they must believe it will be an improvement. Hoping to please a boss may be enough for people to decide the change will improve their situation. Third, they must believe they're capable of making the change.[4]

Gerard ticked off how each condition fit Sylvia, "She knows she has to do something about being late all the time and she knows everyone will benefit if she does. I don't know if she thinks she can get things done on time each and every time though."

"You can help Sylvia meet the third condition by conveying your belief in her ability to change," I responded. "You can emphasize the strengths she has to draw on and take notice every time she successfully meets a deadline."

The goal of feedback, after all, is to encourage the person to consider making a change. You are asking people to undertake new behaviors they may feel uncomfortable with. They are more likely to consider changing if they know you are on their side and believe in them.

CURIOUS ABOUT THE RESEARCH?

The Gallup Organization conducts ongoing research comparing engaged employees (those who "work with passion") with those who were disengaged ("checked out") or actively disengaged ("undermining what engaged employees accomplish"). In their 2005 poll, 77 percent of the engaged employees strongly agreed that their "supervisor focuses on my strengths," while only 23 percent of the not engaged and 4 percent of the actively disengaged strongly agreed with that statement.

Krueger, J., & Killham, E. (2005, December 8). At work, feeling good matters. *Gallup Management Journal Online.* Retrieved November 2, 2006, from http://gmj.gallup.com.

Emphasizing an individual's strengths will also ensure a positive balance in the person's emotional bank account. Popularized by Steven Covey,[5] the concept of an emotional bank account is similar to that of a checking account. One important way to make deposits in a person's emotional bank account is through being strength-focused; you emphasize strengths by giving supportive feedback, encouraging remarks, and expressions of gratitude or appreciation. You make withdrawals through disapproval, harsh criticism, or sarcasm. Sufficient deposits must be made over time to offset withdrawals. Unlike checking accounts, however, the ratio of deposits to withdrawals is not one to one. Rather, more deposits than withdrawals are necessary to maintain a supportive relationship. Why? Negative feedback tends to stick longer and override positive feedback.[6] To make sure others hear and remember your positive feedback, you must provide many times more positives to outweigh the negatives.

CURIOUS ABOUT THE RESEARCH?

In a study of management teams, those with the highest performance levels had slightly more than a 5:1 ratio of positive statements to negative ones. Similarly, in his research on married couples, John Gottman reported that the most satisfying marriages had a 5:1 ratio of positive to negative comments.

Fredrickson, B. L., & Losada, M. F. (2005). Positive affect and the complex dynamics of human flourishing. *American Psychologist, 60*(7), 678–686.

Gottman, J. M., & Levenson, R. W. (1992). Marital processes predictive of later dissolution: Behavior, physiology and health. *Journal of Personality and Social Psychology, 63*(3), 221–233.

You should not, however, give only positive feedback.[7] People have a tendency to believe their performance is higher than it really is;[8] receiving only positive feedback reinforces this misperception. Conversely, focusing only on what is broken sends an incomplete, even inaccurate, message and may trigger a self-fulfilling prophecy.[9] To give effective feedback, you must present the whole picture—in ways that help others see their strengths as well as their weaknesses.

Recognize the Receiver's Choice

"Well, I had my meeting with Sylvia and did what we discussed," Gerard reported a week later. "When she came in, I could see she was scared, but seemed ready to listen. I started by outlining her strengths and telling her how much I appreciated her contributions to the team's efforts."

"Did you find that hard to do?" I asked.

"No, after I calmed down and thought back objectively, I could see that she really has contributed a lot. That fact gets overshadowed, though, by all the times she's late in getting her portion of the work done. And that's what I shared with her next."

"But it didn't work!" Gerard continued. "Two days after our conversation she let me down again."

People too often assume others will change immediately upon receipt of feedback. Yet this is not what most people do. More often, there is a time lag between an initial suggestion to change and when a person actually puts the change into effect.

You are more likely to take others' feedback under advisement than to act on it immediately. Others treat your feedback similarly. At best, they see your feedback as information to consider. Thus, your purpose in giving feedback is not to exert pressure on others (since this is futile) but to provide information so they may learn more about how they are perceived and open a space for change to occur. This small shift in purpose has a big ramification: you recognize that the other person has a choice about whether to use your feedback to change. Communicating your awareness of their power to choose can make a difference in the way they react to you and your feedback.

CURIOUS ABOUT THE RESEARCH?

Some researchers consider self-determination—the freedom to choose—a basic human need. If that need is threatened—by someone pushing us to change in ways we have not yet decided upon—we are likely to react negatively. We balk. The term "psychological reactance" suggests that the source of reaction comes from within—it is part of the makeup of virtually every human being.

Brehm, S., & Brehm, J. W. (1981). *Psychological reactance: A theory of freedom and control.* New York: Academic Press.

"Did you pressure her to change?" I asked Gerard.

He sat up straight. "That's my job, isn't it?"

"How did she respond?"

"She said she would," Gerard responded quickly. "But then she didn't follow through."

"Do you know if she agreed with you that she was late too often? Or if she's been trying to get things done on time but doesn't know how to manage her time?"

Effective feedback takes into account a number of choice points the person receiving the feedback has about whether to:

- *listen* to the feedback;
- *agree* with the feedback;
- *make an initial effort* to change behavior based on the feedback; and
- *stick with efforts* to change over time.

"I assumed she agreed with me, but I must admit I don't know for sure." Gerard began nodding with a knowing look. "You're asking me if I know at which choice point the breakdown occurred, right?"

I smiled. "Exactly. You know she at least listened, but did she agree with the feedback? Did she make the initial effort? Did she do okay with some initial effort but then it broke down? Only if you know the answers to these questions can you be of help to her in changing her behavior."

One clue that something has gone wrong at one or more of these choice points is if you find yourself repeating the same feedback over and over ("How many times do I have to tell you!?!"). When this occurs, you know your demands alone are insufficient to motivate the person to make the change you're hoping for.

"I can see this is more complicated than I'd thought," acknowledged Gerard. "What else is there that I haven't taken into account?"

I smiled at his readiness to assess where we were. "Well, there are a couple more things with regard to effective feedback we haven't talked about yet. One of them is the importance of remaining in the question."

Remain in the Question

While you may have the other person's best interests in mind, your feedback could be off target. After all, there are many ways the feedback could be inaccurate. The person may be working on the problem in innovative ways you have not considered. They may have more information about the particulars of the situation than you do. They may know that the recommended solution could create an even bigger problem. They may be making small gains that are not yet discernable.

Instead of assuming that you have all the facts when giving feedback, consider testing your assumptions. You may uncover unexpected motivations behind the other person's behaviors.

Gerard continued his account of the latest incident with Sylvia. "This time it was some notes I'd asked her to have ready for me in time for an early morning presentation. When I arrived in my office that morning, nothing was waiting for me on my desk. I thought to myself, 'She must deliberately want me to look stupid in front of everyone.' Remembering our discussions about assumptions, though, I realized that I couldn't know this for sure. So I considered whether she might have misunderstood the deadline or thought it was someone else's responsibility. But I'm not sure I buy those explanations."

"How might you find out?" I asked.

"I could ask her, but what would I say? Somehow I don't think asking her if she withheld the notes so I would look stupid in front of the top managers is the best approach."

We both laughed.

"Well," I replied, "that's one way to guarantee a huge withdrawal from Sylvia's emotional bank account." We chuckled again.

"It's all in whether you're truly in the question or in the answer," I responded—more seriously this time. "If you're playing gotcha and want to catch her in the wrong, any question you ask is likely to sound sarcastic. But if you're willing to seriously consider the possibility that there's some kind of misunderstanding, you're likely to uncover more about what's going on with her and obtain hints about how to help her improve. Sylvia's answer, whatever it turns out to be, will likely contain, from her perspective, a logical reason for her behavior. It'll be a step towards understanding the why of her behavior."

"Alright, I'll try it," he said. "But right now, I have to leave for another meeting."

Stay Future-oriented

Later that week, Gerard e-mailed to ask if I was available for a phone consultation—this time about another incident with Ahmed. When we talked, the exuberance in his voice was unmistakable. "I finally seem to have made some headway with Ahmed," he said. "I gave him some corrective feedback and he took it well.

"Here's what happened. We had a team meeting where he had a real opportunity to shine, and instead he just sat there. So after the meeting, I explained to him that during meetings in which we're wrestling with difficult issues, he should speak up more. He admitted that he hadn't said what was on his mind and promised to make an effort to do better."

"Sounds really good, Gerard. What did you say exactly?"

"Well, I told him that initiative and interest in solving problems are what we're looking for in future managers. I suggested he offer to spearhead the assessment and follow-up after the next meeting. I told him that I knew he wants to be considered for promotion at some point, so I was trying to give him pointers."

"Did you tell him you were disappointed that he hadn't spoken up in that meeting?"

"Not in those words. I did point out that he hadn't put forth any of his good ideas in the meeting and that since I knew he had them, he should bring them up."

Gerard did two things well in that interaction with Ahmed. First, he stayed strength-focused, pointing out how Ahmed had good ideas, ones that would benefit the workgroup as well as enhance Ahmed's career. Second, he focused on what Ahmed might accomplish in future meetings—he focused on the future rather staying focused on the past.

"Your feedback to Ahmed gave specific information about what happened in the past but positioned it in terms of how Ahmed might handle a similar situation in the future. That made all the difference. It wasn't about an opportunity lost. It was about a potential benefit to be gained in the future."

There is a difference between a deficit-based approach to giving feedback ("Here's all the things you should change") and a more positive approach ("Given your strengths, here's where you could be"). The latter combines two elements of good feedback: being strength-focused and being future-oriented.

Be Clear about Desired Outcomes

When things go wrong, many people feel they have to stay on top of whomever they believe messed up. If a report goes out with embarrassing errors, the manager begins inspecting every document. If a child brings home a failing grade, the parent begins nagging the child about studying.

In contrast, a basic human need is to feel self-determining, not controlled by others. Thus, feedback is more effective when you provide people with enough information to manage their own future behavior, but leave them free to control it themselves. Producing superior results while being self-determining requires individuals to have a clear understanding of what is expected. By being clear about your desired outcomes, you provide sufficient information for individuals to determine for themselves how they are doing. They can assess themselves against the clear standards of performance you have provided to them, rather than constantly having to rely on others' judgments.

> "I understand the importance of being clear about expectations," interjected Gerard. "But sometimes people accuse me of micro-managing. How am I supposed to know the difference between being clear about what's expected and micromanaging?"

> "What a thoughtful question!" I exclaimed. "What if your feedback to Ahmed had been something like this: 'You've got to learn to do more than sit like a lump when I ask you a question. I want an assessment of our problems with marketing on my desk by tomorrow.' What would've been wrong with that?"

> I could hear Gerard chuckle softly. "Well," he responded, "accusing him of sitting like a lump wouldn't have been strength-focused. And it wouldn't have given him a choice—I'm making demands. It feels very controlling."

> "So far, so good," I said, encouraging him.

> He continued, "I would not be in the question—I'm making no effort to find out what's keeping him from taking more initiative."

> "You're batting a thousand," I interjected.

> He continued, "It *is* future-oriented. I'm talking about what he can do in the future." He paused at that point. "But would it be clear about desired outcomes?" he mused. "I'm not sure. I'm telling him what I expect and when, but I'm not giving him enough information to be able to do it. Is that right?" He paused. I could sense he was figuring it out so I said nothing. "But when I try to give concrete information about how to do something or exactly what the outcome should look like, I'm accused of micromanaging. So I'm not sure." He paused again.

It wasn't surprising that this part was confusing to Gerard. Determining when to offer concrete guidance and when to let the person do their thing is tricky under the best of circumstances. The distinction should be based on the experience and level of sophistication of the other person.[10] A new person might benefit from an outline or samples of previous reports. An experienced person would only require the due date.

> "Does Ahmed know how to do a problem assessment?" I asked.

"Yes, he's actually quite good at it."

"Since you know he understands what a good assessment looks like, you don't have to explain further. To do so would be micromanaging. But if he didn't know, to tell him to have one on your desk without more information would be a disservice. His confidence would be undermined and you'd have to spend time correcting what he'd done wrong. The guideline I use is this: the person should be clear about what the finished product should look like. If he isn't, the manager's job is to clarify it for him. If he is, then the manager should get out of the way and let him do his work."

"But I don't always know if someone reporting to me knows what the finished product looks like," responded Gerard.

Gerard was on the right track. None of us is a mind reader. That's where inquiry and openness come in again. Those who report directly to a manager should learn how to ask, and it's the manager's job to teach them how to do so.

I asked, "Is it safe for people to inquire about the details of how to do a new task? In some organizations, people don't dare ask for this basic information for fear of looking incompetent."

Gerard sounded slightly embarrassed. "Actually, the manager before me used to chew people out if they acted as if they didn't know how to do their jobs, so now people are reluctant to ask questions."

"You do know the implications of this?" I asked.

"Yes, I do. How can we be clear about expectations if people are afraid to say what they're unclear about?"

"Exactly."

"I'm putting this in my Blackberry so I'll remember to address it in my next team meeting," he declared.

"One thing I've noticed," Gerard continued, "is that if someone doesn't know what success looks like, it's easy to assume they don't care. I originally thought this about Ahmed. In fact, I told my boss of my concern about Ahmed's apathy and disinterest in doing even the simplest things without being told. My manager pointed out that Ahmed hasn't had the benefit of the training and mentorship I've had, and what may seem basic to me may be novel to him. It hadn't occurred to me that I was assuming he knew the kinds of behaviors and attitudes we're looking for. I saw then that I had to be clearer about what we expect of our managers—and what we expected of him if he wanted to become one."

"That's terrific!" I replied. "This is another excellent example of being clear about your desired outcomes. The better you become at this, the more Ahmed and other members of your team will benefit."

A final element in improving your feedback skills is learning to handle people's reactions to your feedback. People may have emotional reactions to what you are saying—reactions that may only be indirectly related to the content of the feedback itself.

Avoid Escalation

At our next conference, Gerald began by saying, "I guess I should tell you what happened with Sylvia. I met with her and made a real effort to be strength-focused and future-oriented in my feedback. I did well, if I do say so myself. I thought we'd turned the corner. Then, two days later, she handed in another late assignment. This really ticked me off. I got on her case about being late all the time—even as I was doing so, I knew it wasn't the best approach. She started making excuses and her eyes filled with tears. I could see I wasn't getting through to her, so I ended the conversation."

"The good news is that you called a time-out in the conversation," I responded. "You were wise to realize it was going nowhere. It sounds as though both of you were emotionally flooded."

"Emotionally flooded?"

"Saturated. So upset you were unable to think straight."

Emotionally flooded people are prone to say things they later regret, to selectively hear only what their emotions direct their attention to, and to have a greatly reduced capacity for problem solving and logical thinking.[11]

"Yup, that was me," Gerard agreed. "I was really angry. In bed that night, I was still kicking myself for some of the things I'd said. Finally, I got up and wrote down all the things I was thinking and wanted to say to her—the good, bad, and the ugly—just to get it off my chest. I felt much better after that.

"The next morning, I decided to apologize. I kept thinking I should be the change I want to see. If I lash out at my employees every time they tick me off, how can they trust me enough to seek my help or let me know if something's going wrong? So I told her my reaction was out of line."

"Congratulations!" I exclaimed. "Owning your contribution to what went wrong in that interaction couldn't have been easy."

"No, it wasn't. I just kept thinking about how I'd undermined her trust in me big time. There's no way around it. I couldn't excuse myself. Plus, I found out I had more than that to own."

As I listened, I admired Gerard's ability to self-reflect.

He continued, "I realized that I'd jumped on Sylvia for not getting me the notes, but never gave her a chance to explain what had happened. I didn't go into inquiry. I just accused and blamed. So I apologized for that too and then asked her what happened."

"Another positive score for you. How did she respond?"

"She said she knew I was expecting to have the notes for the meeting and that having to do without them was stressful for me. Then she said the reason she hadn't had them ready was because I hadn't responded to an e-mail she'd sent me the day before asking for clarification of a point. When I didn't respond, she assumed the presentation had been postponed. I had two reactions to this. On the one hand, I was glad she acknowledged the bind she'd put me in. On the other hand, I was appalled that she'd done nothing when she didn't hear from me.

"And then she said something that hit me between the eyes: 'Gerard, I'm doing everything I can to make this team a success. It's you who should check your e-mails and respond to them.'"

Wham! The potential for escalation was apparent. I held my breath, waiting for him to continue.

"I was proud of myself," he acknowledged with a grin. "I knew this was a counter-attack and if I retaliated, we might reach a point of no return. So I deliberately took a couple of deep breaths to cool down. There were several things going on and I wanted to take care of all of them. First, I wanted to let her know that I appreciated her concern. I also wanted to hold her accountable and not let her off the hook for her lack of follow-up on that e-mail. I wasn't going to smooth over how this had impacted me. And third, I wanted to slam her for that snotty remark about my responsibility. Even though I knew slamming doesn't work," he flashed a grin at me here, "I wanted her to know that this approach was inappropriate."

CURIOUS ABOUT THE RESEARCH?

Studies of married couples show that 96 percent of the time, you can predict the outcome of a 15-minute conversation by noting the amount of negativity, blame, and criticism in the first 3 minutes of the interaction.

Gottman, J. M., & DeClaire, J. (2001). *The relationship cure.* New York: Three Rivers Press.

"So the first thing I said was, 'Ouch! I felt that one right in my chest and I don't like being hit in the chest.' I was stern, but not angry. I looked at her and could see she got it. She won't be quick to make that mistake again."

I was amazed that Gerard had responded so authentically. One way to avert reciprocal escalation of accusations when you are under attack is to describe your immediate feelings, just as Gerard had done.

"Then I went on with the rest of what I wanted to say. I let her know how much I appreciated her recognition of the dilemma I was in—a deliberate deposit in her emotional bank account." I smiled and nodded, and he continued, "Then I said I would prefer to have her call me at home the next time there was an urgent deadline and she was waiting on a response from me. I asked if she had any reticence about doing this in the future.

"I do feel somewhat uneasy that I made it all her responsibility to get in touch with me if something goes wrong. At the next staff meeting, we'll come up with a specific plan to handle breakdowns like this. During that discussion, I'll acknowledge that I didn't respond as promptly as I could have to Sylvia. I'd rather handle it that way. If I go back to her now with a third apology, I'd feel like I was undermining my authority. And after her snide comment, I don't have the heart to apologize for another thing."

"Fair enough," I responded. "There's more than one way to handle situations, and you've figured out a way that retains your authority as manager but still lets Sylvia know you recognize her contribution."

Overall, Gerard handled the situation well. He managed to avoid escalation at several points during the interaction.

What are some things that can be learned from this? First, that you must be prepared for others to be unreasonable when you give them feedback. Second, that you should be prepared for individuals to deflect responsibility and instead attack or blame you for what went wrong. If you have learned to clear your emotions and own your culpability, you are likely to have greater success. Third, rather than getting caught up in deciding who is at fault, your focus should be on learning from what happened and taking steps to keep it from happening again.

Delivering Feedback across Differences

Providing feedback to anyone is hard. It is even harder if that feedback is to be delivered across cultural, hierarchical, or gender lines.

Gerard still had concerns about Sylvia and brought her up again during our next weekly conference. His voice was uncertain. "There's something I haven't told you yet. Sylvia's Hispanic and has a chip on her shoulder about it. She thinks we're all racist."

"Everyone?" I asked.

"Well, most of us," he replied. "She certainly thinks I am. That's one reason I have a hard time giving her feedback. Because I know she thinks that."

"Why do you believe she thinks you're racist?" I asked.

"A lot of things," he replied. "The most recent incident was just two days ago. The team was talking about how to expand our services to reach Latino families and she said nothing. The only Latina in the room and she had nothing to say. She looked at us as though we were dunces. It was obvious what she was thinking."

"Anything else?" I asked.

"Well," he sighed, "it happens all the time. We'll be talking about something pertaining to the Latino culture and she all but rolls her eyes. She should be educating us, not condemning us. After all, she's part of the team too."

I decided to use inquiry. "Have you ever been in a situation where you were the only member of your social group and everyone else was a member of a different group?" I asked.

"What do you mean?" he asked.

"I mean, have you been the only male in a group of females or the only staff member in a meeting with senior managers or anything like that?"

"Not that I can think of," he began, "except maybe among my in-laws."

"Tell me about that," I said.

"They're Orthodox Jews, and I was raised Episcopalian. So sometimes, when I attend family gatherings, I feel a little awkward. But I'm very respectful of their religious views and they don't bother me about mine so it works out. Why do you ask?"

"I'm trying to find a parallel situation from your experience that you can relate to Sylvia," I responded. "Have you ever talked about religious differences with your in-laws?"

"Not really," he responded. "The closest was one time at the hospital, when my father-in-law was very sick and we weren't sure he was going to pull through."

"What happened then?"

"The rabbi came and everyone prayed together. Then the strangest thing happened. My mother-in-law asked me if I prayed. It was the first time she'd ever asked me about my religious beliefs. I didn't know how to respond. I mumbled something, but didn't say much that made sense."

"What were you trying to say?"

"Well, it's complicated. There's no easy answer to the question as to whether I pray or not. I'm not an atheist or even an agnostic, but describing my religious views in the context of theirs was simply more than I felt equipped to do on the spot like that."

"Because you thought they wouldn't understand?"

"Yes, and because of the stress everyone was under, and because I didn't want to be misunderstood. They have their scripture, and laws, and rituals, and I have none of that. I grew up Episcopalian, but don't consider myself one anymore. And I'm still trying to sort out the difference between spirituality and religion. It's complicated."

I decided to bring Sylvia back into the conversation. "Do you see any parallels between you in that situation and Sylvia in the staff meetings in which people expect her to describe how to reach out to Latinos?"

"I can't see how it has anything to do with Sylvia," he responded, clearly puzzled. "My situation is personal and about religion. Her situation is work-related and about her ethnicity."

"How did you feel when you were asked about your religious views?" I asked. "I know you said you thought your views were too complicated to explain, but that was a thought. I'm asking what feelings you had."

His answers came slowly, "I felt put on the spot, afraid I might offend since I don't share their religion."

"Did you feel isolated, separate from them, not part of their family?"

"Yes, I did," he responded. Then more thoughtfully, he added, "Are you suggesting that Sylvia feels put on the spot, isolated, not part of the team? It's a possibility I hadn't considered before."

"Can you see how the whole thing about it being complicated applies?"

He was responding more immediately now, as if he had moved past some kind of block. "I imagine she thought it might be too complicated to explain how to reach out to Latinos in the context of that meeting. She would have to feel we had time and interest in actually listening to her."

"Was she right?" I asked gently, aware of how painful this conversation might be for him. "If she'd tried to explain her thoughts about it in that meeting, would all of you have been willing to listen?"

"Well," he responded, "I would love to say yes. But the truth is she can be exasperating to listen to sometimes. When she first started working with us, we asked her about the Latino take on some subject, and she gave such a rambling, off-the-wall response, we just moved on to something else."

"So do you think Sylvia might have felt your reactions to her attempt to explain were racist?"

"I hate to admit it, but I suspect you're right. If I'd tried to explain my views at the hospital and one of my in-laws had cut me off, I'd have assumed they only cared about their religious beliefs and had no interest in mine. And I would have further assumed they didn't care about me. I didn't want to take a chance on that, so I didn't even try."

"Now, how does all this relate to your willingness and ability to give Sylvia accurate feedback?"

"Jean, the whole thing connects together—everything you've been saying about how to give good feedback. I was so sure I knew what Sylvia's problem was that I didn't look at her context. And I certainly haven't been providing her with enough information about how we perceive her or what she (and we) might do to improve the situation."

To understand Sylvia's situation, Gerard had to think about a time when he himself had felt nondominant and outnumbered. "Nondominant" is used as shorthand for the relative position of individuals from social groups different from the societally-defined norm, and who, as a result, have less power and privilege than members of dominant groups. This will be discussed in more depth in the next chapter, but for now simply think about it in terms of Gerard being a spiritual explorer—a person without a religious home. In this society, those without clear religious identities are often regarded as nondominant, especially by members of cohesive and religiously observant groups.

With a little understanding of how Sylvia might feel as a nondominant, it is easier for Gerard to develop the skill of inquiry, test his assumptions with Sylvia, and apply the feedback principles in a more sensitive and respectful manner.

RECEIVING FEEDBACK

There are many reasons for resisting feedback, especially corrective feedback. Having mistakes exposed can be uncomfortable and ego-deflating. You may feel the feedback is simply wrong or unfair. You may think the feedback giver lacks credibility. You may not like the person's tone of voice or word choices. Indeed, the person giving the feedback may not be very good at it.

In all these instances, emotional reactions are common. As the recipient of feedback, you may become angry, hurt, or defensive. To counter the perceived attack, you may list all the reasons the feedback sender is wrong. You may even reverse the action as Sylvia did by blaming the sender: "It's you who should check your e-mails and respond to them."

It is probably safe to assume that most of the feedback you receive will *not* meet the criteria for giving effective feedback. Your job then becomes one of using your relationship skills to convert poorly delivered feedback into information you can use. It is in your best interest to help others give you better feedback so you can use it to improve your performance.

How to do this? Follow the same principles you would use to give effective feedback. If feedback givers are overly negative, ask for positive feedback to balance the negative (focus on strengths). You can assert your right to choose by saying the feedback is thought-provoking, but you would like time to think about how best to use the information (recognize your own choice). You can admit that you may have blind spots and agree to explore them further (remain in the question). You can express regret for what happened in the past and your optimism about future improvements (stay future-oriented). If the person is offering you generalities, you can ask for specific examples. You can go into inquiry to increase your understanding (be clear about outcomes). Asking for time to think and processing your emotions until they lose their charge will reduce your defensiveness and keep you more vigilant to your selective perceptions (avoid escalation).

None of the above mean that you have to agree with the feedback. By understanding the motivation for and content of the feedback, however, you will perhaps feel increased respect for the individual for articulating rather than ignoring the issues. The goal is not agreement, but understanding—and preservation of the relationship.

SEEKING FEEDBACK

The most direct way to get feedback is simply to ask for it. Yet many people are afraid to ask their managers, "How do you think I'm doing? How would you like to see me improve?"

CURIOUS ABOUT THE RESEARCH?

Managers who seek to determine how well they are meeting expectations by direct inquiry or monitoring performance feedback data are regarded as more effective than those who only monitor indirect cues from others' behavior or the environment. Furthermore, those who ask for negative feedback are seen as more effective than those who seek only positive feedback.

Tsui, A. S., Ashford, S. J., St. Clair, L., & Xin, K. R. (1995). Dealing with discrepant expectations: Response strategies and managerial effectiveness. *Academy of Management Journal, 38*(6), 1515–1543.

Sometimes you receive feedback that surprises you. Perhaps someone has said to you, "You shouldn't be so abrasive when you talk." This is unexpected because you see yourself as outspoken but not abrasive.

Before deciding whether to take this feedback to heart, seek feedback from several others. Choose your questions carefully. An open-ended question such as "How do I come across in my communications?" might be misinterpreted as a plea for positive feedback. On the other hand, a question such as, "Do I come across as abrasive to you?" may lead people to reassure you. A better question might be, "How can I improve my communication skills?" With this, people are more likely to think you are seeking feedback for your personal or professional development and to give you an honest answer.

Suppose you get answers like these:

- "You should smile more; you're too serious and unfriendly!"
- "You should be less abrasive."
- "You seem too sure of yourself, as though you know it all."

Notice that only one person described you as abrasive, but there is a pattern in the responses: people are feeling somewhat intimidated by you. In other words, instead of taking each single piece of feedback at its face value, seek feedback from a variety of sources, examine the patterns underlying all the feedback, and test out new behaviors based on the underlying pattern. Continue to seek feedback and test out behaviors until you discern a noticeable difference in how people respond to you or until others tell you they notice a change. Becoming comfortable seeking feedback is a matter of practice.

It is particularly important for members of nondominant groups to learn how to seek feedback, since well-intentioned dominants may simply withhold feedback rather than risk being seen as culturally insensitive. Remember Gerard's discomfort in giving Sylvia feedback because he felt she saw him as racist? This is not uncommon. If Sylvia wants to be certain to get as much feedback as other members of the team, she may have to be more aggressive in seeking it—and help the dominants on her team feel more comfortable in being open and honest in giving it.

CURIOUS ABOUT THE RESEARCH?

In one study, White reviewers provided more lenient feedback to essay writers they believed to be Black than to those they believed to be White.

Harber, K. D. (1998). Feedback to minorities: Evidence of a positive bias, *Journal of Personality and Social Psychology, 74*(3), 622–628.

WHAT IF THE OTHER PERSON REALLY IS THE PROBLEM?

During training sessions on these relationship skills, someone inevitably brings up an individual in his or her life to whom none of what is being said applies. The person being described may be pathological, hopelessly incompetent, insidiously evil, or have some other extreme behavioral or psychological problem. If the person really is pathological, or it is unsafe for you to remain in the relationship, then by all means seek legal or medical advice, leave the relationship, fire or transfer the person, quit the job, or vacate the premises.

However, sometimes the individual presents a persistent, but manageable problem and you choose to remain in the relationship. Even though you may feel you have already tried everything and the other person remains unreasonable, practicing the skills introduced in this book may break the logjam.

You really can be more effective in your relationships by focusing on yourself rather than trying to change others. As you become more open and honest, as you work to accept people and situations as they are rather than trying to change them, as you develop feedback and other skills, your relationships with difficult people in your life can change. We have found that some even make what seem like miraculous turnarounds.

NOTES

1. We are indebted to Chris Argyris and Peter Senge for their development of inquiry and advocacy as critical skills for organizational learning. We use the term "openness" instead of "advocacy" because the term advocacy connotes adversarial relationships in some disciplines.

2. Jaques, E. (2002). Social power and the CEO. *Business Book Review, 21*(26), 1–9.

3. Jaques, E. (1992). Managerial accountability. *Journal for Quality & Participation, 15*(2), 40–44.

4. Murray-Johnson, L., Witte, K., Boulay, M., Figueroa, M. E., Storey, D., & Tweedie, I. (2001). Using health education theories to explain behavior change: A cross-country analysis. *The International Quarterly of Community Health Education, 20*(4), 323–345.

5. Covey, S. R. (1989). *The seven habits of highly effective people.* New York: Simon and Schuster.

6. Roberts, L. M., Spreitzer, G. M., Dutton, J. E., Quinn, R. E,. Heaphy, E., & Barker, B. (2005). How to play to your strengths. *Harvard Business Review, 83*(1), 74–80.

7. Fredrickson, B. L., & Losada, M. F. (2005). Positive affect and the complex dynamics of human flourishing. *American Psychologist, 60*(7), 678–686.

8. Dunning, D., Heath, C., & Suls, J. M. (2004). Flawed self-assessment: Implications for health, education, and the workplace. *Psychological Science in the Public Interest, 5*(3), 69–106.

9. Kim, P. H., Diekmann, K. A., & Tenbrunsel, A. E. (2003). Flattery may get you somewhere: The strategic implications of providing positive vs. negative feedback about ability vs. ethicality in negotiation. *Organizational Behavior and Human Decision Processes, 90*, 225–243.

10. Johansen, C. P. (1990). Situational leadership: A review of the research. *Human Resource Development Quarterly, 1*(1), 73–85.

11. Gottman, J. M., & Silver, N. (1999). *The seven principles for making marriage work.* New York: Three Rivers Press.

CHAPTER 5

Bridging Differences

The emotional undercurrent in the room was riveting. Kate, chair of the board, directed her question toward Derrick, "Why did you think you could just go ahead without our approval? We've talked repeatedly about how important it is to develop this report as a team. Yet you took it upon yourself to make changes and hand it in without getting our okay. You wanted to do it your way and just didn't give a damn about what the rest of us thought!"

At this point, I jumped in. It was only the second time I had met with the board of directors of this non-profit agency, but I knew they were facing several significant hurdles, with ambitious plans for the next year—and, unfortunately, a low level of mutual trust. "The last time we met, most of you agreed to avoid making assumptions about others' motives."

Kate paused. "So this means I should—what did you call it?—go into inquiry with him?" She looked at me questioningly.

I smiled at her, knowing that she knew the answer.

The room was silent. Hesitantly, Kate leaned forward, looked directly at Derrick and asked, "Would you please explain why you didn't call me before sending the report?"

"Wonderful. That puts you in the question rather than the answer," I said.

Derrick paused and then tersely replied, "There wasn't time." I waited to see if he would add anything—he didn't. I looked at Kate, silently coaching her to continue her inquiry.

"Please explain," she said, this time with more patience in her voice.

"At the last minute, I discovered the report had to tie our recommendations to those of the environmental committee. I only heard about this on Friday and the report was due Monday. I called several board members, including three sitting here, and everyone agreed I could just write a paragraph describing the link and hand it in. The change was minor, and I didn't have a lot of time because of personal things that weekend, so I went with it." He fell silent again, staring straight ahead.

Almost in unison, Kate and several others in the room said, "You didn't call me!" They checked among themselves—who had been called and who hadn't? Three people admitted having been contacted, yet rapidly disavowed any connection with Derrick's actions. "I thought he was calling everyone," said one. "I didn't know he'd go with what I said," added another. Derrick's jaw flinched a bit, but otherwise he remained immobile.

At this point, the group was clearly headed for more accusations and negative attributions. An intervention was called for.

"What were your assumptions about Derrick?" I asked. As they named them, I listed them on the flip chart:

- wants to run things his own way
- doesn't care what the rest of us think
- too lazy to check with others

I turned to Derrick. "Derrick, I'm sure there's more to your side of the story. I'll ask for that later. Right now, all I'm asking for is a list of your assumptions about the others."

He rattled off his list immediately:

- have made up their minds about me
- won't listen if I explain
- automatically assume I tried to do them in
- care more about themselves than about the success of the project

I did some quick reflection—internally debating where to lead the group. They had called me in to help them learn to manage their relationship dynamics more effectively. They were a highly diverse group, composed of a near-equal ratio of women and men. There were six Caucasians (including Kate), three African Americans (Derrick was one), two Latinos, one second-generation Japanese American, and one

South Asian. One was an unacknowledged gay person ("everyone knew, but no one talked") and another sat in a wheelchair.

When the chair of the group, Kate, and I had initially set up the contract for this engagement, I suggested that their varied backgrounds would undoubtedly affect the board members' relationship dynamics. For that reason, diversity had been included as a topic, but not until the sixth session. The group was just beginning to take an early step, naming aloud some of the attributions—ingrained assumptions—they covertly held about one another.

The race and gender identities of Kate (White female) and Derrick (Black male) were obvious factors in their assumptions about each other. Another clue was the way in which the attributions voiced fit all too neatly into well-known stereotypes: "too lazy to check with others," "have made up their minds about me." It was a safe bet that race and gender were on everyone's minds, yet the diversity issue was too touchy to be named without prompting.

> "Kate," I said, "I want to ask you a question that may go beyond what we've talked about so far. Is that alright with you?"
>
> "Sure," she responded, looking puzzled.
>
> "Would you describe how you're feeling right now?" I asked.
>
> She paused, looking at me as if to say, "Is it really okay to be honest?" I gave my silent assent, and she said, "I'm thoroughly ticked off. I'm tired of people trying to sabotage my authority as board chair. If he's going to call other people, why not me?"
>
> "Do you sometimes wonder if people don't respect your authority because you're a woman?" I gently asked.
>
> "For sure!" she almost shouted. "That's exactly why! And I'm tired of it!"
>
> I paused to let this sink in with everyone. Greg, one of the White male members of the group, spoke up, "Kate, that's not fair. We're all working together as a team and no one's treating you differently because you're female. We're proud of being such a diverse group and of our ability to work so well together."

I could see the tiniest bit of embarrassment in Kate's face. Had she gone too far and disrupted the group's illusion of harmony with regard to diversity issues?

> I spoke up. "I have two comments. First, we're all entitled to our feelings. If Kate has these feelings, they're coming from someplace, so it makes sense to look at what's going on in the group that may

be contributing to them. She's demonstrating courage by saying these things out loud. Second," and now I addressed Greg directly, "she's expressing a feeling she has as a woman. There's research that people in nondominant groups tend to view interactions with dominant group members based on an accumulation of past experiences in which they felt discounted. People in dominant groups, however, may only look at what's happening within a single interaction."

"Dominant groups? Nondominant groups?" repeated Greg with a hint of sarcasm in his voice. "That's not fair! No one here is dominant. Everyone in this room is equal. What are you talking about?!!!"

Since Kate had opened the door, I felt I could contract with the group to jump ahead of the planned workshop schedule. "I hadn't intended to deal explicitly with diversity issues until later, but since they seem very relevant to the present disagreement, I'd like to move to them now. Will everyone agree to that?"

Greg settled back down. "I think this is a personality issue," he responded, "but if you think it has something to do with diversity, I'm willing to listen." The others agreed, and waited for me to begin.

Quickly, I thought about possible approaches to thinking about differences. I decided that the best place to begin was with their hopes and aspirations. Since they appeared to share strong beliefs about egalitarianism and the value of diversity, then it was a matter of helping them stop pretending they were all the same and instead learn to openly address and benefit from their differences.

"So," I began, "how did you get to be such a diverse board? I see a lot of diversity in a number of ways. How did that happen?"

Kate responded first, "We set out to make it happen. The clients we serve in this organization are from all walks of life—they're male and female, come from different racial and ethnic backgrounds, are rich, poor, and in-between, gay and straight, abled and disabled. We wanted the board to reflect that diversity."

"So is it fair to say that all of you see diversity as a good thing?" I asked. Heads nodded in agreement. "Why did each of you agree to serve on such a diverse board?"

Monica's response was representative: "Personally, I endorse the goals of the organization and want to help it reach out to many different individuals—not just differently abled individuals like myself, but to *all* persons who can benefit from our services. And I wanted to be part of a group that could demonstrate to our clients—and our funders—that diversity works; that you can bring a group of very different people together and make it work."

"In your minds, what are the benefits of having a diverse group? Monica mentioned a couple. What are some others?" I asked.

"Well, I'm not sure I've personally experienced it," offered Ramon, "but I've read that diverse groups are more creative and innovative, that the different backgrounds and experiences of diverse individuals lead to new and different ways of looking at old issues."

CURIOUS ABOUT THE RESEARCH?

Research on the benefits of diversity within organizations has been conducted in both educational and business settings. In college settings, overall benefits to students include a higher level of self-confidence, critical thinking skills, and civic development. In business organizations, work units approaching diversity as an opportunity for greater learning show improved levels of performance.

Gurin, P., Dey, E. L., Hurtado, S., & Gurin, G. (2002). Diversity and higher education: Theory and impact on educational outcomes. *Harvard Educational Review, 72*(3), 330.

Kochan, T., Bezrukova, K., Ely, R., Jackson, S., Joshi, A., Jehn, K., et al. (2003). The effects of diversity on business performance: Report of the diversity research network. *Human Resource Management, 42*(1), 3–21.

"Personally, I'm beginning to wonder if it's worth it," added Derrick rather dryly. "I was under the impression that I was invited to join the board because of my ideas and my skills, my ability to take initiative, and to represent the interests of some of our clients, but I find instead that I'm constantly being brought up short—like with the report."

"It does seem as if we've had more conflict on the board since we've become more diverse," offered Kate. "It wasn't what I expected."

"It doesn't have anything to do with diversity," asserted Greg. "We're just having some personality conflicts that'll eventually work themselves out. Some people are just too sensitive."

"I'm not sure they'll work themselves out," I interjected, "unless you take active steps to acknowledge the differences underlying the conflicts."

Increasingly, organizations are composed of more diverse groups of people than they have been in the past—customers, employees, even leadership itself. Under ideal circumstances, this diversity results in increased innovation and creativity. Yet to promote unity and avoid conflict, leadership teams such as this board often attempt to operate with what sociologists Bernadette Park and Charles Judd call a "color-blind, assimilationist perspective."[1] In such settings, individuals are expected to assimilate their attitudes and habitual actions into the prevailing mindset of the organization. A premium is placed on members' similarities; expressions of differences are deemed irrelevant or even taboo.

It is counterproductive to deliberately add people to an organization because of their diversity and then consider discussion of that diversity off-limits. After all, people have been invited onto the team because they have contributions to make.

The paradoxical solution is to establish a work culture in which unity is built by encouraging diverse viewpoints to be expressed and integrated into the work of the organization.[2] This requires trust, and trust requires open and honest relationships. Yet openness, honesty, and trust are difficult to establish among people who are unequal in status and power, either in the organization or in the larger society. People such as Greg, who staunchly believe in egalitarianism, may find it hard to see how historical power and status in the larger society sometimes play out in what seems to be a simple relationship dispute. Historical status differences may be seen by such people as irrelevant in today's society or too painful to discuss.

> "Let's take a break," I said. I hadn't come to this session prepared to discuss diversity directly, so I wanted some time to formulate my thoughts.

DOMINANTS AND NONDOMINANTS

By the time everyone came back from break, I was ready.

> I wrote the words "Dominants" and "Nondominants" at the top of two columns on a sheet of flip-chart paper and started by saying, "Earlier when I used the terms dominant and nondominant, Greg vehemently objected to applying these terms to this board. His strong reaction, though, tells me that the words themselves have some inherent meaning. What do they mean to you?"
>
> "Well," said Greg, "it doesn't happen here, but it means that some people are treated differently than others."
>
> "Why are some people treated differently?" I asked.
>
> "Because they're not respected or valued as much as others?" Kate suggested.

"Yes, that's right on target," I responded.

Greg's negative reaction to the idea of dominant and nondominant groups was understandable. These terms draw attention to the unequal power and status of people in society based on the groups to which they belong rather than on their individual characteristics. This inequality may get played out in relationship dynamics. The challenge is to become aware of what these dynamics look like when they occur.[3]

"Let's start by identifying which groups are dominant and which are nondominant in this society," I said.

They squirmed uncomfortably, looking at one another. "I know this isn't the way you like to think," I reassured them. "I'm not asking what's in your heart; I'm asking what goes on in society every day. Look at the news. Stand in line at the grocery store. Apply for a loan at a bank. Which groups have more power and status than others?"

"Bosses have more power and status," finally came one response.

"Great!" I exclaimed as I wrote "bosses" in the dominants column. "Okay. Who else?"

Someone said, "Attractive people."

I looked at them and said, "Well, if attractive people are dominants, who is the nondominant group?"

The answer came quickly: "Unattractive people. Average-looking people."

"And who's the nondominant equivalent to the boss?" I asked.

"Subordinates," someone said.

With that, the door was opened and the answers came more quickly—so fast, in fact, that I could hardly keep up. The list on the flip chart soon looked like Table 5.1.

"These are some of the ways people differ from one another," I explained. "There are others. But it's more than just differences in power and status. Nondominants are also targets. They experience others' unintentional discounting, prejudiced thoughts and feelings— and they experience discrimination."

I noticed Derrick and the other African American male glancing at each other knowingly, then turning to me with a cynical look. I knew that look.

Some people become insulted when commonalities among dominance dynamics are discussed. In their minds, such discussions imply

Table 5.1
Dominant and Nondominant Group Members

Dominants	Nondominants
Bosses	Subordinates
Attractive	Unattractive or plain
Physically or mentally abled males	Physically or mentally disabled females
Wealthy	Poor
English-speaking	Non-English speaking
Married	Not married
Christians	Other religions
Right-handed	Left-handed
White	People of color
Middle-aged	Older and younger
Straight	Lesbian, gay, bisexual, transsexual (LGBT)
Thin	Heavy or obese
Tall	Short
Extroverted	Inverted

that discrimination suffered by different nondominant groups is being regarded as equivalent.

> I clarified, "There's a vast difference between recognizing dominance dynamics and assessing the magnitude of an oppression. The oppression historically experienced by Jews, for example, is in no way equivalent to that experienced by left-handed people. Forced enslavement, 300 years of a Jim Crow caste system, and genocide are not the same as being ignored because someone doesn't think you're pretty enough. I'm not equating these at all. What I am saying is that there are patterns to how prejudice and discrimination are manifested and experienced. If you understand the patterns, you can apply them to whatever biases you're talking about."

> I paused, knowing some were still skeptical.

> Kate said out loud what a number of people in the room were probably thinking: "Some of us do feel unfairly treated, but what you're saying implies that everyone is prejudiced. I agree with Greg; I don't think that's true."

In a group full of forward-thinking, community-minded people such as these, an initial hurdle in addressing diversity is distinguishing between individual prejudice and patterns of behavior favoring one group over another.

"You're right," I said. "But let's make a distinction here. I'm assuming you're well-intentioned. You believe prejudice is counterproductive and you consciously work to eliminate or reduce it in your own behavior. You support practices that avoid or reduce discrimination.

"And yes, times have changed," I continued. "We're past segregation. Women and people of color can vote. We have the Equal Rights Act. We even have an African American president. Most people in this society—and especially people in this room—are committed to leveling the playing field."

Heads were nodding in agreement. I glanced around the room, knowing that what I was about to say would challenge many people's image of the way things ought to be. "Your individual attitudes aren't the issue. The issue is whether some groups inherently have more advantages than others. Here's the rub: those starting off with advantages are able to command the power and resources to gain even more advantages. Yet most also discount how much those initial advantages contributed to the successes they enjoy."

People who start off with advantages may indeed work hard for what they have, but they may be unaware of how their group membership has brought them greater opportunities than others. Their individual talent allowed them to exploit those opportunities, yet others with the same talent but lacking in opportunity did not have a similar chance.[4] These status differences translate into how easy or hard it is to go about your daily business—to be paid attention to, listened to, or treated fairly.

"I imagine that most of you know this intuitively without looking at a single piece of research on it," I concluded.

The room was completely still. No one moved. This topic is hard going for any group, but was particularly difficult for this one. They regarded themselves as being on the vanguard of a new era, and they were proud of their individual accomplishments. Yet here I was, telling them that perhaps some of those accomplishments were partly the result of advantages they had inherited rather than earned.

"All things being equal, who's more likely to be paid attention to at a meeting—a handsome person or an average-looking person?" I asked. "An extrovert or an introvert? An able-bodied person or a physically-challenged person? In this society overall, who has more power—women or men? People of color or Whites?"

They listened silently. I knew my questions were rhetorical, but I wanted them to think about the historical patterns of behavior within this society that most people take for granted.

"Please understand. I'm not saying that this is the way any of us want it to be. I *am* suggesting it's the reality. If you're having difficulties in one-on-one or team interactions, begin by expanding your customary view of reality: look for systemic advantages, and then decide whether they have any bearing on the problems you're facing."

Asha, a South Asian woman, was looking intently at the flip chart. "I'm trying to decide whether I'm a dominant or a nondominant. Can one be both?" she asked. "As a professional engineer in my country, I'm definitely a dominant. But as a South Asian immigrant to the United States, most people here consider me nondominant."

"Great observation, Asha," I responded. "Nearly everyone is *both* a dominant and a nondominant. We aren't members of just a single group; we have multiple group memberships. We move from one group membership to another depending on the situation, and as we do, we may shift from being a dominant or nondominant. And these shifts lead to different, but predictable, dynamics."

DOMINANCE DYNAMICS

"In which situations do you have less status as a nondominant, Asha?"

"I'm relatively new to the country, here on a visa," she replied. "I don't know whether I will become a citizen or not, or even if I want to." She looked embarrassed and added, "I hope that doesn't hurt anyone's feelings." They assured her it didn't.

"So you're nondominant compared to U.S. citizens, right, Asha?" She nodded and I established eye contact with her for a moment to prepare her for my next question. "Asha, do you feel you're treated differently than others in discussions within this group?"

"Well," she said hesitantly, "when I speak, sometimes they ignore what I say. It's as though I hadn't said anything at all. Then someone else will say the same thing and everyone will say 'what a great idea.'"

A murmur spread throughout the room. Several people threw their hands in the air in exasperation. No one responded overtly, though.

"That's a very common experience for White women, and men and women of color in groups." I explained. "Even though it may be unintentional, what's valued at the societal level—in this case, speaking with an American accent—gets translated into interpersonal interactions."

Kate jumped in, "Thanks for saying that, Asha. It took courage." She turned to the rest of the group, "This is a difficult conversation and I'm personally proud of us for having it. I think we should commend ourselves."

Kate's comment broke some of the tension and people began patting themselves and each other on the back. I gave the group a thumbs-up and continued.

"What Asha is describing is not something you're consciously doing or intending. These behaviors are ground into us by what we watch on television, what we see done by other people; what's all around us. Asha's feelings, your feelings, Derrick's feelings, Kate's feelings—these all result from things outside this room and affect what goes on inside it. Societal norms and beliefs are always in the room—in silent but pervasive ways.

"Let's go back to an earlier point. I want each of you to think of two social groups to which you belong—one that puts you in the nondominant category and another in which you're a dominant group member."

Scott, another White male, spoke up, "Looking at the groups we've listed so far, I'm a dominant in every dimension."

"We're all nondominant in some way." I responded. "Think back. When have you felt like you've had lower status or power?"

"Well, I went to a public college and my best friend got a scholarship to go to an Ivy League school."

"So what advantages did your friend have that you didn't?"

He responded immediately, "He goes places and people ooh and ah about his having gone to *that* university. People automatically think he's smarter, but he's really not."

"That's what being a nondominant feels like. You see doors opening for others that aren't opening for you."

Scott stared at me blankly. Then almost imperceptibly, he nodded.

"Have the rest of you identified at least one dominant and one nondominant group to which you belong?" They responded affirmatively. "Good," I said. "Now let's list the differences in how dominants and nondominants are treated in this society."

This time it was easy. The two lists paralleled one another (Table 5.2).

"We can see from this list," I summarized, "how initial advantages lead to further ones."

"Are you're saying I should feel guilty because I'm a dominant?" asked Greg. The sarcasm was unmistakable.

Table 5.2
Differential Experiences of Dominants and Nondominants

Nondominants . . .	Dominants . . .
. . . have to prove themselves again and again	. . . are presumed to be competent
. . . cannot assume they will fit in	. . . take for granted that people will make room for them to fit in
. . . often experience physical barriers (e.g., right-handed desks or difficult-to-navigate ramps for wheelchair access)	. . . assume their environment is designed to support them
. . . are often treated as though they are invisible	. . . command attention when speaking
. . . are denied regular access to opportunities dominants take for granted	. . . are more likely to find doors opening to them

"I'm not talking about who's guilty, who's innocent, or who's a victim," I responded. "Let's not even go there. Instead of feeling badly about yourself, I encourage you to feel an increased sense of responsibility for understanding the patterns kept in place through these dominance dynamics. We can all do a lot to help make changes in these societal patterns right where we live and work, if we're willing to take it on."

Doing so, however, requires awareness.

DOMINANTS' BLIND SPOTS

"Look at our list," I suggested. "Dominants and nondominants view the world very differently. Because dominants are likely to take their positions and opportunities for granted, they may fail to see that the situations of nondominants are very different. As a result, they may not think of themselves as advantaged; they simply see their situation as normal."

Organizational scholars Mary Ellen Capek and Molly Mead explain how barriers are unknowingly erected for nondominants by how normal is defined:[5]

What people regard as "normal" assumes the face of neutrality, the appearance of "universal"—generic, genderless, objective, colorblind, and classless (p. 9) .... For those "native" to [and] most in sync with their organization's values, styles, and structures—many of these. . . .

conventions seem so opaque as to be inconsequential. And those not native to the organization's culture, who stumble over these conventions, often are marked as ineffectual and easily marginalized. (p. 52)

A good example is the television voice that dominates in the United States. Many young people start out assuming their spoken voice is normal—everyone else speaks with an accent, they don't. Then they discover, in school or by watching television, that there is a prevailing accent—which may or may not be theirs.[6] In the United States, the predominant accent on television is that spoken in one part of the country: California. People in the rest of the country speak differently. When different accents are heard, they register as regional, while the television voice comes across as neutral or even universal. In fact, the California accent is just one regional voice among many, but carries invisible and unacknowledged status.

Statements by dominants reflecting unawareness of unspoken and unexamined norms are signals of dominance dynamics in play. Dominants often:

- *Justify their attitudes and actions toward nondominants.* Dominants may say: "I'm not prejudiced; they just don't want to work." or "If they were smarter, they would have done better."
- *View nondominants as potential threats or as seeking unfair advantage.* A dominant might say, "I've worked hard for what I have, why should they get away with less?" Bosses accuse employees of whining. Whites accuse Blacks of playing the race card. Working mothers who have difficulty staying late for meetings are accused of not giving their work a high enough priority. Immigrants, whether in the country legally or not, are spoken of as taking over.
- *Minimize or ignore the reality of nondominants.* Dominants often try to play up their similarities with nondominants and inadvertently minimize significant differences: "We're really all the same underneath." If criticized, dominants may assume the primacy of their own good intentions: "I didn't mean any harm; you must be hypersensitive."

What these examples have in common is self-focus on the part of the dominants with little or no consideration given to the perspective or experiences of nondominants.

Dominants who sincerely believe all people should be treated equally may simply have no basis for understanding why some people have less than they do. Instead, they believe a person who has less must deserve less or that a person who is encountering obstacles must simply pull himself up by his bootstraps.[7] Alternatively, dominants may be so busy comparing themselves to people who have even greater status that they do not recognize the degree to which others perceive them as dominant. Without conscious effort, dominants may remain oblivious.

Meanwhile, nondominants are acutely aware of what they don't have. They look at the sturdy boots of the dominants (e.g., the way they are listened to in meetings) and their own shoeless feet (e.g., the way others are given credit for their ideas) and wonder how to bridge the difference.

As I shared some of these thoughts, I noticed people stirring uneasily. Talking about advantages and favoritism goes against the norm of egalitarianism many people hold—the implicit assumption that no matter how rich or poor, no matter how well or poorly-regarded, all are equal in the eyes of morality and the law.

Jill was the first to react. "Let me see if I've got this right. What you're saying is that as a nondominant employee, I can easily see my boss's obnoxious behaviors, but as a dominant White person, I may appear equally abhorrent to people of color and never know it?"

"Exactly," I said.

Monica also responded. "Some things you're saying are hard to take." She began addressing the rest of the group, "As a White person, I didn't like it when Jean said dominants tend to justify their positions and prejudices. I've said some of the things she mentioned and don't especially like being made to feel in the wrong. However, from my nondominant position as a person with disabilities, I can see how many of the things she said were right on target. I've noticed that some physically able White men describe how they got ahead and how hard they had to work, while ignoring additional obstacles White women, individuals with disabilities, and people of color face in these same workplaces. I'm not saying those men didn't work hard or don't deserve what they got. Of course they did. I'm just saying that for some of us, the same level of effort would have gotten us less far."

I intervened. "Before anyone thinks we're dumping on White men or any other group, I want to restate that the behaviors we're talking about may fit any group of people with dominant status. No race, cultural group, gender, or religious group has a monopoly on the ability to fall into dominant behaviors and attitudes beyond their awareness.

"I know people of color who hold religious convictions that homosexuality is a sin," I continued. "They don't think of themselves as dominant because of the historic racial discrimination they've experienced, nor do they connect what they experience based on their race or ethnicity with what gays and lesbians are experiencing by virtue of their sexual orientation. They're not used to seeing dominance dynamics from the perspective of a dominant and miss seeing how oblivious they might appear to others who are nondominant."

No one in the room moved, or even seemed to breathe. People were avoiding looking at one another—a sure sign that this was an undiscussable topic. Finally, Scott spoke up. "I can relate to this, because my brother is gay and people assume he's abnormal and should be straightened out."

I was silent, waiting for others to respond. Finally, LaShunda spoke up. "So let me see if I understand this. You're saying that if I have strong religious beliefs about homosexuality, then I'm a dominant—which means I won't understand the perspective of Scott's brother who is a nondominant gay person. Is this what you're saying?"

Scott interjected, "That's exactly what she's saying."

LaShunda said, "Well, suppose I know I'm right, that my beliefs are right? Suppose his perspective is just wrong? Don't right and wrong have anything to do with it?"

The room was silent again. I stayed silent, too, knowing the group would have to grapple with this question in more depth over a longer period of time: How were they going to respect some people's right to believe as they believe while also supporting others' right to live and love as they live and love?

Looking around the room, I suspected they had strong moral differences on other contentious issues as well.

Around the world, people debate immigration policies, affirmative action, pro-choice/pro-life positions, and the role of religion in public life. These issues are divisive because they cut to the core of people's identities and value systems. There was no easy solution to the group's impasse, yet their ability to work effectively together depended on their having respectful dialogue, even if all they did was to agree to honorably disagree.

I spoke up again. "This is a thorny topic. It's as important and divisive as the Abolitionist movement was in the 18th century, when one side quoted the Bible to justify slavery and the other quoted it in opposition. Both sides thought the Bible justified their beliefs."

Derrick piped up, "Speaking for myself, I'm really glad the Abolitionists won that debate." Even LaShunda laughed.

Scott spoke up. "Here's one thing that puzzles me," he said. "Kate identifies her group as women and Derrick identifies his as African American. My brother identifies with the gay community. What's my group? I'm a White heterosexual male. Why would I want to identify with White males, since we're blamed for all the problems?"

"We're back to pigeon-holing White males as the only bad guys," I responded. "Race and gender are at the core of many of the dominance dynamics in this country. But I want to be clear that this is the situation in this particular country, not everywhere in the world. Think of the Darfur, Rwanda, and Bosnia genocides, or the conflict between North and South Korea. Dominant behaviors are not the exclusive province of White males by any means."

CURIOUS ABOUT THE RESEARCH?

The Minorities at Risk project lists 268 racial-ethnic groups around the world as suffering some form of discrimination or oppression. Sixty-eight groups are at risk of genocide.

Marshall, M. G., & Gurr, T. R. (2005). *Peace and conflict 2005: A global survey of armed conflicts, self-determination movements, and democracy.* College Park, MD: Center for International Development and Conflict Management.

Particularly in the United States, this is often new information. Many groups experiencing oppression around the world are from the same racial background, although their cultures or religions may differ.

Scott replied, "Some of what you say makes sense when I think of my brother. But going back to race and gender issues, we've been dealing with them openly for a very long time. I'm getting tired of all the talk about this group and that group, this race and that race. Why can't we just treat each other as individuals, working together to get something done?" Again, I was silent, waiting for someone in the group to respond.

This time Ramon had something to say. "Last month I went to a seminar on developing intercultural sensitivity. I learned that minimizing differences is a form of ethnocentrism. If I deny or minimize cultural differences between myself and someone else, I'm essentially saying the other person's unique cultural characteristics and experiences are trivial, that the only things important to consider are characteristics and experiences similar to mine.[8] And if I'm in the dominant group, then my cultural characteristics will prevail over those of the nondominants."

"Good point, Ramon!" I commented. "On the one hand, we're all in this together. On the other hand, by dismissing differences, we make them less important than similarities, whether intentionally or not. Here's my definition of cultural competence: seeing people as similar in the ways in which they are similar, and seeing them as different in the ways in which they are different."

Because they hold more power in this society and are often in the numerical majority, dominant group members may simply be unaware that they are looking at things through a dominant lens, and acting in ways that appear to nondominants as taking their advantages for granted and favoring people in their own group.

CURIOUS ABOUT THE RESEARCH?

Researchers have studied high and low-power individuals in a variety of settings using many different groups. Findings include:

- High-power people (dominants) are found to talk, interrupt others, and speak out of turn more than low-power people (nondominants).
- Women (nondominants) are more accurate judges of others' nonverbal behavior than men (dominants).
- Younger siblings (nondominants) are better able than their older siblings (dominants) to imagine the intentions and beliefs of others.

Keltner, D., Gruenfeld, D. H., & Anderson, C. (2003). Power, approach, and inhibition. *Psychological Review, 110*(2), 265–284.

"Most dominants do not deliberately try to get on your nerves," I explained to the board members. "But there's interesting research suggesting that dominants and nondominants may truly be disposed to see the world differently—and perhaps partially for evolutionary reasons.

"Here's an example," I said. "The squirrels in my backyard have set up a hierarchy in terms of access to the feeder. My family calls the top squirrel Midas because he's always hoarding his wares in the feeder.

If some lesser squirrel comes along and tries to encroach on his territory, Midas, as the dominant squirrel, aggressively chases the other squirrel away. In contrast, when the nondominant squirrel experiences threat, it is submissive. Of course we all like to think people can do better than this."

With that, everyone chuckled.

Yet this behavior extends to humans as well. Several studies show that when dominants encounter a threat, they're more likely to become quarrelsome. Threatened nondominants, however, are more likely to become agreeable.[9] While your boss is more likely to quarrel with you than she is to quarrel with her own boss, you are more likely to go along with your boss in order to get along.

Research has established the seductiveness and blindness of power. Over time, as people exercise power, they tend to develop an inflated sense of self-importance, and derogate those with less power than themselves.[10] Unless you make a conscious effort to resist doing so, you are as likely to engage in quarrelsome behavior with subordinates when you feel threatened.

"You don't have to like it," I explained, "but if you recognize that something happens to people as they accumulate more power, you can guard against it and have a greater understanding of others when it happens to them."

"Are you suggesting that if I, as a White male, see things differently from a Black female, for example, I should just take her word for it?" asked Greg, speaking slowly.

"Of course not," I responded. "No one has a monopoly on the truth. But I would invite you to consider the possibility that she has information you don't, information you have no reason to know even exists. The question for you is how to gain that information.

"As a professor in my classroom, I'm the dominant. I believe I know best what I want to teach, but students know best how they learn and whether they're learning. I'd be foolish to ignore any hints that something is getting in the way of their learning. In the same way, I'm not South Asian, as is Asha. If she tells me South Asians take offense at the phrase 'blue sky,' then I won't go around insisting on my right to use that phrase, or claim she's being hypersensitive by objecting to my use of it. I will try to avoid negating her experience in any way.

"The question for me, particularly if I'm conscious of being a dominant, is how to know what I don't know. Dominants pay a huge price: they are unlikely to get accurate information from nondominants, especially if there's a substantial power difference between them."

As I paused, they began to talk among themselves. After a few minutes, I suggested a break. When they returned, I proposed a switch to looking at dominance dynamics from the perspective of nondominants.

ACUTE AWARENESS OF NONDOMINANT STATUS

"Let's look again at the list of nondominants," I said, referring back to the flip chart. "The dilemma is different for them," I began. "No one likes to see themselves as nondominant. It's difficult to accept a world where dominance dynamics operate. But this isn't about inherent worth. It's about patterns of interaction to watch out for, so that you're not caught off-guard."

Research has consistently shown that when members of groups with a history of being set apart from the mainstream—as various ethnic, religious and other groups have been—tend to pay more attention to how their social group is treated than do members of groups without this history. Acts of overt discrimination, as well as small slights based on dominants' blindness, constantly remind nondominants of how their group has historically been excluded. There's even a term for the small affronts: micro inequities.[11]

CURIOUS ABOUT THE RESEARCH?

Research confirms that nondominants are more aware of their group membership than dominants. One study asked individuals to identify which of two artists they preferred and then assigned them to groups in which they were in the numerical minority or majority (based only on their preference for one artist over another). Those assigned to groups in the minority were more preoccupied with their group membership than were those in the majority.

Lücken, M., & Simon, B. (2005). Cognitive and affective experiences of minority and majority members: The role of group size, status, and power. *Journal of Experimental Social Psychology, 41,* 396–413.

Because of their history and experience, nondominants tend to notice possible slights and insults, even when others see none. The question that remains on the table is whether the nondominant individual is being treated with less respect than a dominant person would receive. Declaring "we are all equal" doesn't take away the question if actions suggest otherwise.

> I could see that a tangible example would help. I looked at Kate. "If I understand correctly, you felt Derrick did what he did because as a man, he thought he could just take action and ignore you as a woman."
>
> "Well, I wouldn't put it quite so strongly," she said. "I'm not saying he did it intentionally. I just believe that subconsciously he didn't think about checking in with me as board chair because I'm a woman. In my experience, men are used to doing what they want regardless of what a woman thinks."
>
> A chorus of "That's not fair!" erupted.
>
> "Derrick, what about you?" I asked. "What were you thinking, as a Black man, when Kate accused you of leaving her out of the loop?"
>
> "It felt like déjà vu," he replied. "Here was one more White person accusing me of acting uppity; not knowing my place. It never occurred to her to assume I had good intentions. Had I been White, she would've been more likely to give me the benefit of the doubt."
>
> Again, echoes of "That's not true!" could be heard.
>
> I responded, "Kate has said she often experiences subtle putdowns because she's a woman. Derrick has explained how he regularly gets accused of not acting as a nondominant is supposed to act. Both have had these experiences time and time again. Is this right?" Both nodded agreement. "Past experiences make both more sensitive to the possibility of such things occurring. Again, please be aware that they're not reacting to this one specific incident; their reactions come from prior experiences with many, many similar incidents over a very long period."
>
> Derrick responded quietly, "I think I'm finally past it, and then it happens again."

Management scholars Martin Davidson and Raymond Friedman refer to this as the "persistent injustice effect."[12] In their research, Black managers experienced more unjust acts than did White managers, as well as higher levels of past injustices and expected future injustices.

> I paused for a moment, then asked, "Can anyone give another example of how, as a nondominant, your or someone else's reactions were based on accumulated past experiences, or expected future ones?"

Greg sat back in his chair. "Well, if I think about my own work situation, the vice-presidents are always saying they have an open-door policy, yet whenever someone registers a complaint, they're accused of whining about nothing. The VPs believe they have an open door, but the rest of us see it as slammed shut. The pattern is clear—the VPs ask us to let them know what we think, and when we do, they dismiss it. Then in staff meetings, the VPs ask why we don't speak up with our ideas!"

"That's exactly the same thing. The patterns you've experienced with your VPs lead you to question their present statements."

"And not only with the current VPs," added Greg, visibly getting more agitated. "In the last 10 years, I've only had one boss who actually meant it when she asked for input."

"Okay," I replied. "Your past history causes you to question any boss's statement about wanting your input. But a particular boss may be genuinely puzzled when people don't open up. He doesn't understand how his own behavior is shutting people down. He thinks the issue's your problem, and you believe it's his." I paused, then spoke directly to Greg, "Now apply this to Kate and Derrick."

Greg quickly responded. "Kate is saying that as a woman, she's used to being ignored, so she assumed that's why Derrick left her out of the loop. A good part of her reaction came from an accumulation of previous experiences. Derrick's actions played into that. In the same way, as a Black male, Derrick is regularly accused of being too aggressive. So his reaction, too, was based to a large degree on a whole string of similar incidents."

"Well put!" I agreed. "The interesting thing in this interaction is that both parties were seeing themselves as nondominant. Neither considered the possibility that they themselves were being seen—and reacted to—as a dominant. This is common. As I said before, many nondominants fail to recognize when they're engaging in dominant behavior toward members of other groups. No single group has a corner on dominance behavior."

Nondominants' Justification of the Status Quo

Just as dominants justify their behavior—and thus implicitly rationalize the prejudices and inequities of the system—nondominants often collude in enabling those prejudices and inequities as well. It's a human paradox.[13] You might expect nondominants to flail against the system, trying to change it. Some do—but too often, they think to themselves, "I'm not like those in my group. I'm more like the dominants."

This was another touchy subject. I broached it with a question, "How many of you have heard some White woman or person of color declare, 'No one did me any special favors; I got to where I am in this organization on my own?'"

You could have heard a pin drop. I continued, "When it comes to a choice between identifying with dominants or nondominants, many people go with being a dominant. Why would anyone want to be viewed as oppressed, not-as-good-as, or stigmatized?"

CURIOUS ABOUT THE RESEARCH?

Sociological research suggests that many people feel motivated to preserve the belief that existing social arrangements are fair, legitimate, justifiable and necessary—even in the face of evidence suggesting otherwise, or in contradiction to their own self-interest. As just one example, in a workplace study, low-income employees were found to be more likely than high-income employees to believe large differences in pay were necessary to foster motivation and effort.

Jost, J. T., Pelham, B. W., Sheldon, O., & Sullivan, B. N. (2003). Social inequality and the reduction of ideological dissonance on behalf of the system: evidence of enhanced system justification among the disadvantaged. *European Journal of Social Psychology, 33*(1), 13–36.

Nami, who had been quiet until now, interjected, "In my own family, some of the women have had their eyes Americanized, and my sisters tell me I should spell my name N-a-o-m-i rather than N-a-m-i."

"Exactly," I responded. "Your family is looking at who the winners are in this society, and they want you and your family members to be more like them." She nodded.

Members of nondominant groups may often collude in what is called internalized oppression: accepting society's discriminatory messages and viewing oneself as lesser-than because of nondominant status in their society. From a state of internalized oppression, nondominants perpetuate the same stereotypes toward other members of their group as do dominants—in an attempt to distance themselves from stigma. So for example, welfare recipients denounce the ubiquity of welfare cheats; people of color in an affirmative action organization talk about how they got their jobs on their own and not through affirmative action; fifty year olds talk about how old a friend is looking.

I paused. "Does any of this ring true?"

DeAndre, one of the African American men, spoke up, "This reminds me of my cousin who landscapes for wealthy Whites. He's constantly talking about how rich Whites are so smart and how we as Blacks don't have it together. Is this what you mean by internalized oppression?"

"That's it exactly," I responded.

No Unambiguous Way of Speaking Out

Connor, who had also been silent until now, spoke. "There's something about all this I don't understand. Why don't nondominants speak up for themselves? Earlier, when Asha was talking about being ignored in discussions, I wondered why she hadn't said anything before. If she felt she was being ignored, why didn't she speak up? Personally, I wouldn't put up with it!"

CURIOUS ABOUT THE RESEARCH?

Numerous studies have shown that members of stigmatized groups minimize the extent to which they have been personally discriminated against and are reluctant to acknowledge feelings of discrimination publicly, particularly in the presence of nonstigmatized group members. On the other hand, they may readily acknowledge discrimination against their social group as a whole or against a member of their group whom they believe has been treated unfairly.

Carvallo, M., & Pelham, B. W. (2006). When fiends become friends: The need to belong and perceptions of personal and group discrimination. *Journal of Personality and Social Psychology, 90*(1), 94–108.

Jill jumped in. "That's part of the problem! If Asha complains about being ignored, she'll be seen as a whiny victim."

"Excellent point," I said. "When nondominants complain about subtle putdown behavior directed toward them—or even point it out—they're often viewed as trying to get something for nothing. If Asha were Black, for example, and mentioned that she was frequently interrupted, she might be accused of playing the race card."

One of the problems is that nondominants have no clean way of bringing up the impact of subtle, inadvertent putdowns. They face a litany of denials if they raise the issue. Many dominants truly *do* want to know if there is something in the system or in their own behavior that excludes rather than includes others. Yet nondominants who bring it up risk negative reactions. Dominants who speak up about the same issue are not viewed as having the same self-interest; the group is more likely to hear them.

CURIOUS ABOUT THE RESEARCH?

Because personal responsibility is assigned a high value in this society, people generally react negatively to those who blame negative events on discrimination rather than their own actions. Across racial, gender, and age groups, people within the same social group as the target are as likely to derogate a group member for claiming discrimination as are those in a different social group.

Kaiser, C. R., & Major, B. (2006). A social psychological perspective on perceiving and reporting discrimination. *Law & Social Inquiry, 31*(4), 801–830.

Dominants have to be careful, though, not to speak for nondominants from a place of entitlement or dominance. When dominants assume understanding of nondominants' perspectives without checking, they risk reinforcing their perceived tendency to be naïve and presumptuous.

I reflected back on the earlier conversation regarding Scott's gay brother. "What's the situation for gays and lesbians in this organization?" I asked.

Connor spoke up again. "We have a 'don't ask, don't tell' policy," he said.

"Does this policy work for the organization?" I asked.

"I think it works very well," he responded.

"Connor, I've heard you refer to your wife several times so I assume you're married. Is that correct?"

"Yes," he responded, looking puzzled.

"So, with regard to sexual orientation you're a dominant, right?"

As though anticipating my next statement, his face reddened slightly. "Are you implying that as a dominant, I don't know if it's a problem or not for gays and lesbians?" he asked.

Jill spoke out, "Now I'm confused. You've just said that it's good for dominants to speak up for nondominants since dominants have more credibility. But now you're telling Connor he shouldn't speak up for gays and lesbians in this organization since he's heterosexual and a dominant in terms of sexual orientation."

Kate spoke up. "Here's how I understand it. If nondominants are experiencing a problem—they've tried to bring it forward, but no one seems to be paying attention—then dominants should also speak up, to bring legitimacy to the issue and to help the nondominants be heard. But a dominant should be cautious in saying there's no problem about a particular issue involving nondominants without checking. How would a dominant know if there's a problem? What if the nondominants haven't felt comfortable bringing the issue up?"

CURIOUS ABOUT THE RESEARCH?

One study concluded that dominants may have a unique opportunity to reduce prejudice because their challenges elicit more guilt from participants, yet simultaneously make the participants feel less tense and uneasy than equivalent confrontation by nondominants.

Czopp, A. M., & Monteith, M. J. (2003). Confronting prejudice (literally): Reactions to confrontations of racial and gender bias. *Personality and Social Psychology Bulletin, 29*(4), 532–544.

"Extremely well put," I exclaimed. "I suspect some of your understanding of this once more comes from your experiences as a woman in this society. Am I right about that?"

"Yes!" Kate replied. "I can't tell you how many times I've sat in a room with 10 men and two women and heard one of the men declare there's no gender problem. If that were true, why were there so few women?"

I turned to Connor. "Connor, given this discussion, do you want to revise what you said?" I suspected his regret for his previous statement and wanted to give him a chance to set it right.

"Yes, I do," said Connor. "This has all been quite interesting. I'm going to think about how many times, as a dominant, I declare there's no problem because I'm not personally experiencing the problem or no one has brought it to my attention. So what I want to say instead is that I'm unaware of whether there is a problem or not, but if there is a problem with gays and lesbians not being out in this organization, I wish someone would educate me."

I was pleasantly surprised by his statement. Sexual orientation is a difficult topic in most organizations, and here was someone saying he was willing to talk about it.

"If I were lesbian," said Theresa softly, "I certainly wouldn't feel safe coming out in this group."

"That's ridiculous!" exclaimed DeAndre. "How on Earth are we supposed to get anywhere if we can't talk about tough subjects?"

I was afraid this would shut her down, but Theresa took a deep breath and said, "DeAndre, we're all just learning about this dominance dynamics stuff. Speaking for myself as possibly the youngest person in the room, and certainly one of the newest members of the board, it's sometimes hard for me to sit and listen to the rest of you talking about how open this group is, how willing you are to listen to one another and how it's everyone's individual responsibility to speak up, when half the time I say something I can almost hear you thinking that I'm just a kid and don't know what I'm talking about." She pointed to the nondominants column on the flip chart. "That's me in this group. What I experience here are a lot of unspoken ways of doing things that everyone is supposed to know but no one has told me about. That feels like dominance dynamics to me."

Everyone looked at her. "You're right," DeAndre said. "I've often wondered how you felt in this group. I'm glad you spoke up."

"We'll talk about things you can work on as individuals and as a group," I said. "But before we do, I want to shift gears a little. So far, we've been talking about dominance dynamics as they occur in interpersonal interactions. Some dynamics get played out at the organizational level, too, and these should be considered."

DOMINANCE DYNAMICS AT THE ORGANIZATIONAL LEVEL

Favoritism or even discrimination doesn't have to be deliberate. Both can occur through the tendency of organizations to become more homogeneous over time.

People are attracted to organizations that seem to contain individuals with similar skills, values, and attitudes, even similar demographics.[14] As such, the array of individuals considered for a job is restricted. Once the applicant pool is screened, recruiters are more likely to hire people like themselves: an individual's potential fit with the organization is assessed through the perceptual filters of what is known as similarity bias. Once hired into an organization, those who are considered a good fit are more likely to be promoted and rewarded. Those who don't fit in as well may develop less positive relationships and be more likely to leave.

Unless an organization or a group actively takes steps to make sure its policies and procedures discourage homogeneity, they may look up one day and wonder why everyone is so much alike.

"How did your board get so diverse?" I asked.

Kate responded. "It took a long time and very deliberate effort to attract individuals as diverse as our constituents. At first, we mostly complained about how difficult it was to find and keep diverse board members."

"How did you turn it around?" I asked.

"We got creative. We started looking for potential board members in different places. We went into the community and asked for recommendations and referrals. We didn't give up. We kept going until we started getting the diversity we wanted. And we're still working on it."

Combating the normal drift toward homogeneity should include recruiting and hiring diverse individuals; but to become truly inclusive, organizations and work groups also have to create supportive and cooperative work environments to support diversity.

CURIOUS ABOUT THE RESEARCH?

Simply changing the demographic mix of a work unit is insufficient. A recent study found that increasing the proportion of African Americans in a majority white environment actually led both groups to increasingly "stick to their own," that is, turn to members of their own group for support. An environment of peer support and assistance was critical to improving intergroup relations among racially different employees.

Bacharach, S. B., Bamberger, P. A., & Vashdi, D. (2005). Diversity and homophily at work: Supportive relations among white and African-American peers. *Academy of Management Journal, 48*(4), 619–644.

"I prefer working in a supportive and cooperative organization myself," said Scott.

"Of course," I agreed. "Nearly everyone does. That's the beauty of this work. You think you're doing something for the culturally different person and it ends up benefiting the whole organization."

"Let's look at a scenario," I suggested. "If an Asian American woman who had received sterling ratings on past performance appraisals, was well-known for her collaborative skills, and had been named Employee of the Year was bypassed for a promotion in favor of a White male who'd received mediocre evaluations but was a cousin of the boss, most people would suspect something unfair was going on." They laughed.

"Now suppose that same Asian American woman is up for promotion. The criteria of the White men deciding on the promotion are a take-charge attitude and the ability to socialize with large customers and suppliers. Under such circumstances, her exceptional sales record and organizing ability may not carry as much weight as her competitor's aggressiveness and weekend networking on the golf course. If she were to object, reasonable people might argue that she simply didn't fit the definition of leadership within the company. This is indirect discrimination—especially if her qualities actually have as much impact on revenues and profits as those of her colleague."

Ramon responded thoughtfully, "So you're saying that favoritism can result in indirect discrimination even when no individual has actively discriminated?"

"Exactly," I responded.

People are accustomed to thinking of prejudice and discrimination as something done by an individual to an individual in ways obvious to anyone looking on. What occurs more often today is indirect discrimination—organizational acts with discriminatory outcomes justified for nonracial, nongender, or other non-diversity-related reasons.

"Remember our earlier discussion of unacknowledged ways of doing things that support dominants and exclude nondominants?" I asked. "Indirect discrimination results from those norms in action."

FROM GUILT TO LEARNING AND CONTRIBUTION

Diversity alone is insufficient. Simply adding differences to your group or organization and then pretending those differences don't exist won't get the job done. Instead, the goal must be to learn from the diversity so that people feel their contributions matter. Yes, diversity can bring conflict and tension, but it can also be productive if you consciously seek to achieve a different outcome.

CURIOUS ABOUT THE RESEARCH?

Research on the effects of diversity has yielded paradoxical findings. On the one hand, increased tension and conflict are widely
reported in diverse groups. On the other hand, bringing people
with different perspectives together often results in increased
creativity, innovation, and performance. The key is in learning
how to manage the conflict and to learn from one another.

Kochan, T., Bezrukova, K., Ely, R., Jackson, S., Joshi, A., Jehn, K., et al.
(2003). The effects of diversity on business performance: Report of the
diversity research network. *Human Resource Management, 42*(1), 3–21.

"Here's how I think about it," I explained, writing on the flip chart:

DIVERSITY + LEARNING = INCLUSION

Everyone was silent, carefully avoiding looking at one another or at me.

"You're not looking particularly happy," I commented, knowing conversations like this can be difficult and confronting one's involvement
in dominance dynamics discomfiting.

Finally, Greg spoke up. "Earlier you said you weren't talking about
guilt or innocence, yet here I am feeling guilty as a White heterosexual male. And I'm angry too, because White heterosexual males
have done a lot for this country and I don't think that gets enough
recognition."

Tapping the side of her wheelchair, Monica chimed in, "I'm way past
feeling inferior because of this, yet I'm being reminded that others
may see me as less-than. So I'm not too happy with this conversation
either."

I glanced at the clock, noting that we had about an hour left in the session—
time enough to review how to use this information in positive ways.

"I, too, have various dominant and nondominant roles stemming from
my various statuses in the world," I responded. "Each brings assets
and poses liabilities. You invited me today partly because of my academic background. Yet my education can hinder me from seeing how
I might inadvertently offend or put down someone who hasn't had
the opportunity for the same education. And I would be downright
stupid if I thought my formal education meant I was the smartest person in the room. After being with you for a while, I know very well
I'm not. But I have blind spots I can never fully eradicate—and while

some may draw inspiration from my academic accomplishments, others may regard my very presence as a slap on their face.

"As a Black woman, I'm aware that some segments of society automatically regard me as inferior. I can't change that. I can recognize it for what it is, yet not allow it to limit how I view myself. But I would be foolhardy to pretend it doesn't affect how others may see me. At the same time, when I think of what Black women around the world have accomplished throughout history, I feel enormous joy and satisfaction in being a part of that legacy.

"Bottom-line, I look at myself as both nondominant and dominant and recognize the assets and limitations of both. I use the assets to give me strength and courage, I use the liabilities or limits to provide humility and compassion, and I use both to keep me perpetually in a learning mode. I have learned much from you today. As an academic and as an African American woman, I know what it's like to be vilified and put down. I have never been visibly disabled, but I can empathize with Monica when she talks about the pain of being different in this group. As a Black woman, I also have a sense of standing on the shoulders of many before me who achieved magnificent accomplishments in the face of unimaginable obstacles. So I can identify with Scott's pride in his White male heritage."

"So you're saying it's okay for me to be proud of my White male heritage?" asked Scott.

"Of course," I responded.

"And you're also saying I shouldn't feel guilty and ashamed of some of that same White male heritage?"

People often equate guilt and shame, although researchers make a critical distinction between them. Guilt is about your actions, or actions you have condoned in others. You know you have done something that does not feel right. But you are judging the action, not yourself. Shame is different. Shame is what you feel when you view yourself as fundamentally flawed and unworthy.[15] This can send you into an undeserved spiral of self-condemnation that is disproportionate to the offense you think you have committed or participated in.

Guilt is unavoidable, because everyone makes mistakes, and we all belong to groups that have made tremendous mistakes. A feeling of guilt can motivate you to apologize for those mistakes, or to take steps to make sure you do not engage in or endorse those same behaviors again.

After I explained the difference, I turned to Scott, "To answer your question, I have no interest in encouraging your shame. But if feeling guilty motivates you to do something about it, that's all to the good."

"I can live with that," Scott agreed wryly, "especially since I sense something different going on with my youngest brother. When I was in high school, all the Latinos hung out together, and the Blacks in their group, and the Whites in theirs. But that's not the case with him. He has an appreciation of different cultures and groups that I frankly envy. So maybe we can move past all this."

"I agree that something different is happening with the younger generation. I see it in my family too. I know some of the young adults in my family—and perhaps your brother—are experiencing true multiculturalism in their relationships—where differences are used to promote mutual learning instead of ignored, pretending everyone is the same."

Monica spoke, "I don't say this very often, but sitting in this chair, sometimes unobtrusively, I hear a lot. For whatever reason, people think I'm deaf, so they say things to one another that they might be embarrassed about if they realized I could hear them, really hear them—at least I hope they'd be embarrassed. I've also gained a greater appreciation for the simplest things that the rest of you probably couldn't possibly understand. Now I can see how my Whiteness has brought me advantages. The reason I'm a member of this board is to help open opportunities for others, just as we've been talking about. After today, I see us beginning to use our differences to learn from one another. This is exciting, although a little scary."

I glanced around. Everyone had visibly relaxed. "You're looking better," I commented.

Derrick smiled for the first time all day. "In other words," he said, "all of our dominant and nondominant parts bring strengths and liabilities and we should learn what we can from them and use what we have to help ourselves and others."

"That's all any of us can do, I believe."

I paused to let them think about this before I continued: "We've come full circle, back to the conflict between Derrick and Kate and the rest of you. Let's review how this conflict could've been handled differently using this new information."

BRIDGING DIFFERENCES: ANTIDOTES TO DOMINANCE DYNAMICS

How does a diverse group of well-meaning people move past dominance dynamics and develop the trust so essential to open communications and effective relationships? How does this board build on their similarities and aspirations for unity while taking into account their differences?[16]

There are six antidotes to ameliorate the impact of dominance dynamics and instead promote learning.

1. Test the assumption that a specific interaction reflects personality conflicts.

Could social group memberships and historical backgrounds also be influencing the interaction? Identifying dominance dynamics in an interaction is easier said than done, especially in a society which focuses on individual culpability rather than systemic influences. When you're upset, you can't see society but you *can* see the person right in front of you who is giving you grief. Clearing your emotions may help you test out whether the past is relevant to your present experience.

> Kate interjected immediately. "I was oblivious to Derrick's seeing me as a powerful chair. I assumed instead that he was being a typical male. I could have disputed that assumption and looked for other reasons for his actions—at least giving him the benefit of the doubt."
>
> "And it never occurred to me," added Derrick, looking directly at Kate, "that you may have had a history of having your leadership abilities questioned because you're a woman, or that my actions fed right into that history. That's so ironic, because I know what it feels like to be slighted ever-so-subtly again and again."
>
> Kate flashed him an impish grin and then addressed the group, "Now maybe he *was* acting like a typical male, but at least I could have tested that assumption before getting all worked up about it."
>
> Derrick made a gesture of mock indignation. Their humor signaled that they were beginning to feel more comfortable with the topic.
>
> "This is getting good," I commented. "You deliberately asked people from a variety of cultural backgrounds to join this group. Now that everyone is here, it doesn't make sense to ignore the very backgrounds that led you to bring people together in the first place. Instead, as you're doing now, it makes sense to become aware of some of the red flag items that may have different meaning in one cultural context than another."

2. Acknowledge your and others' blind spots, especially if you are a dominant. Practice focusing on the other's situation and reaction rather than just your own.

Dominants have blind spots to overcome. If you are a dominant in an interaction, it is all too easy for you to think the system is working just fine for everyone—because it *is* working fine for you and members of your group. Christians who work in a government-funded organization, for example, may never question having an Easter Egg Hunt for employees and their families. It may not occur to managers to include lower-level staff members in a meeting, even when task assignments or job responsibilities of these individuals are being considered. You may be genuinely perplexed about the source of complaints voiced by non-dominants, since your own experiences are so different. Seeing one's own advantaged position can be very, very difficult, making it easy to be oblivious to how your verbal and nonverbal reactions and responses affect others.Especially in interactions across differences, your words and actions may have very different meaning for members of other social groups. Deciphering this meaning requires you to seek to understand how the other person might be experiencing the interaction. This is empathy; putting yourself in the other's shoes.

> "Kate thought race wasn't an issue," I suggested, "since she believed she harbored no prejudice. Derrick believed gender wasn't an issue since he believed he respected female leaders. The complexities of the dominance dynamics in play remained hidden until they each began to see things from the other's perspective."
>
> Scott spoke up, "I have another example. Because I have watched my brother's pain, I react whenever someone calls another person a 'wimp.' Now, I know the word doesn't necessarily mean they're putting down gays, but when I hear it, I'm back in high school hearing my brother getting teased relentlessly. This is a huge blind spot for those who freely use that word—maybe they don't even care." He paused and looked around the group, "Hey, that's an assumption I could test, isn't it?" They all grinned at him.

3. Differentiate intent from impact.

Negative impact can be interpreted as deliberate intent. Studies have found that when low-prejudiced dominants are worried about being seen as prejudiced, they may act in tentative and ambiguous ways which can easily be interpreted as prejudicial. Their behaviors are inconsistent with their true attitudes and feelings. It can be difficult for nondominants to differentiate these behaviors from those of more highly prejudiced individuals.[17]

> "No kidding!" responded LaShunda in response to my explanation. "There's a woman at work who acts all nervous around African Americans. Does that mean she may not be prejudiced?"

"Exactly," I responded. "She may indeed harbor some prejudices. Or, she may be so afraid you'll think she's prejudiced that she's acting like she is."

"I will own to that," said Kate unexpectedly. "I was definitely nervous that some of you would think that I was prejudiced because of my reaction to Derrick. But then, I was so mad I had to speak up anyway."

LaShunda responded, "I'm glad you said that, Kate. I think we all worry about whether we'll say the wrong thing."

I turned to Derrick, "Do you remember our earlier conversation about the conflict between you and Kate?" I asked. "When I asked you what you were thinking when Kate accused you of leaving her out of the loop, what did you say?"

"I'm not sure of my exact words," he responded, "but I do know that I'm often accused of being too aggressive, even uppity."

LaShunda added, "You know, my brother is always complaining about something like this. He says he has to walk around at his job on tiptoe, taking care not to assert himself too much lest he scare everybody. He tries smiling and nodding often, doing whatever he can not to intimidate people. He says a lot of his buddies do the same thing because they believe at a subliminal level, people in this country have learned to fear Black men."

"Uppity? Intimidated? What are you talking about?" objected Greg. "I can't believe I'm hearing this. Are you saying our reaction to Derrick's jumping ahead like that has something to do with our stereotyping him as an aggressive Black man? That's crazy!"

"Here's another area where we can benefit from separating intent from impact," I inserted. "I too have heard what LaShunda is describing, from any number of Black men. Their reaction is the impact. And there's research to support it.[18] It's definitely a concern among many Black men I know—not all, but many. It's just not talked about in interracial settings. In fact, I can't recall ever having heard it discussed in a group like this. For your group to do so is to your credit."

With big grins, they patted each other on their backs.

4. Recognize your tendency to automatically stereotype and take active steps to form counter-stereotypes.

"Stereotypes?" exclaimed Ramon after I stated the fourth antidote. "I don't stereotype! That's like saying I'm prejudiced which I'm not." Just about everyone holds unconscious stereotypes toward some social groups, including their own. Social psychologist Patricia Devine refers to these tendencies as "the prejudice habit": the automatic and non-intentional responses that even low-prejudiced individuals have developed through a lifetime of socialization experiences.[19] Even though you believe all people are equal, you may still find yourself forming culturally ingrained, automatic stereotypes about others, or worse—using those stereotypes to justify favoring your own group to the detriment of another.

Jill spoke up. "Well, I'll admit that I do sometimes stereotype others—homeless people and rich people. When I see homeless people, I think they must be too lazy to get a job. And when I see rich people, I think they must have exploited others to get what they have. But then I feel ashamed." As she talked, her face grew red. "This is not how I like to think about myself."

"As I explained before, I have problems with shame if it leads to you feeling fundamentally unworthy," I replied, "but guilt is fine if it motivates you to take action on behalf of those having fewer privileges or opportunities than you. Since you're willing to admit to stereotyping, it sounds as though you're feeling guilty, and using it to hold yourself accountable in a way that leads to change rather than recrimination."

"Oh, alright," said Jill, now mollified. "But what do I do when I make these automatic stereotypes? Just tell myself not to have them?"

"Suppression doesn't work very effectively," I replied. "Fortunately, there are other ways."

CURIOUS ABOUT THE RESEARCH?

Individuals can learn to exert control over prejudiced responses through the use of several methods:

- thinking of what one knows about the individual apart from the stereotyped attributes;
- substituting thoughts of positive attributes of members of this particular group for the negative ones;
- visualizing examples of exemplary members of the particular group.

Monteith, M. J., & Voils, C. J. (2001). Exerting control over prejudiced responses. In G. B. Moskowitz (Ed.), *Cognitive social psychology: The Princeton Symposium on the legacy and future of social cognition* (pp. 375–388), Mahwah, NJ: Lawrence Erlbaum Associates.

If you know you're prone to stereotype a certain group, one approach is to set aside time to visualize a counter-stereotype, and to do this repeatedly until the counter-stereotype automatically occurs along with the stereotype.[20] If you tend to think of Native American women as submissive, for example, you might imagine an assertive and competent Native American woman instead. Dispute the stereotype the same way you would dispute an assumption. For example, you might think, "I remember reading about Wilma Mankiller, the first female chief of the Cherokee Nation. She was a strong leader."[21]

> "Does that really work?" asked Greg. "Just think of a counter-stereotype and then I won't stereotype anyone anymore? That sounds too cut-and-dried to me."

> "It's not quite that easy," I agreed. "But researchers do say that with repeated practice, motivated people can learn to reduce their automatic stereotypes—and the behaviors that follow from them.[22]

> "It does work for me. After much practice, when I find myself stereotyping, I automatically start disputing the stereotype. Eventually I wonder which is correct: my original thought or the disputation."

> Jill commented, "Well, I think most of us already have counter-stereotype ideas about Kate and Derrick. I see her as a strong leader and I see Derrick as friendly and caring. But applying this to people I don't know—that will require practice. I think it's kind of neat, though, and I'm glad to know about it."

> Then she added, "I think I'm usually a dominant when I stereotype others. What about nondominants? Don't they stereotype too?"

5. As a nondominant, stay alert to signs of internalized oppression, i.e., unconscious acceptance of society's discriminatory messages. Instead, consider yourself capable of influencing dominance dynamics.

Jill was right. Nondominants hold stereotypes as well, and these stereotypes often keep them from recognizing their own assets. Statements such as "That's why we never get ahead, we don't know how to act" are rooted in internalized oppression—an assumption that the proper way to act is that of dominants. Sometimes getting ahead does require adopting attitudes and behaviors of the dominants. Other times, however, conforming to dominant norms means rejecting your group in ways that may destroy, rather than enhance, positive aspects of the group.

Internalized oppression is rooted in an assumption that one's own group is inherently powerless or less-than. If Kate actually believed she had power, she might have reacted less emotionally and immediately sought an approach for future situations. If Derrick really believed he was equal, he might have expressed his regrets for having inadvertently slighted others and asked that guidelines be established for handling similar situations.

They seemed intrigued when I explained this. "Give another example," asked LaShunda.

"A friend told me the last Miss Universe contest featured women from all over the world with many features in common. Can you guess what those features were?" I asked.

One by one, they suggested attributes: "Light skin." "Caucasian features." "Long straight hair." "Super-thin."

Greg piped up, "Yes, gorgeous!"

LaShunda crunched a piece of paper and threw it at him. "You think this is a joke?" she asked.

CURIOUS ABOUT THE RESEARCH?

A recent study demonstrated that when people making biased statements were confronted by their targets, they made fewer such statements. However, they also showed more anger and irritation towards the targets who had confronted them.

Czopp, A. M., Monteith, M. J., & Mark, A. Y. (2006). Standing up for a change: Reducing bias through interpersonal confrontation. *Journal of Personality and Social Psychology, 90*(5), 784–803.

I looked directly at Greg, "There's not a woman in this room who matches the physical attributes of Miss Universe, and most don't want to. But many women constantly put themselves down because they don't measure up against that standard—this is internalized oppression. And this negative self-view is perpetuated by the type of jokes that . . ."

Greg interrupted me, clearly contrite. "I get it," he said simply. Looking at his face, I believed him.

6. Create environments where individuals are encouraged to bring positive aspects of their identity into discussions.

A question for the board was how to legitimize such discussions in moving forward. Unless they consciously planned to make such issues part of their conversations, they could easily slip back into overlooking dominance dynamics. One effective practice is to set up an agreed-upon mechanism to alert each other when individuals inadvertently slip into dominance dynamics (as LaShunda did when she threw the paper wad at Greg).

It is not always easy to bridge differences. Even as people work to develop more openness to nondominants in a group, the culture of the dominants tends to retain primacy. Subtle, sometimes nearly imperceptible pressures are exerted on nondominants to conform to dominant norms of thinking and acting. In the extreme, group-based differences can become undiscussable. Nondominants who take pride in their social group identity are not allowed to express that part of themselves; conflict is driven underground. Those with positive social group identities are likely to resist this; they do not want to suppress their own way of thinking in favor of adopting the norms of the dominants.

Adopting a multicultural perspective encourages individuals to bring positive aspects of their identity into discussions. As people talk openly about their attitudes and learn to foster positive relationships and develop trust, they learn to bridge differences and effectively manage conflict. They begin to see differences as contributions, and as a source of learning, rather than impediments to unity.

> I summarized, "You've seen for yourselves a more effective way of handling situations such as the one Derrick and Kate experienced. There are skills you can develop to minimize the threat while staying true to yourself and speaking from your heart about what's troubling you. It's not either shout and scream at someone or make nice and gloss over problems as though they don't matter. You can address real issues. There are skills you can learn to keep the group intact rather than tear it asunder. In fact, I've already noticed you begin to lighten up about issues of difference. That's a good sign."

CURIOUS ABOUT THE RESEARCH?

A study of a 2,062 White adults in the United States found that those favoring multiculturalism (over colorblindness, assimilation, or separatism) expressed lower levels of intergroup bias. Experimental studies have also shown that a multicultural orientation leads to less racial bias than do color-blind or assimilationist perspectives.

Park, B., & Judd, C. M. (2005). Rethinking the link between categorization and prejudice within the social cognition perspective. *Personality and Social Psychology Review, 9*(2), 108–130.

Richeson, J. A., & Nussbaum, R. J. (2004). The impact of multiculturalism versus color-blindness on racial bias. *Journal of Experimental Social Psychology, 40*(3), 417–423.

Greg responded, "Well, I still think Kate and Derrick are being too sensitive, but I haven't been in their shoes, so I'm willing to give them the benefit of the doubt. I also remember how we've talked at length about being strength-focused with one another and if I put that foremost in my mind, I can concentrate more on what they bring to the table—which is a lot." He shyly grinned at both of them.

"Greg has figured out a way to handle his doubt—by increasing his focus on people's strengths instead of questioning their experiences," I commented. "I believe that sets a good standard for this whole board. Approaches like his go a long way toward fostering productive multicultural environments.

"It's not easy work. It may feel awkward at first. But you can take small steps forward. If you have the commitment, and are willing to develop the awareness and skills, you can contribute to building better relationships, better organizations, better communities, and a better world for all. You've already made great strides just in the few hours we've spent together today."

NOTES

1. Park, B., & Judd, C. M. (2005). Rethinking the link between categorization and prejudice within the social cognition perspective. *Personality and Social Psychology Review, 9*(2), 108–130.

2. Ely, R. J., & Thomas, D. A. (2001). Cultural diversity at work: The effects of diversity perspectives on work group processes and outcomes. *Administrative Science Quarterly, 46*(2), 229–273.

3. Calvert, L. M., & Ramsey, V. J. (1996). Speaking as female and white: A nondominant/dominant group standpoint, *Organization, 3*(4), 468–485.

4. Gladwell, M. (2008). *Outliers.* New York: Little, Brown, and Company.

5. Capek, M.E.S., & Mead, M. (2006). *Effective philanthropy: Organizational success through deep diversity and gender equality.* Cambridge, Massachusetts: MIT Press.

6. This example provided by Art Kleiner.

7. Appelbaum, L. D. (2002). Who deserves help? Students' opinions about the deservingness of different groups living in Germany to receive aid. *Social Justice Research, 15*(3), 201–225.

8. Bennett, M. J. (1986). A developmental approach to training for intercultural sensitivity. *International Journal of Intercultural Relations, 10,* 179–196.

9. Fournier, M. A., Moskowitz, D. S., & Zuroff, D. C. (2002). Social rank strategies in hierarchical relationships. *Journal of Personality and Social Psychology, 83*(2), 425–433.

10. Keltner, D., Gruenfeld, D. H., & Anderson, C. (2003). Power, approach, and inhibition. *Psychological Review, 110(2),* 265–284.

11. Beagan, B. (2001). Micro inequities and everyday inequalities: "Race," gender, sexuality and class in medical school. *Canadian Journal of Sociology, 26*(4), 583–610.

12. Davidson, M., & Friedman, R. A. (1998). When excuses don't work: The persistent injustice effect among black managers. *Administrative Science Quarterly, 43*(1), 154–183.

13. Jost, J. T., Banaji, M. R., & Nosak, B. A. (2004). A decade of system justification theory: Accumulated evidence of conscious and unconscious bolstering of the status quo. *Political Psychology, 25*(6), 881–919.

14. Schneider, B., Goldstein, H., & Smith, D. B. (1995). The ASA framework: An update. *Personnel Psychology, 48,* 747–773.

15. Brown, C. B. (2007). *I thought it was just me: Women reclaiming power and courage in a culture of shame.* New York: Gotham.

16. Park, B., & Judd, C. M. (2005). Rethinking the link between categorization and prejudice within the social cognition perspective. *Personality and Social Psychology Review, 9*(2), 108–130.

17. Vorauer, J. D., & Turpie, C. A. (2004). Disruptive effects of vigilance on dominant group members' treatment of outgroup members: Choking versus shining under pressure. *Journal of Personality and Social Psychology, 87*(3), 384–399.

18. Dixon, T. L., & Maddox, K. B. (2005). Skin tone, crime news, and social reality judgments: Priming the stereotype of the dark and dangerous black criminal. *Journal of Applied Social Psychology, 35*(8), 1555–1570.

19. Devine, P. G. (1996). Breaking the prejudice habit. *Psychological Science Agenda 9,* 10–11.

20. Blair, I. V. (2002). The malleability of automatic stereotypes and prejudice. *Personality and Social Psychology Review*, 6(3), 242–261.

21. Mankiller, W., & Wallis, M. (1999). *Mankiller: A chief and her people.* New York: St. Martin's Griffin.

22. Blair, I. V. (2002). The malleability of automatic stereotypes and prejudice. *Personality and Social Psychology Review*, 6(3), 242–261.

CHAPTER 6

Conscious Use of Self

M alinda, a former student, showed up for our meeting right on time.

"In my community development association," she began, "I'm having a serious disagreement with Luis, the chair, about how he introduces me. The organization has members from many different ethnic groups, so our nationality is usually included in introductions. The problem is that Luis continues to refer to me as a Latina, when I have told him over and over again that I prefer to be referred to as Mexican American."

"Why is this so important to you?" I asked.

"I have dual citizenship in the United States and Mexico, and I'm proud to be a Mexican American! I think it's wrong to lump all Latin, Central and South American ethnic identities together as Latino. It disrespects the rich diversity of these cultures."

"And what's Luis's reaction to this?"

"I've tried and tried to educate him about how important it is to acknowledge each as separate cultures, but he pays no attention to me. It's so frustrating! How do I get him to quit doing this?" she asked.

"You can see that reasoning and pleading with him hasn't worked," I said. "Instead of focusing on trying to change Luis, I'm going to suggest you think about how you might change yourself, or more precisely, consciously use yourself to resolve this dilemma."

"Change myself? You've got to be kidding! He's the one at fault here," exclaimed Malinda.

In Malinda's eyes, she is not the problem, so my advice seemed counterintuitive, the opposite of common sense. Yet, in any interpersonal interaction, the only person you can be certain of influencing is yourself.

People who do not consciously use themselves tend to improvise without consideration of how their actions affect others. Individuals skilled in conscious use of self have learned to apply themselves as instruments of change: attending to the ways their presence, thoughts, emotions, and behaviors affect interactions. They choose strategies accordingly. You can be far more influential by altering what you think, feel and do— changing how you show up—than by trying to alter what another person thinks, feels, or does.

CURIOUS ABOUT THE CONCEPT?

Conscious use of self is a term used in social work, organization development, and other helping professions to describe deliberate and facilitative action with others. Elements of conscious use of self include:

- awareness and mastery of your feelings, motivations, and skills
- ability to perceive how others are seeing you, and
- ability to respond appropriately when someone pushes your hot buttons.

Neuman, K. M., & Friedman, B. D. (1997). Process recordings: Fine-turning an old instrument. *Journal of Social Work Education, 33*(2), 237–244.

Guidelines for learning to consciously use yourself as an instrument of change include:

- Get your emotional attachments out of the way.
- Accept responsibility for your own contribution.
- Maintain integrity.
- Focus on the other person's strengths.
- Adopt a learning orientation.
- Seek to understand the other's perspectives.
- Recognize your power and use it responsibly.

I knew that understanding these guidelines would help Malinda figure out how to work more effectively with Luis.

GET YOUR EMOTIONAL ATTACHMENTS OUT OF THE WAY

"Malinda, first let me make sure I understand your position. You believe individual ethnic identities should be distinguished. You're proud of your Mexican American heritage and want others to value and respect it. When others fail to acknowledge it in their introductions of you, it feels like they're being disrespectful. Is this correct?"

"Yes. You're exactly right. That's how I feel."

"Now, can you tell me why Luis feels the way he does?"

"It's perfectly obvious. He's stubborn and wants it to be his way or no way. He refuses to even listen to me or to acknowledge that I could be right."

Malinda was clearly emotionally charged and convinced that Luis was unequivocally wrong.

The challenge was to encourage her to consider other options.

I continued, "You said that Luis was being stubborn. Do you think he experiences *you* as stubborn as well?"

She answered, somewhat reluctantly, "Well, yes, probably."

In asking this question, I wanted Malinda to begin to see how the interactions between her and Luis had become a vicious cycle. The more recalcitrant each became, the less understood the other felt and the harder he or she tried to explain. Instead of bridging the gap, these efforts widened it (Figure 6.1).

As emotions escalate, people's thinking becomes narrower and narrower. It's difficult for someone in such emotional turmoil to see any but their own perspective. And the harder they push their point of view, the more those with different opinions hang onto their own views. It's easy to imagine Luis thinking, "Well, I know a thing or two about culture; how dare Malinda suggest I don't!" Unknowingly, they had both set a self-fulfilling prophecy in motion.

I explained as much to Malinda and then moved on to what I thought might be most difficult of all for her to accept. "Suppose I suggested that your emotional reaction is about you, not Luis." Her eyes widened with surprise.

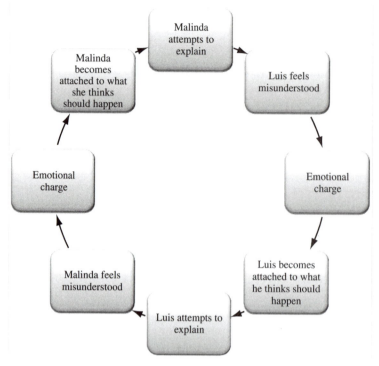

Figure 6.1 © Jean Kantambu Latting & V. Jean Ramsey, 2007–2009.

"How would you have responded if he had insisted Rome was in England, not Italy?" I asked.

She laughed and responded, "I would've told him once or twice that Rome was in Italy and if he didn't agree, I would've dropped it. No big deal."

"So," I said, "it follows that your being so upset and insistent on Luis getting your point is about you being emotionally triggered. Another person might have found the conversation intriguing rather than upsetting."

Malinda was quiet for a long while. "You know, you're right," she said. "I can tell when I get triggered. My voice gets a little higher, I begin to talk a little faster and I get pushy. So yes, as I think about it, I can see that I was triggered."

Malinda's admission represented a huge shift for her. It took courage for her to realize that her emotional response was of her own creation.

This is not to imply that her negative emotions were somehow wrong or bad. To the contrary, if she knew how to use them, her emotions could be quite functional in serving as a red alert that something was going on that warranted her attention.

"All those negative emotions can feel cruddy," I commented, "but they can work for you rather than against you if you view them as a signal for self-reflection. What if you'd asked yourself, 'What is it about me that's stirring up such feelings? Perhaps there's something in this situation reminding me of a pattern in my life.'"

"Is there something about this situation with Luis that's a pattern in my life?" she repeated slowly.

"Yes; have you had similar feelings in other situations? Think back to times when people may have discounted your thoughts and feelings."

She sat silently. Finally, she said, "Okay, now I get it. Here's the pattern. I'm tired of being told that I overreact and am too sensitive. People at work tell me that. When I was a kid, my family used to tell me that all the time. They discounted what I had to say and how I felt. The more I objected, the more they discounted me."

"Like Luis?" I asked.

"Yes!" she said. "Just like Luis!" She paused, seeming to listen to her own words. "So I'm repeating the same pattern with Luis."

I waited.

"But don't I have a right to my thoughts and feelings? I have a right to not be discounted!"

"Certainly, you do," I responded immediately. "This isn't about whether you're right. This is about whether you're interacting effectively with Luis."

"No, I'm not being effective," she admitted. "I'm reacting to him emotionally, just as I did with my family. I'm also doing it with some of my coworkers. It didn't work then and it's not working now."

"Okay, so let's go back to your feeling of being discounted because you believe it's important to respect the richness of the various Latino cultures. How might you have used your emotional reaction as a warning signal?" I asked.

"I guess I could have stopped and noticed my reaction, and wondered where it was coming from. Maybe if I'd done so, I would've seen the pattern sooner."

To respond more effectively to Luis, Malinda could learn to recognize her emotional triggers and refrain from automatically responding to them. Once she is aware that the emotional parts of her brain have overwhelmed the more reflective, thinking parts, she may begin to question her negative assumptions and deliberately release whatever negative emotions have come up. This would allow her to let go of her attachments to what she believes ought to happen and get herself out of the way of what might evolve.

> "Would you consider using an emotional clearing method before you meet with him again?"

> "Jean, I just knew you were going to ask me that. After you taught me how to do it last summer, I kept it up for a few weeks, and then sort of stopped. But it did work for me, and I don't know why I stopped. . . . " Her voice trailed off.

> She continued, "Before, I was having a horrible time with my son and I did a lot of emotional clearing exercises to stay on an even keel with him. It never occurred to me to use it here, but I can see how it might work. I'm definitely willing to commit to doing it again," Malinda assured me. "And afterwards, I'll have another conversation with Luis."

This was progress. She was now seeing that she was emotionally triggered and that she had the capacity to get untriggered. I wanted to remind her, though, that even if she managed to clear herself prior to meeting with Luis again, he could say something to set her right back off.

> "A caution though," I responded. "If the conversation goes south again, you can always call a time out and continue it later."

> "I remember your saying that before," she interjected. "Your exact words were, 'emotional clearing is seldom a one-shot deal.'"

> "I'm glad you remember," I said. "And the good news is that if you can get your emotional attachment out of the way, it'll be easier to focus on both your and Luis's contributions to what's going on."

ACCEPT RESPONSIBILITY FOR YOUR OWN CONTRIBUTION

> Malinda responded immediately and vehemently: "*My* contributions? What do you mean? Any contribution I might have made was *after* he started all the Latino this and Latino that talk. I know I've been short with him, and may even have sniped at him, but I didn't start it. I'm not to blame."[1]

People often try to figure out who is to blame—and are convinced that whoever is the villain, it's not them. Just check out the news when something goes wrong in the world. The newscaster is bound to ask, "Who's to blame?" The assumption seems to be that if blame can be fixed on one guilty person, the problem can be solved or justice served.

"I'm not trying to imply that you're to blame," I said. "I'm just trying to sort out responsibility for how things have unfolded. So, let's talk more about what happened. How did his words and actions affect your reactions?"

"He was being stubborn, so I defended myself and my position."

"And how did your reaction affect his response?" I asked.

"He defended himself and his position," she responded with just a hint of irritation in her voice. "It's like we said before—we were locked in a vicious cycle, a self-fulfilling prophecy."

"And if someone had been watching the interaction between the two of you, who would they think had started it?"

Malinda laughed aloud, "They wouldn't know—or care."

This was progress. Malinda could not learn from her experience with her colleague if she stayed fixed in her assumption that Luis was wrong and she was right. As she was now realizing, an outsider to the conflict would see two people arguing, not one. This awareness laid the groundwork for her willingness to accept responsibility for her own contribution to the conflict.

What might have been Malinda's contribution? Her either/or thinking—insisting she was right and Luis wrong—seemed to be a factor. When people engage in either/or thinking, they end up having to either blame the other person or themselves.

I continued, "Imagine that you both somehow contributed to this upset. You've already told me what he's done. How might you have contributed?"

"What difference does it make???" she exclaimed, no longer hiding her annoyance. "Even if we're both being obstinate, why should I be the one to change?"

People often resist the idea of being the first to change—it feels inherently unfair. Why should they stick their necks out and risk vulnerability while the other person gets off scot-free?

I have a pat answer and a more serious answer," I responded.

"Go for it, Jean," she invited.

"The pat answer is that the person I'm talking with gets to change first. If Luis were sitting here with me, I'd be talking with him about how he might begin to see things differently so he could change. But he's not here, upset about this. You are. So the onus is on you."

"Fair enough. What's the more serious answer?"

"This is about conscious use of self. The person with the greatest capacity to consciously use himself or herself as an instrument of change is the one with the greatest courage and flexibility to pull it off."

She looked at me suspiciously. "Are you trying to butter me up?"

"No, Malinda, I mean every word. In this conversation you've shown the desire to consciously use yourself and you've shown courage and flexibility of thought. You're the logical person to change first, since you've demonstrated that you have what it takes."

"But if I do this . . ." her voice trailed off again. Then she added, "You're not suggesting I be a doormat, are you? That I let Luis introduce me any way he chooses—Latina, Hispanic, Wild Woman, whatever? This really sounds like blaming the victim. My sister works with battered women and tells me that when a woman is being abused, she may feel so defeated that she can't defend herself. Any suggestion that she 'accept her own responsibility' will only do her more harm. It's implying the woman's at fault and deserves the abuse."

Malinda was right: women in abusive situations are often accused of "asking for it" or "deserving what they get." There's a difference between telling someone they are at fault for their past or current situation and suggesting they can do something in the future to improve it. The abused woman is not responsible for being beaten, and she doesn't deserve it. Those in abusive situations may be too worn down and distraught to hear the difference between proactive strategies for the future and accusations of what they woulda/coulda/shoulda done differently in the past. Abused women have few resources and often require strong support before being able to make a change.

Malinda was in a different situation. She had more resources and apparent choices. By insisting that Luis was at fault, she was transferring all responsibility to him, perceiving herself as being victimized by Luis. By accepting her own contribution to this troubled relationship, she stood to gain greater, not lesser, control because she could consciously influence what happened next. I believed that if we kept talking, she would begin to see this.

MAINTAIN INTEGRITY

Consciously using and changing herself does not mean that Malinda should compromise her beliefs or values. Quite the opposite. It is vital to maintain integrity—to clarify and hold fast to one's most important and relevant values—while engaging in self-change. In Malinda's case, this meant remaining loyal to the principles that brought her to the situation in the first place.

CURIOUS ABOUT THE RESEARCH?

Chris Peterson and Martin Seligman define integrity as a pattern of behavior consistent with one's espoused values. People acting in integrity with their beliefs feel better about themselves and come across as more authentic to others. According to Peterson and Seligman's research, authentic people are well-liked and socially supported, and authentic leaders are better able to command respect and trust.

Peterson, C., & Seligman, M.E.P. (2004). *Character strengths and virtues: A handbook and classification.* New York: Oxford University Press.

"Malinda, I know you've been angry with Luis. And you've said you've been less effective with him than you'd have liked. I have another question. Do you feel as though you've acted with integrity in how you've handled your reaction to him?"

"Of course," she declared immediately. "I stood up for my principles."

"I'm not asking you about the substance of what you said to him. I'm asking whether you think you've treated him as you believe people should be treated. Has the way you've treated him been consistent with your core values?"

"Ohhhh. Well, no!" she exclaimed. "I don't like that thought. I don't know if I want to go there." She paused and then admitted, "No, I haven't been consistent. I really do believe that it's important to treat others with respect, and I can see that my knee-jerk reaction to Luis hasn't been respectful. That makes me feel lousy."

"But this keeps coming back to being my fault!" she exclaimed. "I'm not the one creating all these problems. He is!"

When you feel out of integrity, it is easier to believe someone else is the cause of your discomfort. A book called *Leadership and Self-deception* explains how this works, using different terminology.[2] Instead of referring to being "out of integrity," the authors describe a process of self-betrayal. It works like this. First, you betray yourself by doing something to someone that's contrary to what you feel deep down you should do. Then, to justify your actions, you figure out reasons to magnify the other person's faults and your own virtues. In so doing, you deceive yourself.

As I explained the self-betrayal process, Malinda sat silently. I began to feel uneasy, wondering if I was going too far or too fast with her. It's ego-deflating to think about one's own self-deception. Yet I thought she had the emotional maturity to handle it. Leaders who can manage to cross this hurdle can absolutely soar in terms of the moral integrity they can command in their organizations.

"Let me give you an analogy," I suggested.

"Sure," she responded.

"Maintaining integrity requires distinguishing between values and habits: values emerge from your core self while habits are behaviors repeated without conscious thought. For example, you may find your-self driving on a freeway, stuck behind a car going much slower than the speed limit. Perhaps a cliché pops into your head: 'It must be an older driver.' Or you think it must be an Asian driver or a disabled driver or a woman; whichever stereotype is most habitual."

She nodded, "I do that all the time. I usually think it's an immigrant, which is really funny since I come from a family of immigrants."

"Nearly all of us are subject to such automatic thoughts," I assured her. "Your ability to acknowledge it is wonderful! Now, if you're like most of us, those thoughts will be accompanied by feeling irritated or indignant: 'Why won't this driver simply pull over and let others pass?' Does this ring a bell?"

"Absolutely," she responded. "I don't roll down my car window and start screaming, but I do rant and rave to myself." She winced, just thinking about her reactions.

"These thoughts and emotions come automatically—developed through years of stereotypes being pumped into us. Since I know you genuinely value differences, I imagine you may feel guilty when you notice yourself thinking this way. If so, that guilt is a signal that you're out of sync with your integrity."

I paused to give us both a chance to reflect.

She picked up the train of thought. "So, you're saying that I see a slow driver, think about how the person must be an immigrant, feel guilty about it, and then get mad at myself?" She paused then ex-claimed, "No! I get it. I get angry at the driver, not at myself. I put it all on them when the real deal is that I'm feeling guilty! That's what you're saying, isn't it?"

Her emotional and intellectual honesty was stunning to witness and I told her so. Then I asked, "Suppose instead of staying mad at either the driver or yourself, you decide that this is an opportunity to align yourself with your deeper values?"

Her eyes began to soften. "If I saw the whole thing as an opportunity to remind myself of my deep commitment to a society where all kinds of people can work and live together in peace, then my anger dissipates. I still feel a twinge of annoyance, but not like before." As she spoke, she visibly relaxed.

This is self-reflection in action. To maintain integrity, Malinda can make a conscious choice to act on her egalitarian values. Some people derive their core values from their religious convictions or spiritual beliefs. Others recognize them as a deep set of principles reflecting who they are. No matter how you define them, recognizing the difference between feeling emotionally triggered and believing your core values are at stake gives you the freedom and ability to maintain integrity.

I asked Malinda to describe her core values. After we had discussed a few, I added, "Here's why it's useful to list them. Whenever you feel emotionally triggered or sense yourself reacting automatically to some situation, you can instead choose to align yourself with your core values. You can say, 'those other thoughts are not who I am. This is who I am.'"

Malinda responded immediately, "Wow! I can see how that might work." She pondered a bit and then added tentatively, "I suppose my anger at Luis is an automatic reaction that doesn't really reflect my core values. It really is important to me to be respectful toward others."

I waited. She seemed to be testing each idea as she spoke. "And yes, it really is annoying that he disregards my wishes, but the way I've been interacting with him doesn't feel good either. So, when I think he deserves it, I get even more worked up about it. But if I shift the focus to myself, then I can admit that I don't like how I'm treating him. That makes me madder still—how I allow him to get me off-balance like that and violate my own principles. So then, I decide it's all his fault!" She paused again. "But it's not, is it? I'm doing it to myself." She sank back into her chair.

"Discovering how we deceive ourselves can be uncomfortable at first," I acknowledged. "But would you rather believe you're in control of your thoughts and emotions or that Luis is?"

Her head popped up and she stared straight at me. "Why, me, of course!" A moment later, she added, "So, in other words, if I'm doing it to myself, I can undo it to myself!" Then with a big grin she added, "And this is why it's worthwhile to acknowledge my contribution, isn't it? The payoff is that I can do something about it and maintain integrity at the same time!"

She burst into laughter at the idea.

I decided this was a good time for a checkpoint. We had been talking for quite a while. Did she want to take a break now and think about all we had talked about?

"No," she replied. "I'd rather keep going. Some of this has been hard to take, but it's been useful. Let's take a ten-minute break and then see what else emerges."

When she returned, Malinda settled back in her chair and re-opened the conversation. "Alright. I accept that I'm emotionally triggered by this situation. I admit I've been pretty one-sided in my view of Luis and have thus partially contributed to the situation. I also agree that some, but not all, of my anger at Luis stemmed from guilt over how I was treating him. But the fact remains that we disagree sharply on this issue. And I don't know how to go about resolving it."

Malinda was demonstrating a high level of self awareness. The next step was for her to learn what to do with it.

FOCUS ON THE OTHER PERSON'S STRENGTHS

"Up to this point, how have you been trying to motivate Luis to change? By telling him how wrong he is?" I asked rather playfully.

"Well, yes, because he *is* wrong and I'm right," answered Malinda with mock exasperation in her voice. She laughed as she said this, so I knew she was hearing her tendency to see him in simplistic, either/ or terms.

"I gather that as a strategy, it's not working too well. Am I right?" I asked.

"Not so far," she gamely admitted.

Blame-based change strategies seldom work because personal change involves risk. Change can be threatening, especially when individuals don't feel accepted as they are. In contrast, the acceptance implied by a strength-focused approach provides the emotional reservoir required for change—it helps others become more willing to risk change and strengthens their belief that they can do it if they so choose.

CURIOUS ABOUT THE RESEARCH?

Affirming the worth of others, valuing their intrinsic qualities, and working to create contexts that encourage them to reach their own next levels of performance create feelings of safety. The goal of effective interactions becomes to help others feel safe, affirming their worth and value even if you don't understand some things about their words or actions.

Crocker, J., & Nuer, N. (2003). The insatiable quest for self-worth. *Psychological Inquiry 14*(1), 31–34.

Malinda grinned at me, "So if I'm to be strength-focused with Luis, I have to first identify his strengths, right?" I smiled back, enjoying her engagement in thinking it through.

"Well," Malinda replied, "he really has done a good job of involving members of many different ethnic groups in our association. Before he was chair, only a handful of members were persons of color. And under his leadership, there's been much more active membership involvement. He also gives others credit for their contributions."

"So, by and large, you think he's been a pretty effective chair?" Malinda nodded and I continued, "Have you told him how you appreciate the way he's made the association more inclusive?"

"Well, no. Since he doesn't listen to me about how I prefer to be introduced, I assume he's not interested in anything else I have to say. I know now how defensive that sounds, but it's true."

Moving past someone's negative signals and focusing instead on their strengths can be hard to do. It can feel easier to stay angry and pull away. This cycle can be interrupted by getting curious—adopting a learning orientation.

ADOPT A LEARNING ORIENTATION

"Often when I'm frustrated, I look for what's there for me to learn," I said. "For example, during our conversation, you've implied that you don't know for sure why he continues to introduce you as a Latina. Are you at all curious about this?"

"I admit I haven't been. I've been ticked off instead. But even if I were curious, I'm not sure how to go about dredging up questions for him," said Malinda with a mischievous grin.

"Tell you what," I suggested. "Let's generate some questions right now. Pretend you have to write a report on the pros and cons of identifying Latinos as a group versus maintaining distinct country-based identities. What would you want to know from Luis about why he supports the former?"

"I'd want to know whether he realizes he's obliterating whole cultures by lumping them together."

"Good start. Let's work with that," I responded. I knew she was being sarcastic, but at least she was engaged. "From his point of view, would your question suggest you already know the answer or that you have genuine curiosity about his position?"

"It would suggest that I think he's an idiot."

We both laughed. She wasn't making it easy.

"C'mon, Malinda. We both know you can do this."

"Okay, okay. If I were genuinely curious, what would I ask him? Well, I'd ask him about the tradeoffs of the two positions—what he thought were the pros and cons of each approach and what led him to come down on the side he chose."

"What a wonderful question! Do you know how he might answer it?" I asked.

"Actually, no. We've never discussed the pros and cons of our respective positions." Then she added with a smirky grin, "Actually, that might be interesting. I might even learn something."

I smiled broadly at her humor. "Cool! You're in the question, Malinda." I could see she was pleased with herself.

CURIOUS ABOUT THE RESEARCH?

Across four studies, in which people assessed their skill levels in various tasks, participants in the bottom quartile overestimated their performance, thought they were above average, and were unable to judge others' competence. They didn't know what they didn't know. This inability to recognize competence kept them ignorant about their own incompetence.

Kruger, J., & Dunning, D. (1999). Unskilled and unaware of it: How difficulties in recognizing one's own incompetence lead to inflated self-assessments. *Journal of Personality and Social Psychology, 77*(6), 1121–1134.

It requires a certain vulnerability to say, "I don't know and I want to learn." To borrow a well-known saying, a learning orientation provides us with the opportunity to find out what we don't even know we don't know. We open the door to unlearn what we thought we knew and welcome new perspectives.

SEEK TO UNDERSTAND OTHERS' PERSPECTIVES

Malinda had a reflective look on her face. "Jean," she said, "you keep suggesting I do things that I don't really know how to do. What you're saying makes sense, but I don't know how to put it into practice. Luis's position is wrong and I don't understand how to use what you're saying to make him change it."

I mentally ticked off where we were. Malinda was willing to own being emotionally triggered, accept responsibility for having contributed in part to the situation with Luis, had identified core values that enabled her to know when she was out of integrity, had identified some of Luis's strengths, and was willing to learn from him. There were two hurdles to go in consciously using herself in this situation: she needed to gain a better understanding of where he was coming from and recognize that she had power in the situation and could use it more effectively.

First, I wanted her to explore what might be on Luis's mind. "Let's at least consider the possibility that he has valid reasons for his position," I suggested. "Can you think of any rationale for his tendency to introduce you as a Latina?"

"Well, I have heard him say he's frustrated by the deep divisions among people from Mexico and South and Central America."

"Have you tried to find out more about why he holds this position, why it's important to him? Now I'm not asking whether you have argued with him about it. I'm asking whether you have truly engaged with him from a position of curiosity about why he believes what he does—and then listened completely to his response?"

"No, I admit I haven't done that. But why does it matter? I'm all for unity among Latinos. I want unity for the whole world! But I'm not for obliterating all distinctions among people, like he apparently is."

"Malinda," I continued, "I understand why this is an important issue to you. You feel that Mexican Americans should be proud of and maintain their identity as a group."

"I appreciate your understanding that, Jean. If only I could get Luis to!"

"I'm about to ask you a loaded question," I warned. "Did it feel good to have me acknowledge and validate your position?"

"Yes," she responded with a grin. "Yes, it did. It makes me feel like I've been heard, not ignored. I get the point. You're suggesting I should do as much for Luis. The problem is, he might think I agree with him."

"Do you think I agree with your position?"

Her eyes widened with surprise. "I guess I don't really know if you do or not," she admitted. "But even if you don't, I know you at least understand what I'm saying. I guess that's the point, isn't it?"

"Absolutely. Trying to understand others' perspectives is not the same as agreeing with their points of view. If you're listening without discounting their reasons, they may be more likely to reciprocate."

CURIOUS ABOUT THE RESEARCH?

Researchers in multiple settings have found that a primary reason for managerial failure or derailment is failure to understand others' perspectives. Lack of this ability makes it difficult to build a team and get work done through others' efforts.

Hogan, J., & Hogan, R. (2002). Leadership and sociopolitical intelligence. In R. E. Riggio, S. E. Murphy, & F. J. Pirozzola (Eds.), *Multiple intelligences and leadership* (pp. 75–88). Mahwah, NJ: Lawrence Erlbaum Associates Publishers.

"In other words," Malinda concluded, "put yourself in the other's shoes. So simple to say, so hard to do."

RECOGNIZE YOUR OWN POWER AND USE IT RESPONSIBLY

"Okay, the more I think about it, the more curious I get about Luis's perspective," said Malinda reflectively. "That's another hurdle I've crossed." She was obviously mentally ticking off what she could do to improve her relationship with Luis. "But what will I do if he pops off about how I'm really Latina? How do I move past that?"

"Well, let's try looking at the power you have in this situation."

"Power? What power? I'm not the chair!" Malinda countered. "He's the leader of the association. It's his job, not mine, to pull people together for the good of the whole. He's the one who sets agendas for the meetings and assigns people to different committees. People listen to him."

Most people think of power as formal, authorized power—given to people as part of some official responsibility. Informal or personal power can be harder to recognize—until you try to buck someone whose influence reaches well beyond their official position.

"It's clear he does have a lot of formal power," I agreed. "If people listen to him, he probably also has some personal power—ability to influence others. You may not have any formal power in the organization, but I'd bet you have some personal power. What power do you have?" Malinda shrugged her shoulders with a baffled look on her face.

I waited a few seconds to see if she would respond. When she didn't, I continued, "Have you tried to recruit others to your point of view? Have you opposed Luis on this issue, either openly or behind the scenes?"

"Well, yes," admitted Malinda.

"Have you thwarted Luis on unrelated issues because you're annoyed with him? Have you slowed things down in the group?"

The tiniest hint of an impish grin began curling at the corners of Malinda's mouth. "Some of that, yes," she said.

I complimented her on her honesty and self awareness in admitting to such defiant behaviors. "So what power do you have?" I asked again.

After some thought she replied, "I have the power to get in his way."

"Yes, you do. And what other power do you have?"

She paused and said, "I have the ability to influence others in the association—not everyone, but some people now support my point of view."

I nodded in agreement, and then asked, "So, Malinda, do you like how you've been using your power in this relationship? Have you been using your power responsibly?"

There was a long pause. "No," she finally responded. "I haven't been using it very constructively. In fact—and it's embarrassing to admit it—I've been using a sort of back-door power."

"It's not just that he has the title and I don't," she continued. "It's also because he's a man with a title and I'm a woman trying to exert influence, but without any formal authority. Now, don't get me wrong. Everyone, including Luis, has bent over backwards to avoid bringing all the problems other organizations have into this one. But, there's still a subtle difference I can't quite put my finger on. I don't know if it's me or what."

Malinda was right that even today, women have more difficulty being recognized as leaders than men. Yet, she was fortunate to be affiliated with an organization that wanted to eliminate such barriers.

CURIOUS ABOUT THE RESEARCH?

In recent years, negative attitudes toward female leaders have diminished. Yet, women are often placed in a double bind when it comes to their leadership styles. On the one hand, they are expected as women to exhibit kindness, warmth, and concern for others. On the other hand, the typical leader is often stereotyped as aggressive, self-directing and confident. If women act in those ways, they are accused of being too masculine. As a result, some women tend to adopt a coach/teacher leadership style that encourages rather than directs.

Eagly, A. H. (2007). Female leadership advantage and disadvantage: Resolving the contradictions. *Psychology of Women Quarterly, 31*(1), 1–12.

I had a hunch that if Malinda really understood the power she had in the situation with Luis, she would feel greater freedom to work out their differences. Individuals who know how to consciously use themselves in charged situations can have a strong influence, even in situations where they believe the deck is stacked against them.

"Another thing that may be making it difficult for you to embrace your own power is seeing this as an either/or problem. You've told me you disagree with Luis's perspective. Is there any part of his position you could agree with?"

She pondered the question. Finally, she admitted, "Well, actually, I am for Latino unity. It's just that I don't want to give away . . . uh, give away . . . "

"Give away? What?"

"Agreeing with him would be like giving away my power. If he knew I partially agreed with him, he might not ever pay attention to my point of view. It would be all his way."

"So you're afraid that if you let him know that you partially agreed with him, you might give away your power?"

She nodded.

"Would it be fair to say that in a way, you haven't let on how you feel about his position?"

Again, she nodded.

"Would that help explain why you're so angry with him?"

"Yes, Jean. This is so uncomfortable for me, but yes. It all makes sense. I was deceiving him—and myself—about whether I saw any merit in his position. I felt backed into a corner and came out fighting. I've been doing to him what I've been accusing him of doing to me. It's crystal clear now. I haven't been the change I wanted to see; I've been the barrier I didn't want to see."

"Ah, but Malinda, that may've been what you were, but it certainly isn't what you have to remain," I responded. Looking at her, it seemed as though she had grown an inch taller just sitting there. "Do you now feel powerful enough to tell him the parts of his argument you agree with and the parts you don't? Can you partially agree without thinking you're giving away the whole kit and caboodle?"

She took a deep breath, "Of course I can!"

"Great! Now, how do you feel thinking about this?"

She paused and replied softly, "Powerful. Actually, knowing that I can agree with him and still hold to what I believe makes me feel powerful."

We sat silently for a few moments. Finally, she commented, "This is a lot of work! This conscious use of self, as you call it, seems to require a great deal of self-examination."

"It does indeed," I agreed.

"My sister is in Twelve-Step," mused Malinda. "They call this, 'Make a fearless moral inventory' or something like that."

"Yes," I agreed, "that's very similar to what you're doing now."

It was astute of Malinda to connect conscious use of self with the work that the recovering community encourages for their members. Conscious use of self extends beyond the recovering community, though. Executives and managers may learn it with the help of organizational consultants acting as coaches. People in the mental health professions— social workers, therapists, psychologists, psychiatrists—learn how to do it as part of their training. People of all types who want to improve their effectiveness engage in this type of self-examination.

In explaining this, I added, "You're in good company and you certainly seem up to the challenge. You've definitely shown an amazing willingness to face the person in the mirror in our discussion today."

"I have to wonder though," Malinda offered, "Is it worth this much work?"

"For me, it is," I responded. "I know I'm more effective from continuing to do this. Not perfect, mind you. Just consistently more effective, year by year."

She suddenly grinned and sat up straight. "Alright Jean, here's what I'm going to do. I'm going to go home and do some emotional clearing. When I do this, I'll specifically probe to see any other ways I might've violated my sense of integrity. I've already acknowledged some ways I've contributed to this situation; I'll see if I can identify others. After I finish clearing, I'll consciously identify Luis's strengths. Then I'll call him and try to work it out. When I talk with him, I'll go into inquiry about his perspective and be genuinely curious about it. I do indeed recognize my personal power in this situation—even if I don't have a title or any kind of formal power—and I intend to use it more responsibly."

"You are ready, Malinda. You are so ready."

NOTES

1. Stone, D., Patton, B., & Heen, S. (1999). *Difficult conversations: How to discuss what matters most.* New York: Penguin Books.

2. Arbinger Institute. (2000). *Leadership and self-deception: Getting out of the box* (1st ed.). San Francisco: Berrett-Koehler.

CHAPTER 7

Initiating Workplace Change

Gary decided to ask his manager, Jessica, to reschedule late afternoon staff meetings to mornings or early afternoons. After talking with a few coworkers, he raised the issue at the beginning of a staff meeting. "Some of us have child care responsibilities, and others have caretaking responsibility for elderly parents. If the meeting runs past 6 o'clock, we have to pay late day-care fees or overtime to in-home caretakers. We sometimes end up being late to meetings because we have to make alternative arrangements."

Jessica frowned and said sharply, "Let's discuss it later."

Gary felt a tightening in his chest and was unusually quiet for the rest of the meeting. "She obviously doesn't give a damn," he thought. "Anyone with an ounce of concern for her staff would never routinely keep us after 6 P.M. I should have known better than to bring it up. All I've done is make her mad at me."

When Gary came to me with his concerns about this, I began with a question. "How committed are you to the proposed change? There are things you can do immediately towards damage control with your manager, but it may take more time and effort to see a change in staff meeting scheduling."

"Even for a simple thing like a meeting time? We're not talking about scaling Mount Everest!" he exclaimed.

"Even simple routines within the organization may sometimes be difficult to change because they reflect hidden assumptions and habits that maintain the status quo. If you're to see this through," I warned, "you should prepare yourself for the inevitable ups and downs of a change process over a possibly lengthy time period."

You, the reader, may have great ideas about how people and organizations might improve. You see the potential, you recognize change is possible—difficult, perhaps, but possible—and you may be impatient for it to occur. Sometimes you make efforts to induce change: speaking to someone in authority or to your friends and colleagues, pointing out how things are not the way they should be and how they should change. When people listen, you are excited, optimistic, and even proud to have been the initiator of the change.

Before long, however, you discover that your efforts have failed to yield the results you sought. Not everyone listens, or those who do blithely ignore your advice. Alternatively, they listen, try your suggestions, then the whole thing bombs—and you are blamed. Often, you sense the handwriting on the wall and don't even try. You watch others try to bring about change and fail, or hear about others' failures, and decide it is not worth the effort.

This chapter describes what to do when you want something to change and are willing to help make it happen. It deals primarily with change in your work life, but what you learn here will also help you get started in other change efforts—in your community, your home, wherever you find yourself.

Gary mistakenly believed the change he was calling for was a simple one. His assumptions about how to get the staff meeting times changed in his organization illustrate seven myths about how change is induced and sustained (Table 7.1).

Among other things, dominant/nondominant dynamics are at play in Gary and Jessica's interactions. As a subordinate, Gary is acutely aware of how Jessica's dominant managerial status may blind her to realities nondominants experience in the organization. He is likely to focus only on his side of it: "I'm trying to be helpful here, but she hasn't a clue!" Meanwhile, he reminds himself of his desire to maintain a mutually respectful relationship with Jessica as he squelches his impatience with her tone of voice.

Jessica has more power and privilege in this relationship. Nevertheless, she likely has hopes and expectations that her relationship with subordinates will remain congenial and productive; she may even be evaluated on her ability to maintain effective working relationships. Her dominant status may have made her oblivious to how early evening meetings were adversely affecting employees. She may be thinking, "What is it with

Table 7.1
Myths of Workplace Change

It's up to the other person to change.	Gary thought that Jessica, not he, should change.
If I carefully explain my valid reasons and others still won't make the change, they either don't care or are incompetent.	Gary assumed Jessica didn't care since she didn't respond as he wished.
Change isn't possible unless higher-ups support it. If higher-ups don't support the change initially, change is only possible if everyone else supports it.	Gary assumed that if Jessica didn't support the idea, the matter was closed.
Change should happen the way I've decided it should and it should come about as I envision. Otherwise, it's not a real change.	Gary expected an immediate positive response, and when he didn't get it, was disillusioned about the possibility of any change occurring.
If people resist the change initially, they're permanently opposed to the change and there's nothing more I can do. If they say they'll think about the change and don't follow through, they're resisting the change. If they make the change but don't stick with it, they're playing games.	When Jessica said, "Let's discuss it later," Gary interpreted her statement as resistance and assumed she was rejecting the idea completely. This closed the matter as far as he understood.
Upper management lives in a different world. They're oblivious to what's going on and there's no way I can make them understand. If I tell them what's really going on, they'll just get mad.	Gary believed Jessica's dominant status as manager kept her removed from the employees' day-to-day world and precluded her ability to comprehend how the staff felt about late afternoon meetings. He figured there was no way he could ever explain it to her in a way she could understand and accept.
Change will occur quickly, visibly, and within the time frame I think is reasonable.	Gary expected his desired change to be implemented right away. When it wasn't, he assumed the likelihood of change was nil.

Gary? Why is he being so confrontational? Doesn't he know the consequences if we don't meet our performance goals this quarter?"

Clearly, Gary's initial change attempt did not work. What else could he do?

STEPS FOR INITIATING CHANGE

Change efforts are notoriously easy to begin but difficult to complete. You have undoubtedly been involved in numerous change efforts, with varying degrees of success. How many New Year's resolutions have you made, begun, and then abandoned? How often have you decided this is the year the department is finally going to reach its efficiency goals? The fact that you are reading this chapter is a hint that you have not always been as successful in your change efforts as you would like. Change can be hard; long-lasting change is even harder. Change is not impossible, however. It is often worth the effort and patience.

Change does not have to begin at the top of an organization. While this is conventional wisdom, organizational scholars such as Peter Senge, author of the widely acclaimed book, *The Fifth Discipline,* believe otherwise.[1] Successful organizational changes have been launched by low or mid-level staff who were bold enough to try.

Change does not require everyone's agreement or participation; it does not even require a majority. Rather, the goal is for 20 percent to adopt the change. If that many change—a critical mass—a trajectory has been set and change is likely to occur.[2]

CURIOUS ABOUT THE RESEARCH?

Researchers on diffusion of innovation have found that if 10 to 20 percent of people in an organization or community adopt an innovation, it is difficult to stop it from spreading further.

Rogers, E. M. (2003). *Diffusion of innovation.* New York: The Free Press.

Researchers have gone further and classified adopters of change into:[3]

- Innovators—the first 2.5 percent of people in a system to adopt a change or innovation;
- Early adopters—the next 13 percent of people;
- Early majority—the next 34 percent;
- Late majority—the next 34 percent; and
- Laggards—the last 16 percent.

Note that if innovators and early adopters embrace the change, it takes only a small percentage of the early majority to reach the 20 percent goal.

There are several steps to initiating any significant change in an organization. Each of them involves the innovators and early adopters—the people who make an early commitment to the changes and the new ideas represented by them. The steps are:

- Commit to personal change.
- Emphasize changing situational factors, not individuals.
- Gain support from others for the change.
- Set a direction, not fixed outcomes.
- Learn from the resistance.
- Surface undiscussables.

Commit to Personal Change

Our first advice to Gary would be the same as that given throughout this book: to focus on changing himself rather than trying to change his manager. This requires him to consciously monitor his assumptions, emotions, and relationships, particularly with people different from him.

I said as much, "Gary, the first question you should ask yourself is whether you're willing to commit to changing yourself as you work to bring about larger change."

His initial reaction was predictable, "Change myself?! I'm not the one keeping staff stuck at work while the clock is ticking and hungry children are waiting on their parents!"

"Is it in your power to change your manager?" I asked, reminding him of what he already knew.

"Yeah, yeah, yeah," he replied. "I've heard you say this before: I'm the only one whose behavior and attitudes I can change. This is probably why I'm even talking to you. What do you think I should do?"

"I suggest you position yourself mentally as someone who will consciously and strategically use yourself to initiate the desired change. As you change yourself, your goal is to see this change reflected in what's happening around you."

"Are you saying that as I change, so will people around me?"

"Yes, that is what I'm saying. Doing things like getting your emotional attachments out of the way, seeking to understand Jessica's perspective, and adopting a learning orientation will help you become more effective as an agent of change. As you change, others are likely to change in response. As you become more open, you will find that others may be less resistant to your change efforts."

CURIOUS ABOUT THE RESEARCH?

Recent breakthroughs in neuroscientific research suggest a physiological explanation for why someone's personal changes may become subsequently reflected in those around them. Brains have "mirror neurons" that reflect back actions observed in others, causing individuals to mimic others' actions, or at least feel an impulse to do so. Human beings are hard-wired to imitate one another.

Goleman, D. (2006). *Social intelligence: The new science of human relationships.* New York: Bantam Books.

"I may have to think about that for a while," responded Gary. "What else do you suggest?"

Emphasize Changing Situational Factors, not Just Individuals

"Another common mistake we make in initiating change," I continued, "is to focus our change efforts on individuals to the exclusion of systems."

"Systems?"

"Yes, systems. Think of them as those norms, policies, and patterns of interaction that set the rules of the game."

Lasting change requires changing systems, not just changing individual behaviors and attitudes.[4] The word "system" has different meanings, depending on the context. People speak of organizational systems, family systems, biological systems, social systems, and interpersonal systems. No matter the context, the word system implies that parts of a single thing are interrelated—what happens in one part affects the state of the other parts.[5]

In this case, I was referring to organizational systems. Organizational systems include policies, procedures, norms, and *modus operandi* that both help and hinder your actions. These systems set the ground rules for people's behaviors at work. Changes in those systems alter the rules and thereby influence behaviors and attitudes.

It is easier to see individual actions than systemic influences—in this case, the supervisor who schedules late afternoon staff meetings even though she knows employees have after-work responsibilities. From this visible fact, it is easy to conclude that the supervisor, as an individual, is scheduling late meetings out of disrespect, callousness, or ignorance.

If you focus your attention solely on individuals, you may unwittingly fall into the trap of focusing your change efforts only on their attitudes and behaviors. This is a very limited strategy because behaviors and attitudes are difficult to change, and even if you are temporarily successful in doing so, you are likely to have only treated the symptoms, not the underlying causes of the problem. Leaving the underlying conditions or unspoken ground rules intact sets the stage for variations of the same problem to reoccur, no matter how often their resolution is attempted. By focusing on organizational systems—established channels for getting things done—you have a greater chance of uncovering a larger issue that keeps the problem in place. The meeting time issue might well be such a symptom.

> A few days later, Gary called to report that he had met with Jessica and had apologized to her. "I admitted I was out of line at the staff meeting by bringing up the issue of the meeting time without its being on the agenda," he said. "She appreciated that, and said that she hadn't wanted us to get distracted from the already full agenda.
>
> "So I asked her if we could put it on the agenda for the next meeting since these late afternoon meetings were really a problem for some of the staff. Jessica responded by saying 'I'm not convinced a change is needed. We've been round and round on meeting times that work for everyone. And no one else has complained. I don't want to take time to discuss it at a meeting if it's no more than your overreaction to a couple of complainers.'
>
> "I resisted snapping back and asked if it would be okay if I talked to some of the others," Gary continued. "She thought it would be a waste of time, but said she wasn't a micromanager. She said it was up to me how I used my time as long as productivity remains high."
>
> "So how do you feel about your conversation with Jessica overall?"
>
> "I think she's being a jerk about this. Anyone with a grain of sense could see that the meeting times are a problem," replied Gary emphatically. "I've got to do something to change her mind about it."
>
> "I notice you didn't ask her how she really felt about work-family issues."

"The conversation unfolded so quickly that I didn't get a chance to ask her. But I could tell from her response that she isn't very sympathetic. At least, though, she gave me the go-ahead to talk to the other employees about the issue. How do you think I should proceed?"

"Here's what I suggest you consider: before talking with people, figure out which systems might be keeping the late meetings in place and any leverage you might have to affect them."

"Systems again?" retorted Gary. "What do systems have to do with it?"

"Everything," I replied. "Even a simple thing like meeting times exists within a series of overlapping systems supporting the status quo. You mentioned that Jessica said she had trouble finding a meeting time to fit everyone's schedule. That suggests that several systems are in play."

Gary, his co-workers, managers, and other members of the organization are part of overlapping systems of policies and practices, both formal and informal—weekly staff meetings are only one such practice. One way to figure out which systems are involved in a given circumstance is to think about constraints on your options. In this case, performance requirements probably function as a set of constraints on the scheduling of meetings. While everyone in the unit has performance goals, Jessica as manager probably feels more keenly her responsibility for assuring the unit meets its overall performance goals.

Another systems constraint may be the varied job responsibilities of the staff; these may make it difficult to find times earlier in the day to have face-to-face meetings. There may be informal expectations operating, too. Perhaps there is an unspoken understanding in this organization that those who get ahead are the ones most willing to give their all. These unarticulated expectations may have become translated into willingness to stay late for meetings and unknowingly influenced Jessica's view of whether the meeting time was reasonable or not.

Once constraints within a system are identified, the next step is to determine which might be changed and which are sacrosanct. A broader systems approach, for example, might consider whether the face-to-face meetings could be supplemented with or replaced by teleconferences, e-mail discussions, or small group meetings. There might be other ways to generate the same interaction and results. Thus, a systems view might expand their thinking beyond a focus on individuals and encourage the consideration of more options.

Gary had grown more and more animated as we went over the different systems and how each might have affected the meeting time problem. As we concluded, he sat back in his chair and said, "Here's what I get from all this, Jean. It could be that all our grumbling about having to stay late for staff meetings is not the real issue; the real issue may be that we're finding it more and more difficult to meet the demands of our jobs and our families at the same time. We're stretched to the max. Everyone is, including Jessica. Top management keeps expecting more and more of us, but gives us fewer resources to work with. As I think about it, there are other work-family issues creating tension for the employees, and the organization's insensitivity to them is eroding morale."

As Gary was realizing, once you begin to see and understand systems, it becomes more difficult to believe you can address change as a single issue. If you see systemic issues, you recognize that until they are addressed, symptoms of underlying problems will continue to reappear. By focusing on changing systems, you seek to alter conditions that give rise to behavior.

Concentrating on systemic change also increases the likelihood of getting others to support your efforts to initiate change. Individuals may resist letting others push them into change, but may be willing to help alter systems they find constraining. Trying to get Jessica to see the light about meeting times may not be nearly as effective as inviting her to examine the systemic pressures negatively impacting everyone's work. Has increased pressure for productivity led to increased stress, less flexibility, and perceptions that the organization does not care about employees? Is concern about the meeting time symbolic of a larger issue?

Gain Support from Others for the Change

"Okay," continued Gary after further reflection. "I'm convinced that this thing may be bigger than just the meeting times. But all this talk about systems seems very grandiose. I've talked to LaTisha and Shawn about their situations, and they're looking to me to take the initiative. You tell me I can't change another person—how is changing a system going to be any easier? Where do I start?"

"You've already begun the process," I told him, "by listening to LaTisha and Shawn. You can continue it by talking with others. Asking others about their views will help you gain a clearer understanding of the issues and garner additional support for change. You begin changing the system by talking with one person at a time."

Systems are not nameless, faceless objects floating out in the organization or environment somewhere. People and relationships are key elements of systems. Every person who joins the change effort has the opportunity to influence others in her or his relationship network.

CURIOUS ABOUT THE RESEARCH?

Everett Rogers has investigated hundreds of cases around the world in which innovation spread throughout a community. He sees diffusion as a social process: people talk about new ideas in order to give them meaning before adopting change.

Rogers, E. M. (2003). *Diffusion of innovation.* New York: The Free Press.

It begins with one person talking with another. As you talk with others, your goal is to stimulate an image of what might be possible if change were to occur. It also means listening to others to determine how they see the current reality and what they imagine is possible. If you share your thinking with others and encourage them to articulate their desires, they are more likely to do the same. And on and on it will go. Within a few weeks, dozens of people around the organization could be talking about the possibilities, with the number growing exponentially.

Noting a disgusted look on Gary's face, I asked, "Is something bothering you about this?"

"I'm just annoyed that this has to be so complicated. I have a lot on my plate right now and don't have a lot of extra time. All we want is a simple little change in the meeting time. Is that so much to ask?"

"Do you think you might benefit from releasing some of your annoyance, using one of the emotional clearing processes we've discussed in earlier conversations? I'm guessing that if you tried rallying support right away, you'd end up complaining about Jessica and the situation instead of inspiring a vision of what might be possible."

He agreed, somewhat reluctantly: "I suppose you're right. I may not be completely clear-headed about this at the moment."

"Once you've cleared some of your strong feelings around the issue, you'll be in a better position to discover how your coworkers feel about the timing of staff meetings, as well as whether other work-family issues are important to them."

The next day, Gary called me with a brief update. "I did as you suggested, Jean," he began. "I used the Sedona Method to release some of my anger towards Jessica and the situation. I think I can now be more effective in engaging in inquiry with the rest of the staff. I'm going to talk with as many people as I can over the next few weeks. I've begun to get excited about the possibilities."

Some people may be reluctant to join you in your change efforts without full support from top management, particularly if what you are proposing is a dramatic change. They may not want to stick their necks out. Some may immediately cite reasons why the whole thing is not worth the effort. Do not let their initial resistance dissuade you. Remember, you are not looking for support from everyone; you are only seeking a group of innovators to strategize with you on how to effect the change. With the support of the innovators, early adopters may also join you, and eventually enough of the early majority for momentum to begin. Go back to the naysayers a second time. Some may change their position given more information or time. As Herb Cohen explained in his book, *You Can Negotiate Anything*, "'No' is a reaction, not a position."[6] A negative response is often a knee-jerk reaction to the unfamiliar.

How you approach others will affect their response to you. More effective questions inquire about hopes and dreams as well as barriers. Questions about hopes and dreams ("What would life in this organization be like if . . .?") inspire momentum toward change. Questions about barriers seek to identify obstacles ("Are there particular reasons you don't want to participate right now?"). The questions leave the door open for the person to participate later and are deliberately intended to avoid blame. Your goal is to inquire in a genuine manner about the other person's situation and attitudes.

In your early discussions, your task is to make the unfamiliar familiar. The more conversation generated about a potential change, the more familiar the topic will become. The more familiar it is, the more feasible it seems. Your goal is to keep talking about possibilities until people get used to the idea and join in.

CURIOUS ABOUT THE RESEARCH?

Kimberlee Weaver and her colleagues found that an opinion's popularity is affected by its familiarity—even if the reason for its familiarity is that only one person has expressed it repeatedly.

Weaver, K., Garcia, S. M., Schwarz, N., & Miller, D. T. (2007). Inferring the popularity of an opinion from its familiarity: A repetitive voice can sound like a chorus. *Journal of Personality and Social Psychology, 92*(5), 821–833.

Set a Direction, not Fixed Outcomes

Vision for change emerges from the involvement and commitment of those affected. Rather than attempting to sell predetermined solutions, shared solutions—as well as shared definitions of the problem—are sought. In this way, others help define the outcomes. This means truly involving others in the change effort.

A week later, Gary called me with excitement in his voice. "I am so glad I 'stayed in the question,' as you put it, about the solutions that might work best for everyone!" he exclaimed. "For one thing, I checked to see what other companies were doing and discovered they were experimenting with flextime, job sharing, telecommuting, leave for new fathers and adoptive parents, on-site childcare centers—all kind of things.

"When I asked people point-blank if they thought our work environment was family-friendly, I uncovered a lot of different issues. One of my coworkers, Maria, said she'd really like to have the opportunity to work more flexible hours. She'd be willing to begin her day at 6:30 A.M. and take only a half-hour lunch in order to get off at 3:00 P.M. so she could be home when her children arrived from school. This was something she'd been secretly hoping for but felt she didn't dare bring up since Jessica was holding these late afternoon meetings.

"And James, a worker in the unit next to ours, wants paternity leave, so he can bond with the newborn they're expecting in a few months. Porscha wants the organization to consider an adoption-leave policy. Vashon thought it would be a good idea to begin a 'daughter-son at work day' during which children could learn more about what their parents do. All were more than willing to support a shift in staff meeting times if their coworkers would consider these other changes.

"I'm amazed at what you can find out by just asking questions," he concluded.

"Well, you didn't just ask questions," I emphasized. "You articulated a direction and then solicited others' involvement in what the details of desired change might look like. Checking what innovative companies in your industry were doing was really doing your homework."

"And, you know what?" he continued. "As I thought about it and learned more, I realized that changing the meeting times wasn't really my goal. What I really want is to find a way to keep my staff from burning out under the tension between work and home life." I could almost hear him grin over the telephone.

Setting a general direction or strategy for change, rather than a specific one, is counter to common advice to begin with an end already in mind. Had Gary concentrated on imposing his narrow vision of changing the meeting hour, he would have precluded the larger vision that was beginning to emerge from discussions with his colleagues. For authentic shared vision to occur, others must be involved in creating it. Creating a vision or goal and then trying to sell it is more likely to trigger reaction and resistance.[7]

Learn from the Resistance

There is considerable evidence that people *do* embrace change. People want to grow and develop. Margaret Wheatley, in *Leadership and the New Science*, said that "Change is not foreign. In the natural world change is not a singular event you try to live through, it's just the way things are."[8]

Yet the common wisdom is that everyone resists change. Why the inconsistency? It comes back to choice. People do not resist change, they resist being changed. People want to change on their own terms, not someone else's.

CURIOUS ABOUT THE RESEARCH?

The human brain is a pattern-making organ with an innate desire to create novel connections. It is thought that hard-wired neural pathways resist being told what to do—stress and discomfort are experienced. When people solve problems on their own, however, their brains release a rush of neurotransmitters such as adrenaline.

Rock, D., & Schwartz, J. (2006). The neuroscience of leadership. *Strategy + Business, 43*(Summer), 72–81.

People's resistance to change can be a source of learning. Although counterintuitive, embracing the resistance, exploring it, even welcoming it, will allow you to learn from it and be more effective in your change efforts. Discovering what resisters are concerned about—what it is they are trying to protect—requires showing respect for the resisters. Listening deeply and with an open heart and mind allows you to learn the "reasons beneath the reasons—the things those who resist say to each other when you are not around."[9]

When I suggested this to Gary, he arched his eyebrows and raised his voice a little. "But resistance is very real!" he said. "And I don't know how to get past it. My experience with conflict is that no one really ever listens to the other side—and few ever change their minds. We end up wasting a lot of time in endless debate."

"You've put your finger on a key problem," I responded. "We don't know how to listen to one another. Writing off others' dissenting opinions as unreasonable resistance merely fuels the conflict. Let me give you an example."

I told him a story about the faculty at a school for deaf children. "Faculty were considering whether to open admission to hearing children whose parents wanted them to learn sign language. The group became split over the issue; they disagreed so heatedly that one teacher described them as being 'at each others' throats.'

"Some thought the change would provide a new source of revenue and expose the deaf children to the hearing world and vice versa. Others feared the admission of hearing children would dilute their mandate of service to deaf children.

"Because it involved a particular student's application, the decision had to be made quickly. The issue was so contentious that they brought in an outside facilitator to help them set ground rules for a meeting to hash it out and to keep them on track. The first step of the process was to fully describe all aspects of the situation. As new information was added, no one could contradict what had already been said.

"After about a half hour, they agreed the complete story had been told. They could then see that there were essentially two groups in the room: advocates for change on one side, and protectors of the mission of the school on the other."

"You mean the resisters," Gary said.

"Well, they didn't accept that label. In fact, no one really resists change itself. Rather, they resist losing what is of value to them. So, the key is to discover the underlying value people wish to protect and then figure out a way to preserve that value within the context of the change. When someone suggested the word 'protectors' to describe them at this meeting, the group liked it so much they applauded."

I went on to describe what had happened next: "People stood up from each group and made statements supporting their position. An advocate for change talked about the isolation many deaf children feel and how important it is for them to have opportunities to interact with the hearing world. A protector said simply, 'I'm afraid we're going to give the school away to the hearing community.' Each individual wrote a one-sentence summary of what he or she had said on flip chart paper posted around the room. Ultimately, there were many one-sentence perspectives on both sides of the issue.

"Next, everyone milled around and looked at what others had written. This time the ground rule was that if anyone disagreed with a statement, he must put his comment in the form of a question, rather than a refutation. For example, one of the protectors wrote, 'How do we avoid sacrificing the needs of our primary population, deaf children, to the needs of the hearing children?'

"By now, there were statements and questions posted all around the room. As the group milled around, they talked with one another and were able to answer the questions instead of defending their positions.

"When the group came back together as a whole, both sides understood the reasons why the other held their position so strongly. 'I thought I knew the protectors' position," one advocate said, 'but I'd never really heard it until now.'

"They were now able to hammer out an agreement fairly quickly, and put in some safeguards to protect the school's mission. Of these, the most important was that hearing children could never make up more than 20 percent of the school's population. At the start of the session, no one thought the group would be able to come to an agreement. But once they found a structure by which they could really listen to and learn from one another, their commitment to the school and their natural humanity took over."

When I paused, Gary joked, "Hey, does that place have any openings? Maybe I can go work there." Then, more seriously, he mused, "So that means I have to be in the question when I talk to Jessica again."

"Yes," I responded. "You want to go into the meeting to listen and learn, not to sell your position. If you find that Jessica is opposed to the ideas you've collected to provide more work-family balance, including changing the meeting times, you'll want to discover why and what it is she wishes to protect by rejecting your suggestions."

"Okay, I can see that," said Gary more confidently. "But before I talk to Jessica again, I'm thinking that I should talk to some of the staff who've remained silent so far, and maybe go back to others who put me off. Maybe some of them are protectors—and I just couldn't see it before."

"What a great insight! Let me know what you learn."

Surface Undiscussables

Several weeks later, Gary called to report significant progress in talking with his coworkers about the kinds of policies and practices they would like the organization to consider.

> Gary's voice hardened a bit, though, when he said, "But one person will hardly talk to me about the topic. Stacy says she doesn't believe the organization is serious about any of this. And that only a few will benefit! She says she doesn't want to waste her time talking about it. What makes this puzzling is that usually she's at the forefront of organizational change efforts. She's become a legend around here because of her extraordinary leadership of the relief effort for the Hurricane Katrina evacuees. People know she really cares about others and often follow her lead. She would be a good one to have on board, but every time I broach the topic, she brushes me off."
>
> I thought about what Gary said for a moment and then asked, "Is it possible there are any undiscussables standing in the way of having an open and honest conversation with Stacy?"
>
> "What's an undiscussable?" Gary asked.
>
> "The term," I said, "comes from Chris Argyris, a pioneer in organizational learning.[10] He believes that most people have been socialized to cover up threatening issues. When a threatening issue is concealed, it becomes undiscussable: people don't talk about it, and more importantly, they don't talk about the fact that they don't talk about it. When a topic involving an undiscussable comes up, individuals shut down."
>
> "Welllll . . ." Gary said hesitantly. "I have heard that Stacy is lesbian, but I don't know that for sure, since no one talks about sexual orientation in our organization. Everyone has their private suspicions, but no one asks questions. But I don't know what sexual orientation would have to do with issues related to work-life balance, anyway."

People are often unwilling to discuss issues that make them feel uncomfortable. Fear of embarrassment or hurting others keeps undiscussables from being discussed. People are afraid of looking stupid, or appearing unknowledgeable or unsophisticated. It may feel easier to remain silent than risk isolation from friends, family or organization members.[11]

> "Undiscussables don't have to be socially sensitive issues," I said to Gary. "They can be any issue that makes one of the parties to the

interaction uncomfortable. For example, how long have people been coming to the late afternoon meetings and feeling secretly resentful?"

"At least two months," he replied thoughtfully.

"Has anyone raised the issue before? Or done anything besides grumble under their breath?"

"No," he admitted. "I guess that would make it an undiscussable."

"Yes, organizations have lots of undiscussables—big ones and little ones. No matter their import, undiscussables are damaging to open and honest relationships and impede a group's ability to function."

Undiscussables particularly impede change, because change is a social process. Anything undiscussable is unchangeable. If people cannot talk about it, how will they be able to change it? Indeed, sometimes the underlying reason an individual has for rejecting a change is undiscussable. In that case, the group will not be able to talk about the real issue—whatever the protectors are protecting—and the change process will come to a halt.

To be sure, conversations about undiscussables may feel uncomfortable. There is a saying that you cannot expect to step from one rowboat to the next without rocking. If you want change, you can predict that there will be a time of feeling unsteady on your feet, one foot in each boat. Expect a temporary feeling of lack of safety. Naming the elephant in the room can, however, be an act of caring and can free up more space for inquiry and openness.

"This all sounds good," responded Gary. "But I don't even know how to start."

"One way to begin a conversation about an undiscussable is to state your feelings of discomfort openly," I told Gary. "For example, you could begin to raise the issue with Stacy by saying 'I'm feeling uncomfortable here and I'm frankly concerned about what you might be experiencing and how best to support you. Is there something I'm missing? Or something I'm not hearing? Or that is difficult to talk about? I really would like your honest input on this issue. And I want to be sure I'm doing everything I can to help make that happen.'

"In just a few sentences, you could describe your in-the-moment reaction to a difficult situation, express your support and empathy, state your ambivalence and uncertainty about the situation, engage in inquiry, and focus on a desirable future. Most importantly, you would only say what is unarguable and say it without blame. Then you should be quiet and wait for a response, leaving room for Stacy to react without defensiveness."

The conversation Gary wants to have with Stacy will require some forethought and maybe even rehearsal. He must avoid any preconceptions about what Stacy should do or say. He should take care to be concise, instead of trying to cover his discomfort with a lot of words. He should not accuse Stacy of making him uncomfortable, or lecture her on how important it is for her to be open and forthcoming with him. He should honestly inquire about the problem (and solution) Stacy sees instead of maintaining a preconceived idea of the solution she should accept.

Finally, even the best-designed effort to surface an undiscussable in this way may catch the other person unaware. Stacy may still respond defensively.

> I could tell he had continuing doubts and invited him to challenge or question any part of what I was saying. He did so with vehemence: "Suppose she responds by saying, 'I don't know what you're talking about! There's nothing wrong. Do I have to have an opinion about everything?' What do I do then?"
>
> "Good question," I said. "A possible response could be: 'Of course you don't. But I still feel uneasy and uncertain about the cause of that uneasiness. I want this to work out for all of us.'"
>
> "In other words, don't give up?" he asked.
>
> "Exactly," I replied. "Your feelings are your feelings and cannot be disputed. As long you're not putting attributions on her, you have a right to your own feelings."

Using this approach, Gary would not demand a change or assert that he has the right answer. He would instead stay firmly in the stance of disliking the situation and not being sure how to work it out. His job at this point is not to solve the problem, but to remain grounded in the idea that there is a solution. Through his demeanor, his statements, and his questions, he provides reassurance to Stacy.

Undiscussables are usually made so because they are emotionally laden. Feelings of discomfort are to be expected, but before deciding to surface an undiscussable, clear your emotions sufficiently around the issue to maintain a sincere position of inquiry and curiosity. If you feel yourself triggered emotionally, either by the issue or the other person's defensive response, call for a time out. Engage in emotional clearing and return when you can be an active and engaged listener.

Another week went by before I heard from Gary again. He said that Stacy—who had never officially come out as lesbian at work—was indeed concerned about issues related to sexual identity. Once she felt he would really listen to her, she had spoken frankly.

> "She told me that all the discussion of family-friendly policies so far had assumed heterosexuality," Gary related. "It was as if same-sex relationships didn't—or more importantly, shouldn't—exist. No one was considering the impact of these heterosexual assumptions on the policies and practices being discussed.
>
> "This opened up a whole new set of possibilities to consider. Just a brief search of the Internet educated me about the ways in which same-sex partners are often overlooked by standard benefit plans like health, dental or life insurance. This adds a new dimension to what we've been considering. So there were two good outcomes of this: Stacy is now on board and I've learned something."

"I'm glad to hear it!" I responded. "Another way to surface an undiscussable when a problem exists in the organization or community is to ask about positive exceptions."

"How do you mean?"

"If Stacy is in the closet, then you already know it's not your place to out her. So, how will you bring up the issue of how employees in same-sex relationships are treated? This can be a big undiscussable at the organizational level. A strength-focused way to do this is to inquire about positive exceptions to the norm either within your organization or within other organizations. The question here is what distinguishes the companies offering same-sex domestic partner benefits. Is there something about them worth emulating? Within your own company, you might inquire whether there are employees in a few work units who are out, and whether everyone is comfortable with them being so. If so, then the question becomes; what is different about those work units that might be transferrable to the larger organization?"

CURIOUS ABOUT THE RESEARCH?

Richard Pascale and Jerry Sternin investigated situations in which organizational or community change was initiated by surfacing undiscussables through inquiry. The key question in each case was whether pockets of people existed within the organization or community who had successfully overcome a problem. These exceptions were then used to prove that a different approach was possible.

Pascale, R. T., & Sternin, J. (2005). Your company's secret change agents. *Harvard Business Review, 83*(5), 72–81.

"Wow!" responded Gary. "That certainly gives me more to chew on."

MOVING FORWARD: A SEQUENCE
OF SMALL WINS

Surfacing undiscussables may be one of a long series of steps toward change. Some of these may feel like steps forward, where you are making progress; others may feel like steps backward. Change is not a linear process, nor does it happen all at once.

As change begins to occur within a system, a strength-based perspective is once more helpful. In this case, focusing on strengths means seeking out and rewarding things that go right, even if they are only small wins. Too often, change initiators give up because they do not immediately see results from their actions. They may, however, be looking for the wrong thing: evidence of big change instead of small incremental adjustments in the desired direction.

By acknowledging small wins during each small step of the process, you remind yourself of your progress, however slow the pace. Recognizing small wins or strengths in every situation takes practice, however. It is so much easier to see what remains to be done than what has already been accomplished.

> "Hmmmm," said Gary. "In other words, when Jessica said she wouldn't stand in the way of talking with others about work-family issues, I was disappointed that she wasn't wildly enthusiastic about the idea. Instead, I could have considered her reaction a small win."

Gary called me a week later. As it turned out, when he finally had his meeting with Jessica, he was amazed at her response.

> "Remember we talked about finding small pockets of positive change within the organization or elsewhere and following their lead?" he asked. "I discovered that Jessica had already been thinking about exploring work-family issues within the organization because she'd heard about another work unit in which employees had greater flexibility in their work hours, but kept it quiet because they didn't want top management to come down on them. She hadn't said anything because she didn't want to expose them and she wasn't ready to try it out with us or to approach the VP for permission. What I'd interpreted as disinterest during our one-on-one interaction was really reaction to pressure she'd been experiencing recently from top management for increased productivity. Look, Jean, you've emphasized that if someone has a negative impact on me, I should test the assumption that they actually intended it. This is another case where

it turned out that the person's intent didn't match her impact—she didn't mean to put me off!

"Actually, she thought dealing only with staff meeting times was short-sighted—there were many other issues to be considered, such as how to introduce flex-time and extend parental leave and health benefits to domestic partners—and how lack of attention to these might be leading to lowered productivity. It turns out that while I was out talking with coworkers about their desired changes, she was debating how to tackle the larger issues. The upshot of our meeting was that she asked me to head up a task force to prepare a set of formal recommendations she could take to the execs and possibly the board."

A few months later, Gary called again to report that the meeting times for staff meetings had changed and they were experimenting with teleconferencing to accommodate people's schedules.

"We've gone way beyond the original concern," he said. "I admit there've been ups and downs, though. Some parts of the organization have adopted flex-time while others seem to be dragging their feet, claiming it won't work in their areas. There are charges of unfairness, of the changes accommodating certain individuals or groups and ignoring others. Competition has increased and sales are down, and the organization is looking for ways to cut costs. We'd been talking about expanding health care benefits to accommodate domestic partners, but now I don't know what will happen. Some of these new programs look like they may be candidates for cutbacks. That would be a real mistake, because such programs have sometimes reduced rather than added costs, but the execs are worried about their numbers. It's touch and go."

The key is to focus on what is going right—or may do so—instead of what is going wrong. The small wins to celebrate are those changes that have taken hold. The executives were willing to experiment with flex-time. They were willing to consider same-sex benefits. They should be congratulated and praised for each positive step, no matter how small.

The small wins approach provides constant reminders that gains are possible. A focus on small wins increases a group's confidence in its ability to attain and sustain the change. This influences their staying power—and resistance to discouragement—in the face of opposition or failure to get quick results.[12] If change is to be ongoing and enduring, change participants must be committed for the long haul, not just during the easy short-term beginning.

The middle phase of change can be marked by confusion between the old way and the new one. Doubt surfaces about whether the change will actually occur, whether top management will support it, or whether people can sustain it. There may be vacillation between action and relapse. This can be a period of intense confusion within an organization.

One element in successful change efforts often overlooked is the role of ongoing support for change initiators.

> "Who do you have to talk with about this?" I asked Gary. "How do you take care of yourself through all these ups and downs?"
>
> "Well, we have a 'merry band of family-friendly door-openers'— that's what we call ourselves," laughed Gary. "We're a small group, but tight. We support each other. We make sure we don't take on more than we have energy to sustain, and try to figure out in advance the impact of each step we take. We're also gathering resources.[13] We found an expert in work-family balance who sent us materials and information on the benefits and costs of these policies."

The middle phase of change can tax more than your staying power. It can also severely test your skills in managing your emotions, testing your assumptions, developing effective relationships, bridging differences, and discerning an appropriate strategy for whatever is confronting you in the moment. This is where your small group of committed innovators comes in handy—they help support you and you do the same for them.

Do not try to go it alone. Find caring and competent support and treat these individuals as the valuable resources they are. They can act as truth-tellers, helping you identify what you are doing that is working, how you might be contributing to the problem rather than alleviating it, and how you might change your attitudes, behaviors, or strategy to achieve greater success. Last but not least, it is also good to have at least one organizational strategist adept at diagnosing systems and relationships within those systems to help you think through the next steps.

The approach described here contradicts the way most people in organizations think about change. They tend to seek change by challenging others to change through logical reasoning, proselytizing, or admonition. When change does not occur as rapidly as they expect or in the way they want, they give up and silently collude in the status quo.

It may help to revisit the myths of change introduced at the beginning of the chapter and look at how the recommended steps for initiating change counter those myths (Table 7.2).

The goal in initiating change is to set a trajectory in the direction of the desired change. You are throwing a stone into a pond, creating a ripple, which extends into a lake, which flows into an ocean. Initiating change is throwing the first pebble into the pond. You may not see the result. You may not even get credit for having thrown the stone. In fact, if you are truly successful, others will rightfully claim credit for their contributions to the ripple that eventually reaches the ocean.

Table 7.2
Myths of Workplace Change Revisited

Myths of Change	*Steps for Initiating Change*
It's up to the other person to change.	Commit to personal change.
If I carefully explain my valid reasons and others still won't make the change, they either don't care or are incompetent.	Emphasize changing systems, not individuals.
Change isn't possible unless the higher-ups support it. If higher-ups don't support the change initially, change is only possible if everyone else supports it.	Gain support from others for the change, one person or small group at a time.
Change should happen the way I've decided it should and come about as I envision. Otherwise, it's not a real change.	Set a direction, not fixed outcomes.
If people resist the change initially, they're permanently opposed to the change and there's nothing more I can do. If they say they'll think about the change and don't follow through, they're resisting the change. If they make the change but don't stick with it, they're playing games.	Learn from the resistance.
Upper management lives in a different world. They're oblivious to what's going on and there's no way I can make them understand. If I tell them what's really going on, they'll just get mad.	Surface undiscussables.
Change will occur quickly, visibly, and within the time frame I think is reasonable.	Persevere through the time lag of change; recognize small wins along the way.

© Jean Kantambu Latting & V. Jean Ramsey, 2007–2009.

CURIOUS ABOUT THE RESEARCH?

Complexity theory suggests that individual change spawns a ripple effect of successive changes in surrounding environments. Over time, members of individuals' social networks may respond to new behaviors with their own changes. These shifts may prompt changes in this new set of social networks, which then transfer to still other interconnecting networks.

Marion, R., & Uhl-Bien, M. (2001). Leadership in complex organizations. *Leadership Quarterly, 12,* 389–418.

NOTES

1. Senge, P. M., Kleiner, A., Roberts, C., Ross, R. B., Roth, G., & Smith, B. J. (1999). *The dance of change.* New York: Currency Doubleday.

2. Rogers, E. M. (2003). *Diffusion of innovation.* New York: The Free Press.

3. Rogers, E. M. (2003). *Diffusion of innovation.* New York: The Free Press.

4. Vohra-Gupta, S., & Latting, J. K. (2007). Promoting women's empowerment in patriarchal societies through triple loop action learning. unpublished manuscript.

5. Schaefer, M. (1974). Concepts of general systems theory applied to administration. In M. Schaefer (Ed.), *Administration of environmental health programmes: A systems view* (pp. 33–59). Geneva: World Health Organization.

6. Cohen, H. (1980). *You can negotiate anything* (1st ed, p.105.). Secaucus, NJ: L. Stuart.

7. Senge, P. M., Roberts, C., Ross, R. B., Smith, B. J., & Kleiner, A. (1994). *The fifth discipline fieldbook.* New York: Doubleday.

8. Wheatley, M. (1996). Natural change: An interview with Margaret Wheatley. In R. Maurer, *Beyond the wall of resistance: Unconventional strategies that build support for change* (pp.50–51). Austin, TX: Bard Press.

9. Maurer, R. (1996). *Beyond the wall of resistance: Unconventional strategies that build support for change* (p.57). Austin, TX: Bard Press.

10. Argyris, C. (1999). *On organizational learning.* Malden, MA: Blackwell Publishers, Inc.

11. Bowen, F., & Blackmon, K. (2003). Spirals of silence: The dynamic effects of diversity on organizational voice. *Journal of Management Studies, 40*(6), 1393–1417.

12. Bandura, A. (2000). Exercise of human agency through collective efficacy. *Current Directions in Psychological Science, 9*(3), 75–78.

13. Brager, G. A., & Jorrin, V. (1969). Bargaining: A method in community change. *Social Work, 14*(4), 73–83.

CHAPTER 8

Matt's Story Redux

Remember Matt in Chapter 1? In this final chapter, his story is revisited and the many principles discussed throughout the previous chapters are used to suggest what he might do to bring people together in his organization to improve their situation.

Despite Matt's objections, his director had ordered staff members to take down pictures covering the glass on their office doors. When asked for an explanation, the director said that reducing the staff members' privacy would keep them from thinking they were "too important." Matt thought the director was engaging in divide-and-conquer tactics by deliberately cultivating the favor of the managers while minimizing the contributions of the front-line staff. Matt also noted that the director came from a country outside the United States in which people higher in authority were obeyed without question. Although Matt felt he had accurately assessed the situation, he felt powerless to change it.

Several years before, Matt had taken a class from me that covered much of the content of the previous chapters. He was calling now for advice on how to more effectively address this difficult situation. If you have read these previous chapters—or even glanced at the table of contents—you may anticipate that my recommendations will be that Matt:

- *Identify and test his assumptions about what is driving the director's behavior;*

- *Clear his negative emotions* about the unfairness of his director's motives and actions;
- *Seek to build a more effective relationship* with his director by focusing on the director's strengths and engaging in powerful listening, inquiry, openness, and feedback;
- *Bridge the power and status differences* between them by recognizing the likelihood that the director has a blind spot about how she is wielding her power in the situation, and that Matt himself is minimizing his potential influence;
- *Consciously use himself* by deliberately choosing thoughts, emotions, and actions to positively improve the situation while maintaining his sense of personal integrity; and
- *Initiate workplace change* by taking a broader look at the situation and how the director's actions are being supported by the larger system.

These are the elements of Conscious Change. The principles will be used to help Matt sort out his situation and think through his responses.

Throughout this book, emphasis has been given to the importance of looking beyond individual actions to consider workplace policies and practices that constrain people's behavior. Before Matt acts, he would benefit from looking beyond his assumption that the director's personality is the sole cause of the problem. A broader view—focused on situational factors—might reveal how current relationships, unspoken and contradictory norms, and established ways of doing things within the overall system interact to provide a context for the director's actions.

At the moment, however, Matt's perspective is more limited, as summarized in Table 8.1.

When we left the phone conversation with Matt in Chapter 1, Matt had explained the situation and ended by saying that he felt he didn't have the power to improve things.

"Matt," I began, "you're far from powerless in this situation."

"What do you mean?" he asked.

"Here's how you've used your power. For two weeks, you managed to postpone having the pictures removed from the staff's doors. You weren't able to keep it from happening altogether, but you held the director off for all that time. You've managed to earn your staff's respect; they trust you enough to tell you how unhappy they are. And you're providing them with reassurance that they aren't crazy for

Table 8.1
Matt's Current Perspective

Matt's assumptions	Matt believes the director is unpleasant, unreasonable, and insecure. He sees the director as using her rank in the organization to drive a wedge between the managers and staff members. For the most part, Matt is in the answer, not in the question. He *is* in the question about one aspect of the situation: whether the director's upbringing in a more hierarchically-oriented culture is impacting her behavior.
Matt's emotions	Matt is angry and frustrated that the staff are not valued, and concerned that the director will turn on him.
Matt's efforts to build effective relationships	He has spoken up to the director, trying to explain without offending. He is sympathetic with his staff, telling them he sees the director's actions as unfair. Yet, he believes he has been ineffective with the director and only partially effective with the staff.
Matt's efforts to bridge the power and status differences between himself and the director	Despite Matt's best efforts, the director still took down the staff's pictures. As a nondominant in this situation, he feels stumped and powerless.
Matt's conscious use of self	He is making every effort to retain his integrity by being truthful with the director, but does not see how he himself may be contributing to the situation. He has not considered his director's perspective or strengths. Asking for help is a sign that he is willing to learn from the situation.
Matt's view of the organizational system	He has not fully considered the organizational context. Since problems have occurred with the past few directors, something may be off kilter at the organizational level.

being upset with what's happening. Meanwhile, the director obviously respects you. These are all sources of power."

Recognize your power and use it responsibly.

Matt jumped in. "She values me now, yes, but that could change. As I said, I've watched several other managers under her supervision leave in the last six months—one was fired and the others made so miserable they left on their own. So, she could come after me too. I feel as though I have to watch my back."

"Yes," I replied, "and you're doing an effective job of it, even as you're speaking your mind to her. You haven't been fired, she's coming to you for reassurance, and she's giving you raises and new equipment. So something you're doing is working."

In saying this, I wasn't just trying to make Matt feel better. I had a more deliberate objective: to show him the power he had in this situation and get him to think about how he might use that power more effectively. He had not achieved the goal he wanted—to stop the director's abusive behavior—but he had achieved some limited success, and had the potential for greater influence.

As a nondominant, ferret out any tendency toward internalized oppression and views of the dominants as a monolithic, all-powerful group.

I also had a second objective: to help Matt re-frame his thoughts so he might consciously deploy his own presence more powerfully to get the results he wanted on behalf of his staff and the organization.

Thus far, Matt's thoughts had been based on a simplistic, polarized, and personalized perception of the situation: he saw the director as morally weak, yet politically strong. In contrast, he saw himself as morally strong, but politically weak. By not looking beyond these initial assumptions, Matt over-simplified the situation and was unable to accurately see workplace factors that may have constrained the director's behavior, much less his own potential levers of influence.

Avoid either/or thinking; look for multiple points of view.

An initial step toward seeing that the reasons for the director's actions may not be as simple as they seemed was to ask Matt to expand his view of the director—to look at the director's strengths; not just her weaknesses.

FOCUSING ON STRENGTHS

"So what is good about your director?" I asked. "What does she do well?"

Focus on the other person's strengths.

"Do well?" Matt repeated. "Do well?! I've been so busy being angry about what she's doing wrong, I haven't really thought about what she's doing well."

I waited.

Matt repeated my question, this time more slowly. "What's she good at? It's hard to think of anything because she's so horrible. But if I'm honest, I have to admit she has vision and plans for how we can grow. She understands the scope of our work and how all the parts fit together. She has innovative ideas."

"Those are excellent strengths," I replied. "I'm impressed with your ability to identify them even though you're angry. That's a strength on your part: to be able to see past the anger to what she's doing right."

"Now, let's consider how her strengths might factor into your choices," I went on. "She was willing to pay attention to your initial objections to uncovering the staff's glass panes for a while, but they weren't enough to hold her off for good. So, suppose you'd taken a different approach—instead of blaming your director for poor judgment or character, what if you'd focused on her strengths and her concerns?

"Suppose you'd said this: 'You want them to take down their pictures because you feel some people think they're too important? Well, it isn't necessary to have them take down their pictures to fix that! If someone has been insubordinate, or done something that implied they don't respect you or the other managers, we should address that head on. Taking down their pictures is a back-door approach to the problem. A more direct approach is to make sure all the staff know what we managers are doing, and specifically, what you as director are doing to provide us with a vision and generate clients and opportunities.'"

I stopped and asked, "Matt, suppose you'd said something like this, what would her reaction have been?"

"It might have worked," he responded, seeming to ponder every word. "She really is insecure."

"Would you have felt dishonest if you'd said that?"

"Well, I'm so mad at her that I might've felt deceitful or manipulative. But when I think about it, nothing you said was untrue. So, yes, I could've been alright with saying it."

"Okay then," I said, "She has strengths and you believe you could acknowledge them without compromising your integrity."

Maintain integrity.

Matt was silent for a minute and then said, "Yes, I could do that. But I'm not sure I want to."

I wasn't surprised. People often feel like gagging when a strength-focused approach is suggested, particularly with dominants with whom they are angry. You may question whether it is your role to offer reassurance and empathy to those in superior positions. However, there is far more to be gained than lost by this approach—which starts by showing people you understand the nature of their authority, self-worth, and strengths.

Most individuals are willing to change only if they feel valued. They resist evidence that undermines their sense of self-worth. If you give people feedback that makes them feel inadequate, most will automatically reject it, even if it is good advice.

If instead you encourage individuals to think positively about a value they hold or to reflect on a success, they are more likely to be open to what might otherwise be threatening information. Despite the director's power and position in the organization, there is evidence that she feels insecure. Indeed, many leaders do. The director might not engage in as many self-protective actions that are hurtful to others if Matt could help her reconnect to her own considerable assets and her sense of self-worth.

BEING IN THE QUESTION

Certain that Matt understood the importance of being strength-focused, even if he wasn't ready yet to take that step, I moved on. "Now, here's another question."

I paused as I knew this one might be tough to take.

"Tell me about her country of origin and what you think it means to be from that country."

"I know where you're going, Jean. I can hear it in your tone of voice. You're wondering if I have a stereotype about her because her country is so hierarchical."

> **Check to see if you are making cultural assumptions.**

I burst into laughter. "Yup. That's exactly where I was going."

"Well, I thought about that, and realized that it is my assumption. I freely own it."

"Has she said anything to contradict such an assumption? As we've talked about already, there's a difference between a cultural norm and a stereotype. It's only a stereotype if you are thinking the cultural norm is true for each and every individual from that country."

> **Develop awareness of your own stereotyping tendencies and biases and learn how to manage them.**

"She seldom talks about her country," Matt responded reflectively. "However, she did once say that she left it because she felt stifled as a woman. She said women were just coming into their own, and she decided the changes were occurring too slowly, so when she had a chance to come to the United States, she did."

"What do you think are the implications of this for how she's managing now?"

> **Move out of the answer and into the question.**

"Good question. She may have learned how to act hierarchically from watching the male managers in her country, but that doesn't mean it's how she wants to be. She simply may not have any models for behaving differently. Maybe it means she doesn't really know how she's coming across."

Matt was making some astute connections here, identifying assumptions he might later test. He understood that his director may have been modeling behavior she had witnessed growing up in her country. Even if his assumption proved to be true, it may not be her intention to replicate that behavior with her staff. Matt was separating intent from impact.

> **Distinguish intent from impact.**

"How can you test your assumptions? How might you determine what her views are on hierarchy in organizations?"

Matt laughed. "I suppose I could just ask her. We've had philosophical conversations before. I could ask her what differences she's experienced in how managers governed in her country and how she functions here. But then again, maybe not. She might think it's a loaded question."

Test your assumptions about others.

He began thinking out loud: "Maybe I can do it in the context of a movie I saw the other night. Yes, that would work. I know how I can do it without acting like I'm setting her up."

"It's important to not set her up," I agreed, "and it sounds as though you've figured out a way to avoid doing that."

Develop skills in inquiry and openness.

I switched gears. "Matt, can you imagine how awful it might be to hold the title of director and feel disrespected by the staff?"

"Well, if she feels that way, she ought to!" Matt exclaimed. "Who can respect someone who acts as underhanded as she does—even if she doesn't mean to do it??!"

"Fair enough," I responded. "I'm not asking whether her actions warranted it. I'm asking whether you can imagine how awful it might feel."

Seek to understand others' perspectives;
put yourself in their shoes.

Matt was quiet for a moment. Then, he reluctantly acknowledged, "I can see that. I certainly wouldn't like it. But if she wants to be treated with respect, she might start by treating us that way."

BUILDING RELATIONSHIPS AND BRIDGING DIFFERENCES

I responded, "My experience, unfortunately, has been that generally when dominants don't feel valued or respected, they may tend to become more controlling. I've seen it time and again. They assert their authority in some way and then get outraged when nondominants resist. The resistance increases the dominants' anger, which translates into clamping down harder, all the while firmly believing the behavior of the nondominants requires them to be more controlling."

Learn to recognize dominant/nondominant dynamics.

"That's what's happening here," responded Matt.

"It's a blind spot many dominants have," I continued. "They don't see the connection between their actions and the nondominants' reactions."

***As a nondominant, recognize that dominants
may have blind spots about the impact of
their behavior on nondominants.***

Matt was silent so I asked again, "Can you imagine how alone she might feel?"

"Jean, your naming this as a blind spot dominants tend to have helps me better understand it. And yes, I can see how lonely that might be. Maybe that's why she keeps trying to bribe the managers: she wants us on her side."

"That's certainly a possibility," I agreed. "There's something else that may be going on too. Would it be fair to say that your unconscious strategy for changing your director's behavior so far has been to point out to her how wrong she is and exhort her to change?"

"Yes, that's fair," acknowledged Matt.

"I'm afraid it's a doomed strategy. Do you remember when we talked in class about 'psychological reactance'? That describes people's reactions to threatened loss of freedom. Even though your suggestions to your director are rationally correct, and following your advice would be in her best interest, I'm not at all surprised she resisted."

While the director initially acquiesced to Matt and left the pictures alone for a few days, Matt may have inadvertently stirred up the director's psychological reactance. To have any hope of continued success, Matt must choose a new strategy, one more respectful of the director's need for authority and autonomy. He could begin by putting himself in a learning mode. Rather than making assumptions about the director's motivations, Matt might simply ask the director for more information. What had her experiences been since joining the organization? What was it about the staff's behavior that bothered her? Had Matt himself done something that annoyed her?

Learn from resistance.

When I suggested these questions to Matt, he immediately interjected, "Are you suggesting I ask her to criticize *me*?"

"Well, you could look at it that way. I prefer to think of it as seeking feedback. How would you like it if she asked you how she might improve as a director?"

"I'd love it!" Matt exclaimed.

"Yes, most of us would love for people in our everyday lives to ask that question. So, if you would like her to ask that question, could you do it as well?"

"She won't ask that question," Matt responded sardonically.

"Maybe not. But will you?"

Learn how to give, receive, and seek feedback.

After a brief moment, Matt added, "Okay, right now I'm inclined to ask her, but I'm not making any promises. I remember when you had us do it with each other in class. Talk about feeling awkward."

"Sure, as we're learning how to skillfully give, receive, and seek feedback, it does feel quite awkward. With practice, though, it becomes easier and feels more natural."

"Well, that's what happened with the class, I remember. We really bonded afterwards—once we got over the shock of that level of honesty. We stopped tip-toeing around one another. We felt freer to be who we were. The class got more fun."

"Do you remember how we did it?"

"Yes, we stayed strength-focused and we listened intently to one another. That's what made it work. We knew that people were telling each other what they really valued about one another and what they wished would improve. We didn't pressure anyone to change. Our focus was on listening to one another's stories and experiences."

Engage in powerful listening.

"I call that powerful listening."

"Yes, I remember," Matt responded in a reflective tone. He paused and then added, "Okay, I'll probably do it—but I'm not making promises."

"Fair enough," I responded. "I appreciate your being straight with me. I'm glad you're not making promises you don't intend to keep."

"Oh, I won't do that!" laughed Matt. "But this has got me thinking. I would love for the director to ask me how she might improve in her job. I wonder if my staff would like me to ask them that same question? Maybe they're sitting on stuff I don't know anything about. I'm thinking the director has blind spots—maybe I have some of my own. It's uncomfortable to think about, but maybe I do."

As a dominant, recognize that you may have blind spots as to your own behavior and systemic biases.

"Just hearing you say that, Matt, reminds me of how committed you are to your own development," I commented.

"It's not just for me that I'd do this, Jean. It's for my staff and our clients. If I'm keeping us from achieving what we're capable of, I want to know about it."

In a nutshell, Matt was explaining the value of feedback. If the flow of information is blocked, people cannot perform at optimal levels.

"I'll have to go back to my notes on how to seek and receive feedback, but I can honestly say that I'll probably ask my staff," Matt continued. "Staff members are under such stress now, I want to make sure I'm not doing anything to add to it. I may not agree with everything they suggest, but I should at least know what's on their minds. Maybe we can all agree to have a feedback session with one another."

"That sounds wise to me," I agreed.

"I have to think about whether I want to ask my director for feedback, though," he added. "Right now, I can see the benefits, but I don't want to give her the satisfaction. I know how that sounds, Jean, but I really don't."

I could feel how upset he was. I suspected that before he could consider approaching his director for feedback, he had to take a more systemic approach as well as clear some of his negative emotions about her.

SEEING SITUATIONAL FACTORS, NOT JUST INDIVIDUALS

Up to this point, we had been talking about the situation from Matt's personal point of view—like a snapshot of a complex scene from a single camera angle. Matt was seeing the director as the person in the organization most capable of independent action: the director could influence Matt, and Matt might have some minor influence on the staff, but there was no consideration of how the director might have been affected by others. I drew a diagram of the situation for myself (Figure 8.1).

> Then I said, "Workplace dynamics are seldom this simple. The direc-tor's move—ordering staff to take down their pictures—was not an isolated power play, occurring in a vacuum. It's more likely to have been a reaction to one or more interactions she'd experienced within the organization."
>
> "It sounds like you're making excuses for her," said Matt, a little testily.
>
> "No, I'm not trying to excuse her behavior, but I *am* trying to under-stand it. Your director's actions seem out of proportion to any actual problems staff members might have created. And her explanation sounds heartfelt, but logically inconsistent. If the staff members truly felt they were too important, they would have expressed those feel-ings in ways other than quitting or covering the glass on their office doors."
>
> I asked Matt who could potentially influence the director's actions. My diagram then looked like Figure 8.2.
>
> "My guess is that your director's response is a reaction to some other provocation. Perhaps something happened which led her to perceive

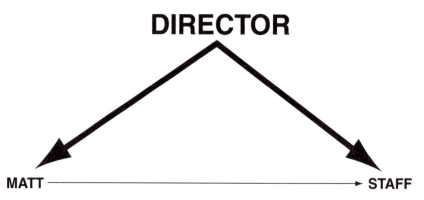

Figure 8.1

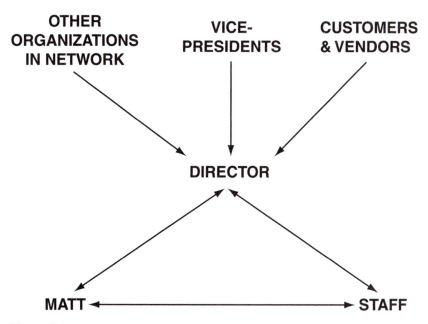

Figure 8.2

an attack on her authority, or even her sense of self-worth. Perhaps a staff member inadvertently said something the director perceived as insulting. Perhaps someone outside your work unit suggested that the director lacked sufficient authority or competence."

"How could I know that?" asked Matt.

"You can't know the specific source of what provoked the director," I replied, "but a broader view of the director's place in the organization suggests that there could be many more possibilities to consider.

"Worrying about staff members feeling 'too important' is so illogical, I just naturally wonder what is going on in the larger organizational context. You say she has a vision for the organization's future. I'm actively wondering 'What is she trying to protect?' It might be her own position or reputation or it could be that her hopes for the organization have been threatened somehow. Is it possible that something more complex is going on—something that might help explain, but not excuse, her actions?"

"All this speculation is well and good, but what do I tell my staff when they come to me demoralized?"

"Okay," I said. "Let me illustrate my response with an example. Let's take a father with a son who has a disability—a problem with his left foot. The child comes home crying because kids at school teased him on the playground, calling him 'club foot' and other stuff. The father sympathizes with him and says he has every right to feel horrible about it. But that's all that is said.

"Now consider a second father, with a similarly disabled son, who comes home crying about the same situation. This father says, 'Those kids teased you?!! Well, that's terrible!! What did you say to them? Let's talk about how you might respond to them so you'll be ready for them tomorrow if they tease you again. Let's make sure you know how to handle this situation, because it's probably going to happen again!' Which child will be better off?"

Matt responded thoughtfully, "So I should help my staff learn skills for dealing with her?"

As a dominant, provide support to nondominants in your group.

"Absolutely. There are millions of people just like you, trying to do their jobs and have a good life while they're treading through sludge, trying to deal with all the crappy things going on around them. And they feel stuck just as you feel stuck. So yes, your staff needs skills to handle misguided, unfair, oppressive situations and people. Otherwise, this situation will continue to repeat itself over and over again, whether with this director or some future one."

He was silent again, so I kept going. "The fallacy is believing things are going to automatically be good and people will automatically act the way we want them to and that we shouldn't have to work at it. The truth is, if we want a good life, we can't expect it to be handed to us on a silver platter. We have to learn how to respond to what feel like horrid situations in ways that support and sustain rather than demoralize us. You said you can't afford to quit right now, so you might as well use the situation as a learning laboratory. Later, if you're no longer learning from the situation, you might rethink whether it's worthwhile to stay."

Adopt a learning orientation.

"Your director is providing an unusually blatant example of an unfair and unreasonable person. Yet, I'd bet you and your staff are also dealing with other people who routinely behave irresponsibly or hurtfully—and create enormous problems as a result. All of you could benefit from developing skills to help you handle such situations."

"That's true," he said.

CLEARING EMOTIONS

"But here's the catch, Matt. You won't be able to help your staff learn these skills as long as you're so angry. As far as I can tell, your anger comes from your feelings of powerlessness. You can't make your director stop, so you get angry with her for putting you in this situation. The good news is: even though you're livid, you're managing to speak to her without blowing up. That's something you're doing right. You know that blowing up at her wouldn't be effective."

"No, it wouldn't," he agreed, "although I've had to walk out of her office several times because I didn't trust myself not to say something stupid. I didn't want to get fired; but more than that, I just don't believe in dumping my stuff on people. I don't want people to do it to me and I don't want to do it to others."

Identify with your values, not your emotions.

"That's awesome," I exclaimed. "You used the strength of your convictions and emotional self-awareness to walk out of her office. That's a real plus. The next step is to learn how to clear your emotions so you can stay and respond effectively."

"Well, I can't just tell myself not to be angry."

Avoid emotional suppression.

"Of course not," I agreed. "That's another fallacy. People think they should just be able to order their strong emotions away. People think that if they can just learn to accentuate the positive, all the negative gunk will disappear. It's not that simple. Clearing one's emotions is a skill. There are methods available to help you clear your emotions, but it takes practice, patience, practice, patience. And then one day, you'll be in her office and she'll tell you she's going to take away their pens and paper and make them write with pencils and little tablets, and you'll be able to look at her and respond effectively and without rancor."

Get your emotional attachments out of the way.

I could almost hear him smiling, so I continued. "Most of us are simply not good enough actors to be able to point out someone's strengths and appear genuine with our teeth clenched. Even though you know intellectually that you need to be strength-focused, your anger will simply get in the way."

Clear negative emotions.

"Furthermore, as long as you're angry, you're in no position to help your staff learn how to better deal with any emotional darts they receive from her—or, for that matter, from clients, the public, or each other. For you to help them learn how to interact effectively with others, you must first be effective. And this goes back to managing your anger—processing it until it no longer drives your actions."

Matt interjected. "So you're saying the first step is for me to learn how to clear my emotions?"

"I don't know a better way. And it's also the most efficient way, although taking time out to do it may seem to waste time at the moment. Some years ago, before I knew how to clear my emotions, I had a serious run-in with someone. The conflict itself lasted six months, it took two years for me to get over being mad at the person, and another four years before our relationship got back on an even keel."

"Today," I continued, "I would use some of the tools I've adopted for emotional clearing and continue processing my emotions until I achieved clarity. Of course, I'd still see the rotten things she did. But I'd also start seeing her multi-dimensionally—as a full human being with strengths and weaknesses, just like the rest of us."

"So you're saying yet again that I should be the first to change," Matt said softly.

He was clearly reflecting on the class he had taken with me in which self-change had been a recurring theme.

CHANGING WORKPLACE DYNAMICS AND RELATIONSHIPS THROUGH CHANGING ONESELF

"Have you been successful in changing your director?" I asked, knowing he knew the answer.

"I know, I know," he responded with mock exasperation. "I can't change anyone else. I can only change me. It gets tiresome, though, and seems so unfair. I'm not creating the havoc; she is. Still, what

I've tried so far hasn't worked—or at least not for very long—and sometimes I wonder if I've made things worse."

Accept responsibility for your own contribution.

"You know, Matt, so far, you've been looking at your director as if she were Attila the Hun and you say it hasn't worked. You also said you could acknowledge her strengths without compromising your integrity. Are you willing to try a strength-focused approach: to look at her strengths, to see the good she brings, to see her as a worthwhile human being in her own right, as someone who has a wonderful vision and innovative ideas to contribute? If you can hold that image of her in your mind, you can speak to her strengths, not her weaknesses. This means changing yourself.

People look at other people or at situations and think, 'this is awful'; then they feel justified in being angry and upset. And so, we end up with broken friendships, divorces, dysfunctional organizations, even wars. The most effective place to start change is not the people or situations out there, it's with yourself. Changing the self first involves asking whether your actions are producing the desired results and whether they're consistent with your values.

"I certainly feel justified in ranting and raving," admitted Matt. "That's why I don't want to ask her for feedback. But I admit I've been myopic in focusing only on what's wrong with her and not putting it in the context of what's also right. I certainly didn't consider her strengths or her desires."

He paused, and then continued, "So, am I willing to try a different approach? To take the focus off how she needs to change and put it on myself instead?" I could tell he was genuinely asking himself that question, checking to make sure he meant every word as he said it. After a long pause, he answered, "Yes, I will. I commit to it."

Commit to personal change.

Many people are unfamiliar with the power they can wield by changing themselves before trying to change others. Matt's director certainly exhibits some behaviors that are not working. However, so does Matt. He has been ineffective in motivating or pushing his director to change. Matt can gain far more leverage in this situation by changing his own strategy—which is more under his control, after all. Changing his strategy, and experiencing a corresponding change in his own behavior, will take him a long way toward being able to more effectively influence people around him.

> After another long pause, Matt asked, "But what about the staff? I've been focused on how I might change, but I haven't considered what this means for them. How does my changing make it better for them? Will they think I've sold out?"

> "Could you explain to them what you're doing and why?" I asked. "Yes, if they see you treating her differently without explanation, they'll wonder about it. If you explain why you're changing your strategy and they understand it, they may be tempted to emulate your approach—especially if you provide them with some concrete skills on clearing emotions, building effective relationships, and so forth.

Gain support for the change one person or small group at a time.

> "As they begin to make changes, their new attitudes and behaviors will influence others. Rather than trying to change the director, you'll be changing the patterns of interaction among the people in your division. Then these changes may ripple out through the organization in unexpected ways.

> "If you start responding to your director differently and train your staff to do the same, all of you will be in a much better position to handle her—or, for that matter, any person who comes along and tries the same thing. Eventually, your director will find herself in a work setting where her old shenanigans won't work. She won't have a receptive audience for them. She may continue throwing darts, but there won't be a target to receive them. At that point, she'll have a choice: either change or leave."

Changing patterns of interaction is an important part of changing workplace dynamics, but not the only part. I was curious about structures within the organization that allowed the director to make such an arbitrary decision.

> "Do you have a Department of Human Resources?" I asked. "Are they aware of what's happening in your division?"

> "They pretty much only handle routine stuff," Matt responded. "You know: hiring, transfers, health insurance, that sort of thing. We don't go to them about problems with our managers."

"Is there a reason for that?"

"We're not sure we can trust them, for one thing."

"Do you know you can't?"

"No, not really. But I've heard rumors that they've leaked things told to them in confidence. Although I don't know this firsthand since I've never gone to them for anything like this."

"Are you willing to talk to them and tell them frankly that you have a delicate matter to discuss and want to know if they'll keep it confidential?"

"If I ask that, they'd know that I think they aren't trustworthy. That could get me into trouble."

"Well, maybe yes, maybe no. Right now, you're saying people aren't going to HR with problems because of a suspicion that they can't be trusted. It's a huge elephant in the room, an undiscussable. But if you don't discuss it, how can they know it's an image blocking their effectiveness?"

Surface undiscussables.

"Why should I care?!" Matt interjected. Before I could respond, he added, "Well, if I could trust them, and if people around the organization could trust them, then maybe we wouldn't have some of these problems. If HR knew about it, maybe they could figure out a way to help us. This is another example of how blocking the flow of information within an organization can keep people from coming together to achieve what they're capable of, isn't it?"

"Yes, indeedy," I responded. "However, it's your job on the line, not mine, so I encourage you to trust your instincts about this. My experience, though, is that undiscussables are what keep poorly functioning systems intact, and apparently some people in your organization harbor a big undiscussable about how HR is functioning. When an elephant is undiscussable, it overpowers the room. People try to walk around it and then wonder why they're not getting things done the way they'd like—or why they're so unhappy in such a stinky room."

We both laughed. Then, switching gears, I added, "You said she's the third director who's acted this way. This implies that something in the system is supporting her behavior. So, unless the system changes and all of you learn to deal with the situation more effectively, the next director may well walk in and see a cowed staff waiting to be exploited."

Emphasize changing systems, not just individuals.

"I have another question," I continued. "The fact that this is the third director within such a short time also suggests the absence of a good mechanism for giving managers feedback on their performance. Is this true?"

"Yes, that's right. Her VP rates her. We don't have anything to do with it."

"Does her VP know how your director is managing her people?"

"I have no idea. He never asks us."

"Well, Matt, this seems like it's close to the root of the problem from an organizational point of view. You have an HR department, but staff are afraid to go to them about problems. You have a performance review system, but the review is all top-down with no input from the staff. It seems as though members of upper management are making decisions without access to information from those at your level and below. Does this also affect your services?"

"Does it ever!" Matt exclaimed. "We have ideas, we're in contact with other organizations in our network, we know what's going on day-to-day, yet the VPs never ask us anything!"

"So you're saying there are information and feedback gaps throughout the organization?"

"Absolutely."

"I understand why you might not feel comfortable going to HR and saying that the director is driving you batty. But could you go to them and say you'd like to discuss ways of increasing feedback and information sharing across the organization? Would you feel in jeopardy for suggesting something like this?"

"Oh! Now that's something to think about. If we had a way of giving the VPs information about our work and our clients, they could plan better; and meanwhile, we'd have a way of letting them know what's not working for us. I'm not talking about subverting the hierarchy, but it would seem reasonable that they'd want to hear directly from us, at least once in a while. I wonder if HR would listen to us about something like that?"

I nodded, "As far as I know, in many organizations, this is HR's job—to look at reporting lines and feedback mechanisms to make sure accurate information is getting where it's supposed to go. Your director making staff take the pictures off their glass door panes isn't just an individual issue. It may also be a symptom of problems at the organizational level—a disconnect between those working on the front lines, HR, and top decision-makers."

"This is so cool, Jean," responded Matt. "Yes, I can see that it goes beyond my or the staff's angry and hurt feelings. This really does impact how effective we are in our jobs. If we have no way of telling anyone how her management style is affecting our productivity or willingness to offer our suggestions for improving services, then we're functioning with one hand tied behind our backs. I'll think about this and maybe talk to some other managers and let you know how it turns out. And maybe, somehow, I can figure out how to work in a conversation about the stinky elephant."

In the latter part of the conversation, we had moved away from simply a diagnosis of Matt's current reality. We were now talking about a potentially different kind of workplace with a new, more positive set of policies and practices involving Matt, his staff, his director, and the organization as a whole. But to get there, Matt would need to accept a new set of attitudes and attributes. One of these is patience—a lot of patience.

"One last thing, Matt," I added. "I want to caution you about what to expect if you decide to go the route we've been talking about. You already know it won't be easy. What I want you to understand is that we're not talking about a quick fix. You can expect reversals and setbacks and stalemates. But there will be small wins along the way. If you make a point to identify each small win—no matter how tiny— this will go a long way toward helping keep your spirits up."

Persevere through the time lag of change;
recognize small wins along the way.

When change is slow, people forget how it was when they first started and only look at what has *not* happened rather than at the gains they've made and how far they've come. One way to stay focused on gains is to keep a journal to chronicle the small wins along the way. This will help build your positive emotions about what is happening; in turn, positive emotions will give you the energy to persevere through setbacks and stalemates.

"That's interesting," said Matt, as I explained the benefits of journaling. "I don't remember you talking about keeping a change journal in class, but this does remind me of a weight loss program I used to be in. They had us record our baseline weight and weigh ourselves daily so we could keep track of our progress."

"Yes, that's the same idea!" I exclaimed. "Keep track of your small wins so you can maintain a positive attitude toward the change, however slowly it occurs."

Build positive emotions.

Change normally occurs far more gradually than most people wish. The deeper and more profound the desired change, the greater the time lag between efforts to initiate change and signs that it has actually taken hold. Learning to recognize small wins can alert you that change really is occurring, albeit one small step at a time. If Matt is willing to stay the course, the Conscious Change approach will steer him through the inevitable ups and downs of the change process (Table 8.2).

Table 8.2
A Shift in Perspective

	Original Perspective	*New Perspective*
Matt's assumptions	Matt believes the director is unpleasant, unreasonable, and insecure. He sees the director as using her rank in the organization to drive a wedge between the managers and staff members. For the most part, Matt is in the answer, not in the question. He *is* in the question about one aspect of the situation: whether the director's upbringing in a more hierarchically-oriented culture is impacting her behavior.	Matt has moved beyond either/or thinking about his director to seeing her as a person with both strengths and weaknesses. He is also now in the question as to whether some of his cultural assumptions about the director are correct.
Matt's emotions	Matt is angry and frustrated that the staff are not valued, and concerned that the director will turn on him.	Matt can learn how to clear his emotions. This will put him in a better position to use a strength-focused approach and maintain his integrity. Emotional clearing may help him think more clearly, allowing him to explore new avenues for relating to the director and other key individuals in the organization.

Table 8.2
A Shift in Perspective (*Continued*)

	Original Perspective	New Perspective
Matt's efforts to build effective relationships	He has spoken up to the director, trying to explain without offending. He is sympathetic with his staff, telling them he sees the director's actions as unfair. Yet, he believes he has been ineffective with his director and only partially effective with his staff.	Matt has decided to change to a more strength-focused approach with his director. He also plans to help his staff learn skills that will allow them to respond more effectively to the director without being insubordinate. He will seek feedback from his staff on how to im-prove his effectiveness as their manager and will consider asking the direc-tor for feedback as well.
Matt's efforts to bridge the power and status differences between himself and the director	Despite Matt's best efforts, the director still took down the staff's pictures. As a nondominant in this situation, he feels stumped and powerless.	There is still reason for anger, frustration, and fear, but Matt no longer feels powerless. He has the beginnings of a plan and sees possibilities for securing additional support from his staff and HR.
Matt's conscious use of self	He is making every effort to retain his integrity by being truthful with the director, but does not see how he himself may be contributing to the situation. He has not considered his director's perspective or strengths. Asking for help is a sign that he is willing to learn from the situation.	Matt understands how his anger may have blocked him from seeing ways to act more effectively in the situation. He plans to be more conscious of the strengths of others, and to remain aware that he can-not force anyone in the organization to do what he suggests. He will take steps to learn more about the director, the organiza-tion, and how he might effectively use his power.
Matt's view of the organiza-tional system	He has not fully considered the organizational context. Since the problems have occurred with the past few directors, something may be off kilter at the organizational level	Matt has a broader view of the organizational context, including possible pressures on the director and an expanded role for HR.

At this point, Matt's flight was announced and our conversation ended. But the story didn't. He began to experiment with consciously using himself to initiate workplace change.

ALLOWING THE UNEXPECTED TO EMERGE

A few weeks later, Matt called again, this time to report a frank conversation he had had with someone he trusted in HR. Apparently, HR had considered revisions in how the organization was soliciting and handling feedback from employees, but the idea had been languishing on the back burner. Because of suggestions from employees around the company, including Matt, HR was now actively investigating 360-degree performance feedback plans. They were realizing that having only top-down reviews was limiting the breadth of information that a diversity of perspectives could provide.

Address underlying systemic biases.

"We still have to go through our managers to get our suggestions to the VP," Matt said, "but they're talking about beefing up the defunct open door policy. So it's a start."

I was surprised when a week later, Matt called again. "I just had to tell you this, Jean. Attila the Hun has left! We aren't sure what happened; she left very abruptly. We'd started responding to her differently. Here's how I'd been handling the situation. I worked very hard to encourage all of us to demonstrate respect and emphasize each other's strengths where we could, and to extend this to her and everyone we worked with. We also talked frankly about her unreasonable demands and agreed to join forces and say 'we can't do that' when she asked us to do something that was blatantly over the top. I could tell she wasn't sure what was going on, but we were all beginning to feel better about our jobs and get more done since we weren't spending so much time griping and complaining about her—or each other for that matter. And now she's gone! We don't know if she left because of us, HR, or what. But she's gone! She's gone!"

"That's wonderful, Matt!" I responded. "Did you anticipate that this would happen?"

"Not in the least, Jean. We were prepared to just stick it out, stay strength-focused and stick together. It worked far better than I could've hoped for."

"I can hear that in your voice," I agreed. "And that's the beauty of it. Here's why I think what you did worked so well. You didn't set out with a particular fixed outcome in mind. You set a direction instead. You knew you wanted people to stick together and be strength-focused, as you said, but you didn't deliberately try to get her fired or get anything set in stone. You didn't limit what was possible. You simply wanted your group to move in the direction of health."

Set a direction, not fixed outcomes.

"And we're doing it!" Matt exclaimed. "That's exactly right. We aimed to become healthier, but we didn't declare that such-and-such had to happen by this or that date. And now that the director is gone, it opens everything up. I feel as though I can breathe again!"

Matt was exuberant, yet his efforts to initiate change were not over, even though "Attila the Hun" had left the organization. To believe that would be to believe all the problems were caused solely by the director in the first place. Many Attilas in workplaces, homes, and other shared spaces are supported by established policies and practices and people who endure or even collude with them.

"Matt, what do you know about the new person?" I asked.

"Not much. He's coming in from out of state."

"Do you have reason to believe he will be any better than your former director?"

I could hear him catch his breath. "No, I don't. He couldn't be as bad as the previous one, could he? Could he?"

"What I know is that organizations have a way of attracting personnel who fit their stage of growth. Think of how many people have a series of problematic personal relationships, each time promising they'll avoid the same pitfalls and yet each time, they end up with a replica of the person they'd just broken up with."

"My brother does that," Matt said reflectively. "But what does it mean for our unit?"

"There's no way to know until you meet the new person. For now, plan on maintaining an open conversation with your staff about the kind of relationship you want to have with the new director. Just keep in mind that the long-established habits of people in your organization may act as a self-fulfilling prophecy and steer him into reenacting similar behaviors as his predecessor. The trick is for you and your staff to monitor any backsliding on your part."

Matt was on the right track in urging the staff to develop a strength-focused work culture, yet resist submission to unreasonable authority without exploring other avenues. Maintaining that demeanor would be an essential step in helping to set a positive tone for the new director.

CONCLUSION: SUSTAINING HOPE

Time and again, we, the authors, have heard stories similar to Matt's and those in the other chapters from our students and organizational clients. In these stories, the provocations may have been relatively mundane, but they were heart-wrenching experiences for those facing them. Exacerbating these situations were power and status differences stemming from job rank, demographics, or worldview orientations. In these and similar circumstances, a different trajectory can be set if those experiencing such problems make a deliberate choice to speak up as constructively as they are able, and to encourage others within their sphere of influence to respond constructively as well. As happened with Matt, a ripple effect occurs so that individual actions, joined with those of others, prompt significant changes in workplace relationships.

Does this mean that you will not face additional trials and tribulations as you attempt to navigate the difficult terrain of personal, interpersonal, and workplace change? Obviously not. The question is not whether there will be travails; the question is how you will handle them as they occur. A deeper question is how can you develop and maintain the courage and will to persist despite the inevitable setbacks? This is not a simple question to answer. For many, including the two of us as authors, it is also a highly personal question. Anyone who has attempted to bring people together to embark on any form of change effort knows it is easier to initiate change than to see it all the way through.

At the beginning of the change effort, there is a honeymoon period, where the vision of what might be propels us forward. After the honeymoon, however, the real work begins as you experience the inevitable setbacks in the course of a change effort. Obstacles can be threatening and frightening. "Too risky!" you tell yourself, or others tell you, and your emotions agree. The more threatened you feel, the fewer alternatives you can fathom. Your vision and hope for what might be possible erodes.

It is hard work to sustain hope. Fear is more automatic and spontaneous; hope has to be worked at. Fear is unintentional; hope has to be consciously maintained. Hope involves effort; it requires consciously using yourself to overcome fear and other negative emotions and thoughts.

Often, the actual obstacles are not the most formidable impediments to change; rather, it is negative emotions in the face of such obstacles that deflate your energy and cause you to lower your initial hopes. When fear overtakes hope, perseverance requires a conscious decision to reactivate hope. You have a choice between fear and hope, the past or the future, sticking with the status quo or taking a chance that a new way might be found.[1]

There are tools in this book to help you maintain hope. The chapter on emotions, for example, provided a number of techniques to reverse the ratio of positive to negative emotions by clearing negative emotions and enhancing positive ones. By clearing your negative emotions, you alleviate the stranglehold fear can have on your thought processes. Enhancing your positive emotions allows you to find new strategies to deal with immediate threats, and hold on to images of future possibilities. Consider this as a form of self-care, taking care of yourself as the instrument of change.

Speaking personally, here's what we do to avoid getting discouraged as we work to bring about change. First, we have both developed support networks of people who share our commitment to healing divisiveness and generating more positive connections among people. We turn to our networks whenever things get rough or just to recharge our batteries; many of these individuals are recognized in the acknowledgments.

We also believe in savoring small wins, appreciating with gratitude hidden gifts that come along the way. When we deliberately search for them, we repeatedly find pearls among broken rocks and sludge.

We have daily practices of clearing our negative emotions and amplifying our positive ones. Jean L. uses a form of daily meditation that allows her to eliminate "the churning inside." She also employs several of the emotional clearing techniques described in this book that require vivid imagery and rehearsal. She deliberately cultivates sensations of gratitude, caring, and well-being until she feels at peace. Jean R. uses daily journaling and an active yoga practice to maintain equanimity.

Both of us have abiding faith in the human spirit's desire to grow, develop, and contribute to humankind. We believe people wish to realize their potential, both individually and collectively. We also believe the use of the principles of Conscious Change will help you tap into that potential and will lead to positive energy and beneficial results. This has been our continuing experience.

Negativity, cynicism, and sheer meanness do abound. Too often, people separate into warring factions and refuse to let go of their animosities. In their separate groups or even as individuals, good people can be tempted or pushed into doing horrific things.

Yet, we believe people are increasingly motivated to unite with others to grow toward some ultimate good. The personal growth movement is alive and well. Social networking and advocacy groups are growing exponentially as people seek likeminded others at work, in their communities, and on the web with whom to work, play, and make a difference in the world. People are volunteering in their churches, food shelters, and other nonprofits at higher rates than ever before. And marketers estimate that nearly 60 million adults in the United States are now willing to pay up to 20% more than the current market price for products that will help sustain the planet, promote fair trade, and promote healthy living.[2]

You are not the only one in your organization who wants to bring people together to make a difference, but you *are* the only one who can take the first step of leaving your safe and known ways of operating and venturing into the unknown new land of greater self-knowledge and initiation of workplace change. Along the way, we encourage you to seek companions for the journey to enhance your likelihood for success. They are there.

NOTES

1. Jarymowicz, M., & Bar-Tal, D. (2006). The dominance of fear over hope in the life of individuals and collectives. *European Journal of Social Psychology, 36*(3), 367–392.
2. Everage, L. (2002). Understanding the LOHAS lifestyle. *Gourmet Retailer, 23*(10), 82.

APPENDIX

Principles for Conscious Change

Testing assumptions	1. Move out of the answer and into the question.
	2. Avoid either/or thinking; look for multiple points of view.
	3. Test your assumptions about others.
	4. Check to see if you are making cultural assumptions.
Clearing emotions	5. Identify with your values, not your emotions.
	6. Avoid emotional suppression.
	7. Clear negative emotions.
	8. Build positive emotions.
Building effective relationships	9. Engage in powerful listening.
	10. Develop skills in inquiry and openness.
	11. Learn how to give, receive, and seek feedback.
	12. Distinguish intent from impact.

Bridging differences	13. Learn to recognize dominant/nondominant dynamics.
	14. Develop an awareness of your own stereotyping tendencies and biases and learn how to manage them.
	15. Address underlying systemic biases.
	16. As a dominant,
	a. Recognize that you may have blind spots as to your own behavior and systemic biases;
	b. Provide support to nondominants in your group.
	17. As a nondominant,
	a. Recognize that dominants may have blind spots about the impact of their behavior on nondominants;
	b. Ferret out any tendency toward internalized oppression and views of the dominants as a monolithic, all-powerful group.
Conscious use of self	18. Get your emotional attachments out of the way.
	19. Accept responsibility for your own contribution.
	20. Maintain integrity.
	21. Seek to understand others' perspectives; put yourself in their shoes.
	22. Focus on the other person's strengths.
	23. Adopt a learning orientation.
	24. Recognize your power and use it responsibly.
Initiating workplace change	25. Commit to personal change.
	26. Emphasize changing systems, not just individuals.
	27. Gain support for the change one person or small group at a time.
	28. Set a direction, not fixed outcomes.
	29. Learn from resistance.
	30. Surface undiscussables.
	31. Persevere through the time lag of change; recognize small wins along the way.

Index

About the Authors

JEAN KANTAMBU LATTING, DrPH, LMSW, is an organizational consultant, Professor of Leadership and Change Emeritus, Graduate College of Social Work, University of Houston and Co-Director of Leading Consciously. Dr. Latting is the author of over 25 refereed journal articles and book chapters on workplace dynamics, cultural competence, and promoting change.

V. JEAN RAMSEY, PhD, is retired as Professor of Management at the Jesse H. Jones School of Business, Texas Southern University and Co-Director of Leading Consciously. She is the author of *Teaching Diversity: Listening to the Soul, Speaking from the Heart* (Jossey-Bass), and *Preparing Professional Women for the Future: Resources for Teachers and Trainers* (University of Michigan), as well as several dozen articles on teaching, diversity and other topics.